29.95

B
785
·F433
T4813
2001
v.6

D1124483

THE I TATTI
RENAISSANCE LIBRARY

James Hankins, General Editor

# FICINO

# PLATONIC THEOLOGY

VOLUME 6

ITRL 23

THE I TATTI RENAISSANCE LIBRARY

James Hankins, General Editor

*Editorial Board*

Michael J. B. Allen
Brian P. Copenhaver
Vincenzo Fera
Julia Haig Gaisser
Claudio Leonardi
Walther Ludwig
Nicholas Mann
Silvia Rizzo

*Advisory Committee*

Joseph Connors, Chairman

Francesco Bausi
Robert Black
Virginia Brown
Caroline Elam
Arthur Field
Anthony Grafton
Hanna Gray
Ralph Hexter
Jill Kraye
Marc Laureys
Francesco Lo Monaco
David Marsh

John Monfasani
John O'Malley
Marianne Pade
David Quint
Christine Smith
Rita Sturlese
Francesco Tateo
Mirko Tavoni
†J. B. Trapp
Carlo Vecce
Ronald Witt
Jan Ziolkowski

# MARSILIO FICINO

✦ ✦ ✦

# PLATONIC THEOLOGY

VOLUME 6 ✦ BOOKS XVII–XVIII

ENGLISH TRANSLATION BY

MICHAEL J. B. ALLEN

LATIN TEXT EDITED BY

JAMES HANKINS

with William Bowen

THE I TATTI RENAISSANCE LIBRARY
HARVARD UNIVERSITY PRESS
CAMBRIDGE, MASSACHUSETTS
LONDON, ENGLAND

2006

Colo. Christian Univ. Library
8787 W. Alameda Ave.
Lakewood, CO 80226

Copyright © 2006 by the President and Fellows of Harvard College
All rights reserved
Printed in the United States of America

Series design by Dean Bornstein

*Library of Congress Cataloging-in-Publication Data*

Ficino, Marsilio, 1433–1499.
[Theologia Platonica. English & Latin]
Platonic theology / Marsilio Ficino ; English translation by Michael J.B. Allen
with John Warden ; Latin text edited by James Hankins with William Bowen.
p.    cm. — (The I Tatti Renaissance library ; 2)
Includes bibliographical references (v. 1, p.    ) and index.
Contents: v. 1. Books I–IV. v. 2. Books V–VIII.
v. 3. Books IX–XI. v. 4. Books XII–XIV.
v. 5 Books XV–XVI. v. 6. Books XVII–XVIII.
ISBN 0-674-00345-4 (v. 1 : alk. paper)
ISBN 0-674-00764-6 (v. 2 : alk. paper)
ISBN 0-674-01065-5 (v. 3 : alk. paper)
ISBN 0-674-01482-0 (v. 4 : alk. paper)
ISBN 0-674-01719-6 (v. 5 : alk. paper)
ISBN 0-674-01986-5 (v. 6 : alk. paper)
1. Plato.    2. Soul.    3. Immortality.    I. Allen, Michael J. B.
II. Warden, John, 1936–    III. Hankins, James.
IV. Bowen, William R.    V. Title.    VI. Series.
B785.F433 T53 2001
186.'4 — dc21        00-053491

# Contents

ஜஜஜ

# Prefatory Note

❦

This is the final volume in the I Tatti Renaissance Library's six-volume edition and translation of Ficino's eighteen-book *Platonic Theology*. It also includes his brief Introduction or *argumentum* (see Note on the Text). As in the previous volumes, Michael Allen is responsible for the English translation and notes, and James Hankins for editing the Latin text, though each has gone over the other's work. While some corrections to the first five volumes have come to our attention and are listed in the Corrigenda in this volume, we anticipate that other scholars will enrich our understanding of this monumental work's varied sources and debts, particularly, one suspects, to Aristotle, Augustine, Proclus, Averroes, and the Scholastics, as they look beyond the network of identifications attempted here.

We wish to thank Patrick Baker for helping us to compile the concordance and the cumulative indices of names and of sources; Lys Ann Weiss for her cumulative subject index; and William Bowen for supplying us (as in the previous volumes) with an electronic copy of Marcel's Latin text as the starting point for a fresh collation of the principal witnesses.

Above all we wish to take this opportunity of again thanking John Warden for his drafts of books I–XII, and Wendy Helleman for her drafts of books XV and XVI. They gave us the courage to begin what we knew would be a long and arduous climb up one of the loftiest peaks of Renaissance thought. The result for us at least has been an alpine view of horizons as far as Mt. Ventoux, of reasoning's escarpments and faith's plunging ravines. Our hope now is that others will explore this whole magnificent terrain.

M. A. and J. H.

# THEOLOGIA PLATONICA
# DE IMMORTALITATE
# ANIMORUM

2

*The Theology on the Immortality of Souls*
*by Marsilio Ficino the Florentine*
*Divided into Eighteen Books:*
*Chapter Headings*

Seventeenth book. This resolves the [five] platonic questions.[1]
The fifth question: What is the soul's status before it approaches
the body, and what after it leaves?

Eighteenth book. This gives a view of the soul drawn from a
consensus common to all theologians.

3

FINIS

THE END

# LIBER SEPTIMUS DECIMUS[1]

## : I :

*Quinta quaestio.*
*Qualis sit animae status antequam ad corpus accedat,*
*qualis etiam post discessum.*[2]

1  Sed iam disputationem quintam aggrediamur per quam quaestio illa solvatur quae interrogabat: qualis sit animae status priusquam accedat ad corpus, qualis etiam cum discesserit?

2  In rebus his quae ad theologiam pertinent, sex olim summi theologi consenserunt, quorum primus fuisse traditur Zoroaster, Magorum caput, secundus Mercurius Trismegistus, princeps sacerdotum Aegyptiorum. Mercurio successit Orpheus. Orphei sacris initiatus fuit Aglaophemus. Aglaophemo successit in theologia Pythagoras, Pythagorae Plato, qui universam eorum sapientiam suis litteris comprehendit, auxit,[3] illustravit. Quoniam vero ii omnes sacra divinorum mysteria, ne prophanis communia fierent, poeticis umbraculis obtegebant, factum est ut successores eorum alii aliter theologiam interpretarentur. Hinc turba Platonicorum interpretum in sex academias se divisit, quarum tres Atticae fuerunt, reliquae peregrinae. Atticarum vetus sub Xenocrate[4] floruit, media sub Archesila, sub Carneade nova; peregrinarum Aegyptia sub Ammonio, Romana sub Plotino, sub Proculo Lycia. Verum cum sex fuerint scholae Platonicorum, tres illae Atticae simul atque Aegyptia, quaecumque de animarum circuitu scripta sunt a

# BOOK XVII

*The fifth question: What is the soul's status
before it approaches the body,
and what after it leaves?*

Let us now come to the fifth argument that resolves the question 1
people have raised: What is the soul's status before it approaches
the body and what after it has left?

With regard to these matters pertaining to theology, six theo- 2
logians, once supreme, were in mutual accord. The first is said
to have been Zoroaster, the chief of the Magi, and the second
Mercurius Trismegistus, the prince of the Egyptian priests. Succeeding him was Orpheus, and then Aglaophemus was initiated
into the sacred [mysteries] of Orpheus. In theology Pythagoras
came after Aglaophemus; and after Pythagoras came Plato who
embraced the universal wisdom of all of them and enhanced and
illuminated it in his writings. But since they all wrapped the sacred mysteries of these matters divine in poetic veils to prevent
them becoming mixed up with matters profane, the outcome was
that various of their successors interpreted that theology in various
ways. Hence the host of Platonic interpreters divided itself into six
academies, three of which were Greek, three foreign. Of the Greek
the old academy flourished under Xenocrates, the middle under
Archesilas, the new under Carneades; of the foreign, the Egyptian
academy flourished under Ammonius, the Roman under Plotinus,
and the Lycian under Proclus.[1] But since there were six schools of
Platonists, the three Greek schools along with the Egyptian school
accepted whatever had been written down by Plato about the cir-

7

Platone, aliter quam verba sonarent accipiebant; duae vero sequentes ipsam verborum faciem curiosius observarunt.

3    Quo autem modo hae duae platonica exponant mysteria diligenter recenseamus.


## : II :

*Expositio Platonis de anima secundum duas academias ultimas.*
*De compositione animae.*


1  Plato in *Parmenide* quidem deum vocat infinitum, in *Philebo* vero nominat terminum. Infinitum scilicet, quia nullum aliunde accipit terminum; terminum autem, quia formis quasi mensuris passim distributis omnia terminat. Hinc Platonici disputant, quatenus deus tamquam infinitus omnem a se excludit terminum, eatenus ferme ex eo quasi umbram pendere potentiam quandam quasi materialem termini cuiuslibet indigam informemque natura sua et, ut ita loquar, indefinitam. At vero quatenus deus tamquam terminus umbram suam respicit tamquam speculum, eatenus in umbra iam velut imaginem resultare infinitatemque ipsam, id est materiam communissimam, formis ordinatissime terminari.

2  Idem rursus ita confirmant. Si in deo semper est universi faciendi potestas, merito semper extra deum universi, ut ita loquar, fiendi potentia. Non enim facere ille semper omnia posset, ut opinantur, nisi semper fieri omnia possent. Potentiam eiusmodi materiam communissimam, id est vim formarum omnium aequaliter receptricem nominant, quae natura sua neque ad ipsum esse ver-

cuit of souls in a non-literal way, but the two schools succeeding them observed the literal sense of Plato's words more fussily.[2]

Let us carefully review the manner in which these last two ex- 3 plain the Platonic mysteries.


: II :

*Plato's account of the soul according to*
*the last two academies.*
*On the soul's composition.*


In the *Parmenides* Plato calls God infinite,[3] in the *Philebus* he calls 1 Him the limit:[4] infinite because He accepts no limit at all from anywhere, but the limit because He limits all things with forms, with measures as it were distributed everywhere. Hence the Platonists argue that to the extent God as infinite excludes all limit from Himself, so depending on Him almost like a shadow is a sort of material potentiality devoid of any term, naturally formless, and so to speak indefinite. But to the extent God as the limit looks back to His own shadow as a mirror [of Himself], so is He reflected in the shadow like an image; and then that infinity, that matter common to all, is limited by forms in a supremely ordered way.[5]

The following argument proves the same thing. If the power to 2 make the universe is always within God, it duly follows that the universe's power to be made must always be, in a manner of speaking, outside God. For God could not always make all things, so they believe, unless all things could always be made. They call this power—namely, the potency that is equally receptive of all the forms—the matter common to all. Of its own nature it tends neither towards being itself, for if it did it would not need a supernal

gat, alioquin superno formatore non indigeret, neque ad non esse, alioquin formatori non obediret, sed ad esse pariter atque non esse; item ad formas tales aut tales quasi medium quoddam aeque se habeat atque a formatore determinetur. Sit quoque in omnibus una, non numero, non specie, non genere, sed analogia et proportione quadam potius, scilicet quoniam ab Uno dependet atque unius dei infinitatem, utcumque potest, modo quodam umbratili repraesentat, quemadmodum et actus quodammodo unus in omnibus nominatur, quoniam ab uno terminatore et unius terminationem imaginarie refert. Atque actus huiusmodi potentiam superat, propterea quod a deo manat non fugiente ulterius, sed iam respiciente materiam. Huiusmodi potentia in spiritibus nonnihil corporis habere videtur, siquidem in mentibus habet corporum rationes, in animabus insuper motiones, in utrisque formabilem facultatem. Rursus in corporibus incorporei nonnihil videtur habere, quia et dum antecedit quantitatem, indivisibilis apparet, et semper vires quasdam quodammodo incorporeas sustinet. Ex hac infinitate, ex hoc termino, id est potentia receptrice formabilique atque actu formali constare sub deo omnia putant.

3    Quod Maurus Avicebron in libro *Fontis vitae* forte significat, atque theologi nostri breviter ita confirmant. Si creatura et quaelibet et universa esse sortitur a deo, certe ex se non est, atque ab illo destituta iam ultra non esset. Quapropter esse potest atque non esse. Igitur non est ipsum esse suum, immo ad ipsum potentia est. Nihil vero ad se ipsum est potentia vel suscipit semetipsum. Semper enim agens, dum agit, quod potentia tale est, efficit actu tale.

form-giver, nor towards non-being, otherwise it would not obey the form-giver; but it is equally disposed towards being and non-being. Likewise it is equally poised as a mean between various forms and it is limited by the form-giver. This power is also one in all things, not one numerically or in terms of species or genus, but analogically and in terms of a certain proportion; this is because it depends on [something] one and represents the one God's infinity, insofar as it can, in a shadowy manner. Similarly, the [form-giving] act is called one in a way in all things because it comes from the one giver of limit, and reflects in the manner of an image the limiting of that one giver. And such an act overcomes the [receptive] power precisely because it emanates from God not as He flees ever farther from matter but as He looks back even now towards it. In spirits, on the one hand, this power is seen to have something of the corporeal, since in minds it has the rational principles of bodies and in souls it has motions besides; and existing in both is the ability to be formed. In bodies, on the other hand, this power is seen to possess something of the incorporeal, since it appears indivisible when it precedes quantity, and it is always sustaining certain incorporeal powers in some manner. From this infinity and from this limit, that is, from the receptive and formable power and from the form-giving act, Platonists[6] believe all things exist under God.

In his book, *The Fountain of Life*, Avicebron the Moor signifies 3 this perhaps;[7] and our own theologians briefly confirm it as follows. If a creature, whether any individual creature or the universal, is allotted being by God, it certainly does not exist of itself; and were it abandoned by God, it would no longer exist. So it can exist and can not exist. Therefore it is not its being per se, rather it is the potentiality for it. But nothing exists as a potentiality for itself or receives itself. For an agent when it acts always makes what is potentially such actually such. So a creature is produced not because a potentiality is imprinted on a potentiality (otherwise noth-

Quamobrem creatura producitur non ex eo quod potentiae potentia imprimatur, alioquin nondum quicquam ederetur in actum, neque ex eo quod actus actui infundatur vel idem sibi ipsi concilietur, alioquin quod producitur esset antequam esset, sed in ipsa productione proprie actus potentiae adhibetur. Atque haec ipsa duo in creatura necessario distinguuntur, alioquin esse ipsum creaturae, quia in se ipso subsisteret, esset penitus infinitum. Cum igitur esse ab essentia differat, numquid fit ab essentia? Minime. Nihil enim tamquam efficiens potest sibimet esse tribuere. Itaque aliunde accipit esse. Hinc ergo, prout capit, potentia est. Quod vero capitur, actus cognominatur. Quare quicquid producitur ex potentia et actu, scilicet essentia et esse componitur.

4      Essentiam quidem potentiamque ad infinitatem, esse vero et actum ad terminum Platonici referunt. Proinde in *Sophista* et *Parmenide* et[5] in *Timaeo* quinque rerum numerantur genera, ex quibus praeter primum omnia componuntur, scilicet essentia, idem, alterum et status et motus. Essentia quidem manifeste significat rationem rei cuiusque formalem; innuit quoque esse tamquam actum essentiae proprium. Idem vero dicitur, quoniam quodlibet et secum in primis et cum aliis congruit. Rursus additur alterum, quia quandam, tum intra se tum ad alia[6] differentiam habet. Praeterea status, quippe cum aliquandiu suam retineat unitatem. Denique motus hoc in loco exitum quendam ex potentia in actum sive essendo sive quomodolibet intrinsecus extrinsecusve agendo significat. Quamobrem divinae infinitati ac divino termino hinc rerum infinitas, inde rerum terminus subditur. Deinde ad rerum infinitatem tria potissimum, scilicet essentiam et alterum motumque referimus. Ad ipsum vero rerum terminum tria similiter, scilicet esse, idem, statum pariter distribuendo reducimus. Quod autem in *Par-*

ing would ever be led into act), nor because act is poured into act or the same [act] would unite with itself (otherwise what is produced would exist before it existed). Rather in this producing of a creature, act is properly brought to potentiality. And necessarily these two are distinguished in a creature, otherwise a creature's true being, since it subsists in itself, would be entirely infinite. Though being differs from essence, therefore, does it come from essence? No. For nothing [created] can give itself being as the efficient cause. So it receives being from elsewhere. Insofar as it receives, accordingly, from this source it is potentiality; but what it receives is called act. So whatever is produced is composed from potentiality and act, that is, from essence and from being.[8]

The Platonists relate essence and potentiality to infinity, but being and act to the limit. Hence in the *Sophist*, the *Parmenides*, and the *Timaeus* the universal genera are listed as five and all things except the very first [i.e. the One] are compounded from them: essence, identity, otherness, rest, and motion.[9] Manifestly, essence signifies the formal rational principle of each thing; but it also implies being as the proper act of essence. Identity is mentioned because anything whatsoever agrees with itself in the first place and then with others. And otherness is added because anything possesses some difference both within itself and with regard to others. And rest is added, since anything whatsoever retains its unity for a while. Finally motion in this context signifies a departure from potentiality into act whether by existing, or by acting in some way (internally or externally). So to the divine infinity and the divine limit are subject things' infinity on the one hand and their limit on the other. Then to things' infinity we chiefly relate three of the [universal] genera: essence, otherness, and motion. But to things' limit we distribute equally the [other] three: being, identity, and rest.[10] What is called in the *Parmenides* the one and the many[11] is called the indivisible and the divisible in the *Timaeus*[12]; and this must be taken to mean that the one and the indivisible accord-

4

*menide* quidem unum et multa, in *Timaeo* vero impartibile et partibile dicitur, sic accipiendum est, ut unum et impartibile secundum terminum; rursus multitudo et partibile secundum infinitatem per sua passim genera propagentur. Quamvis autem singula praeter primum ex iis quasi seminibus elementisque componantur, incorporea[7] tamen consonantiori seminum mixtione quam corporea[8] conflari dicuntur. Quam ob causam illa magis indissoluta permanere putantur.

5      Missam[9] in praesentia faciam ceterarum rerum commixtionem, et qua ratione ex[10] his generibus animam Pythagorici et Platonici misceant, mox exponam, si prius admonuero, ne forte putemus, etsi animam semper fuisse horum plerique dicunt, eam tamen illos omnino ex se esse putare. Cum enim non totam operationem suam anima, per quam semper operatur, simul explicet, sed paulatim, constat eam hanc infinitam semper operandi virtutem haud totam simul habere. Si enim totam simul haberet, ederet quoque totam simul et unicam. Omnis enim, ut aiunt, potentiae operatio, una unius. Igitur semper accipit virtutem semper agendi. Propterea non similiter semper, sed alias aliter agit, ut summatim dici possit, quicquid temporaliter agit, sive corpus sive anima, accipere quidem continue paulatim operandi virtutem; numquam vero simul totam penitus possidere.

6      Quamobrem anima non solum semper esse, sed etiam gigni semper a Platonicis iudicatur, scilicet quatenus vim suam haurit paulatim et formas intrinsecus alias aliter explicat atque affectus actionesque continue variat. Igitur quatenus vitalis ipsa sui motus causa est, quodammodo sibimet essentialem interminatamque[11]

ing to the limit, and the many and the divisible according to the infinite are everywhere propagated through their genera. But although individual things, with the exception of the very first [i.e. the One], are compounded from the genera as from seeds and elements, yet incorporeal things are said to be produced from a more harmonious mixing of [these] seeds than corporeal things are. For this reason they are thought to endure longer in an undissolved state.

For the moment let me set aside the commingling of other 5 things and let me straightway explain why the Pythagoreans and Platonists mix the soul from these [six] genera. First, however, I have to warn us against perhaps supposing, even though the majority of them declare that the soul has always existed, that they believe the soul is entirely self-created. For since the soul does not unfold its whole activity (the activity through which it is always acting) all at once but little by little, obviously it does not possess this infinite power of always acting all at the same time. For if it did possess it all simultaneously, it would also produce it all simultaneously and as one. For all the activity of a power, as they say, is the one activity of that one power. So the soul is always accepting the power of always acting. On this account it does not always act in the same way, but does various things in various ways, to the point that it can be summarily said that whatever acts in time, whether it is a body or a soul, continually receives the power of acting little by little, but never possesses this whole power completely and simultaneously.

So the soul, in the Platonists' view, not only always exists but is 6 always being born; that is, insofar as it draws little by little upon its own power, it also unfolds various other forms within in various ways and continually varies its feelings and actions. Therefore to the extent that it is the vital cause of its own motion, the soul supplies itself in a way with essential and limitless life, and is thought to exist as such; but to the extent it unfolds it in infinite

suppeditat vitam, atque ita esse censetur; quatenus vero infinito id explicat tempore vimque eiusmodi paulatim a superioribus accipit, nimirum gigni perpetuo ab alio iudicatur. Accedit ad haec quod principium rerum summum rebus omnibus adest, adeo ut singula principii pro natura sua ubique participent, alioquin subito evanescerent. Anima vero non adest omnibus. Non enim omnia vivunt.

7     Item primum omnino ipsum unum esse oportet. Nam si multitudo[12] quaedem esset, proculdubio super se causam suae unionis haberet, quippe cum unire non multitudinis sit, immo unitatis, officium; esse vero primum multitudinem sparsam dictu nefas. Anima tamen omnis est multitudo. Rursus primum super omnem essentiam cogitatur, cum omnis essentia in se multitudinem patiatur, saltem qualem in superioribus numeravimus. Anima vero essentia quaedam est, vitalis scilicet atque vivifica. Denique primum neque usquam neque unquam neque ullo pacto contaminari potest. Animae tamen permultae quandoque et alicubi et certo quodam modo inficiuntur. Quamobrem anima necessario a superiore principio suo quodam pacto compositam habet essentiam.

8     Ceterum in rebus super animam a deo compositis munera, quae ad terminum spectant, longissimo intervallo opposita genera superant. In rebus vero sequentibus animam contra contingit. At vero in anima componenda genera generibus aequalius concinnunt. Cum enim anima verissimum omnium, quae a deo componuntur, medium sit, consentaneum est eam media quadam aequalissimaque, quoad fieri potest, ratione esse compositam. Igitur in ea, ut cetera praetermittam, partibile impartibili, alterum eodem, motus statu quasi acutum gravi harmonice temperatur.

9     Profecto in his, quae super animam sunt, tria potissimum cogitantur: essentia, vita, intellegentia. In his quoque, quae sunt infra

time and accepts such a power little by little from those above, it is certainly judged to be born perpetually from another. Moreover, the highest universal principle is present to all things in such a way that single things everywhere participate in that principle, each according to its nature, otherwise they would suddenly vanish away. But the soul is not present to all things; for not all things are alive.

Again, the absolutely first must be one. For were it a multitude, 7 it would undoubtedly have the cause of its own union [existing] above it, since to unite is not the duty of a multitude but of [a] unity; but it would be sacrilegious to say that the first being is a dispersed multitude. All soul is, however, a multitude. Again, the first is deemed to be above all essence, since all essence endures the many in itself, the many at least as we have enumerated it earlier. The soul by contrast is an essence, a living and life-giving one. Finally the first cannot be contaminated anywhere, at any time, or in any way. But very many souls are infected at a particular time, in a particular place, and in a particular way. So from its higher principle the soul necessarily has an essence that is in a way compounded.

Moreover, in things compounded by God above the soul the 8 gifts [i.e. the genera] that look to the limit utterly surpass the opposite genera. But in things subsequent to the soul the reverse happens. In the compounding of the soul, however, the two sets of genera chime in more equal measure. Since the soul is the truest mean of all things that are compounded by God, it is appropriate that it be compounded by a mean rational principle — one that is as perfectly positioned in the middle as it can possibly be. So in the soul, to leave aside the remaining creatures, the divisible is harmoniously tempered with the indivisible, the different with the same, and motion with rest, as the high-pitched with the bass.

Certainly, in the things that are above the soul, we must chiefly 9 consider three attributes — essence, life, and understanding; and also in the things that are below the soul, consider three [other]

animam, tria vicissim: qualitas, natura, sensus, ut sensus intellegentiae, natura vitae similitudo sit, qualitas denique essentiae ultima sit imago. In superioribus quidem secundum essentiam et vitam et intellegentiam impartibile partibile superat, idem quoque excedit alterum statusque motum. In inferioribus autem omnino contra contigit. In anima vero, utpote omnium media, modus per omnia quasi medius observatur. Proinde sive eam ad extrema mundi conferas — inter mentes tamquam admodum impartibiles et qualitates tamquam omnino, id est tempore locoque partibiles — media iudicatur. Sive ad sui ipsius extrema, scilicet ad mentem hinc suam atque inde ad vitam corpori mersam, similiter inter individuum et dividuum media pariter esse censetur. Sive ad ipsum sui ipsius medium, scilicet rationem denique conferas,[13] etiam haec ipsa ratio, quando ad intellectum et universalia surgit, dicitur impartibilis. Quando vero ad sensus singulaque declinat, partibilis nuncupatur, atque illic identitatem, ut ita loquar, statumque consequitur; hic vero vicissim alteritatem subit et motum. Ac dum in aeternis considerandis quodammodo ipsa discurrit, individuo statui[14] divisibilem permiscet motum. Contra vero dum in temporalibus attingendis quodammodo in se ipsa consistit, motum vicissim divisibilem in dividuo[15] quodam statu[16] contemperat.

10 Praeterea sicut anima mundi in movendo quidem caelo, quod *aplane*,[17] id est inerraticum dicitur, in eodem ostendit alterum; in planetis vero quodammodo erraticis moderandis per ipsum motionis ordinem in altero vicissim idem servare videtur, sed hactenus idem superat alterum. Denique in inferioribus gubernandis idem iam ab altero superari permittit. Similiter hominis anima circa tria

attributes in turn—quality, nature, and sense, with sense as the image of understanding, nature as the image of life, and quality finally as the ultimate image of essence. In things superior to the soul, the indivisible surpasses the divisible according to essence, life, and understanding; the same exceeds the other; and rest exceeds motion. But in things inferior to the soul the completely opposite happens. In the soul, however, being the universal mean, we see a middle way as it were through them all. Accordingly, if you compare the soul to the universe's extremes, that is, locate it between minds (insofar as they are virtually indivisible) and qualities (insofar as they are entirely divisible in time and place), then it is adjudged the mean. If you compare it to its own extremes, that is, to its own mind on the one hand, and to its own life immersed in the body on the other, it is similarly adjudged the exact mean between the undivided and the divided. And finally, if you compare the soul to its own mean, that is, to its reason, then when this reason rises up towards the intellect and universals it is also called indivisible, but when it sinks down towards the senses and individuals it is called divisible. There it attains identity, so to speak, and rest, and here it submits in turn to otherness and to motion. And when, in considering things eternal, this reason proceeds in a way discursively, with undivided rest it mixes divisible motion; but when, to the contrary, in touching on things temporal, in a way it stays steadfastly in itself, it tempers divisible motion in turn with a sort of divided rest.

Take the World-Soul moreover. In moving heaven itself, which 10 is called *aplanes* (i.e. non-wandering),[13] it reveals otherness in identity. But in moderating the planets (wandering in a way as they do), it seems in turn to preserve (by way of the order itself of motion) identity in otherness—and thus far identity rules over otherness. Finally in governing lower things, it allows identity to be overruled now by otherness. Similarly, man's soul seems to be concerned with three vehicles as it were, the aethereal, the airy, and

quasi vehicula, scilicet aethereum, aereum, compositum corpus se habere videtur. Iam igitur quid sibi Timaeus velit, ubi in anima componenda musicis proportionibus utitur, satis intellegi potest. Nihil enim aliud sibi vult quam animam tum ex ipsis rerum generibus tum ex viribus suis ita componi, ut ideae suae in primis, deinde sibi ipsi, tertio rebus aliis aptissime congruat.

II  Solent Pythagorici in anima figuranda mathematicis tam figuris quam numeris uti, quoniam sicut mathematica, sic et animae inter naturales divinasque formas medium obtinent.[18] Constituunt ergo triangulum, in cuius apice locata sit unitas, a qua terni utrinque numeri profluant, hinc pares, inde similiter impares, hac videlicet ratione, ut a parte altera primum duo, deinde quatuor, demum octo, altera ex parte primum tria, deinde novem, postremo septem atque viginti. His vero censent omnes animae partes, vires, officia designari. Quae enim super animam sunt, unita potius quam numerosa putantur. Quae vero sub anima, numerosa quidem, sed per se maxime dissona. Verum anima primum[19] numerosa ideo dicitur, quoniam cum proxima sit multiplicitati corporeae, iam intellegitur tam motionibus quam viribus multiplex esse. Deinde vero cum ordinatae motionis generationisque proximum sit principium, probabili ratione concluditur numerositatem eius esse maxime consonantem, a cuius consonantia corporis continue tum caelestis tum elementalis consonantia non aliter pendeat quam ab ipsa quae in musici mente harmonia est, illa deinceps, quae in vocibus et quae in sonis harmonia sentitur, et fluere[20] soleat. Proinde Philolaus, cum deum unitatem more pythagorico nominasset, mox extensam materiam dualitatem cognominavit, propterea quod quemadmodum dualitas ipsa prima inter numeros divisio est, sic materiae dimensio causa est in primis ut formae distractae[21] inter se repugnantesque evadant.

the compound body. We are now in a good enough position, therefore, to understand what Timaeus intends when he uses musical proportions in compounding the soul.[14] For he means nothing other than that the soul is compounded so well from the universal genera and its own powers that it is in perfect accord first with its Idea, then with itself, and thirdly with other things.

Customarily the Pythagoreans use mathematical figures and numbers alike in figuring forth the soul, because, like mathematical objects, souls occupy the middle position between the natural forms and the divine forms.[15] The Pythagoreans therefore establish a triangle: in its apex is located the number one (the unity), and from the apex three numbers descend on each side, on the one side three even numbers, on the other likewise three odd, and with this logic: down one side first comes 2, then 4, then 8; down the other side 3, 9, and finally 27.[16] They suppose that all the soul's parts, powers, and offices are designated by these numbers. For things above the soul they think of as united rather than numbered, but things under the soul as indeed numbered but totally discordant among themselves. The soul, however, is first said to be numbered because, since it is closest to corporeal multiplicity, it is understood to be multiple in its motions and powers alike. But then, since it is the immediate principle of ordered motion and of generation, probability leads us to the conclusion that its being numbered is concordant to the maximum degree; and from its concord continually depends the concord of its celestial body and of its elemental body alike. In exactly the same way, from the harmony in a musician's mind there customarily arises the harmony heard both in vocal and in instrumental music. Hence Philolaus, having in the Pythagorean manner called God unity, straightway called extended matter duality, because, just as duality is the first division among numbers, so is matter's dimension the cause in the first place that the forms emerge as estranged from and opposed to each other.[17]

12    Itaque animam ab unitate divina pendentem sese in materiam quasi in dualitatem infundere putant, non aliter quam triangulus ab angulo summo in duos similiter desinat angulos. Itaque in corpore composito distrahi semper et perturbari. Merito igitur anima triangulo figuratur. Septem vero deinde huic triangulo numerorum terminos adhibent. Nempe cum videamus rerum generationem septenario planetarum numero gubernari summumque planetarum Saturnum septimo quolibet anno mutationes in vita hominum facere, lunam quoque, planetarum infimam, septimo quovis die tum in se ipsa tum in humoribus mutationem inducere, merito animam motionis generationisque originem septenario numero describere iudicantur. Sunt etiam qui foetum in alvo perfici septenariis et natum extra alvum per aetates duci similiter arbitrentur. Afferunt insuper utrinque numeros, et pares et impares, ut per pares animam ex natura dividua, per impares ex individua commixtam esse declarent.

13    Rursus numeros lineares superficialesque et solidos addunt, ut appareat animam per longitudinem, latitudinem, profunditatem corporis sese facillime fundere. Eligunt autem illos dumtaxat numeros, quorum proportionibus mutuis musica consonantia constat, ut ostendant animam, concinne compositam, concinne cuncta disponere atque movere. Sane inter quatuor ac tria sesquitertia proportio est, ex qua nascitur harmonia, quam Graeci nominant diatessaron. Sed inter tria et duo est proportio sexquialtera; haec procreat harmoniam, quam nuncupant diapenten. Praeterea inter

So the Pythagoreans think that the soul, depending on the di- 12
vine unity, pours itself into matter as into duality, just as a triangle
similarly descends from the angle at its apex to end in the two an-
gles at its base; and thus the soul is always estranged and perturbed in the composite body. With justice then they figure the
soul as a triangle.[18] But they then apportion seven numbers as its
terms to this triangle.[19] Certainly, since we see that the generation
of things is governed by the sevenfold number of the planets, and
that the highest of the planets, Saturn, causes mutations in human
life every seventh year, and the lowest of the planets, the moon, introduces change both in itself and in the bodily humors every seventh day, we deem it appropriate that they deploy seven terms to
describe the soul, the soul being the origin of motion and generation. There are thinkers too who suppose that the fetus is perfected in the womb in sets of seven and that having issued from
the womb it similarly lives through seven ages.[20] They introduce
the two sets of numbers on either side [of the triangle], the even
and the odd, in order to declare, moreover, that the soul through
the even is blended from the divided nature, and through the odd
from the undivided nature.[21]

Furthermore, they introduce linear numbers, plane numbers, 13
and solid numbers[22] in order to clarify how the soul extends itself
with greatest ease through the length, breadth, and depth of the
body. But they elect only those numbers from whose mutual proportions issues a musical harmony in order to show that the soul
is harmoniously compounded, and that it disposes and moves all
things harmoniously. The ratio between 4 and 3 is the sesquitertial
proportion, and from this is born the harmony which the Greeks
call the *diatesseron* [the fourth]. But the ratio between 3 and 2 is the
sesquialteral proportion; and this produces the harmony they call
the *diapente* [the fifth]. The ratio between 4 and 2 or between 4
and 8 is the double proportion that produces the harmony of the
*diapason* [the octave].[23] Between 1 and 3 or between 3 and 9 or be-

quatuor atque duo sive quatuor et octo proportio dupla, quae diapason conficit consonantiam. Inter unum vero et tria, sive tria inter et novem, sive inter novem atque viginti septem proportio tri-
pla, a qua melodia diapason diapente componitur. Proinde inter
quatuor et unum, sive duo inter et octo, quadrupla proportio nascitur, quae disdiapason generat harmoniam.[22] Denique inter octo
ac novem fit epogdous, quo constat tonus. Sonum vero tono re-
missiorem hemitonum nominant. Quamobrem omnes quas narravimus proportiones arti musicae potissimum necessariae ab illis
fiunt numeris, qui in figura animae describuntur. Per quos animae
tum naturalis compositio tum motio actioque naturalis maxime
omnium esse tam consonans quam numerosa significetur. Neque
desunt qui sphaerarum quoque caelestium magnitudines inter se
intervallaque et motus planetarumque habitus et aspectus proportionibus paene similibus metiantur; spiritum quoque vitalem simili qualitatum suarum temperatione disponant.

14    Missa non absque ratione facio multa, quae multi hac in parte
de fictis numerorum figurarumque virtutibus tam leviter quam
curiose pertractant. Haec est mysterii pythagorei[23] et platonici
summa. Mitto quod solent intelligentiam, quoniam per simplicem
fit intuitum, saepe unitatem cognominare; scientiam vero dualitatem, quoniam ex principio probat conclusionem; sed opinionem
trinitatem, quia insuper conclusionis oppositum ambiguitate quadam affert in medium; sensum postremo quaternitatem,[24] propterea quod circa composita ex quatuor elementis plurimum versari
videtur. Mitto rursus, quod animam ideo currum vocant, quia motus efficit circulares, quodve in ea lineam ponunt quodammodo
rectam, quantum corpora movet et respicit; deinde circulum
quendam inferiorem, quasi planetarum orbem, quando redit in se-
metipsam; circulum quoque superiorem, quasi stellarum orbem

tween 9 and 27 is the triple proportion from which is compounded the melody called the *diapason diapente*. So from the ratio between 4 and 1 or between 2 and 8 emerges the quadruple proportion that generates the harmony of the *disdiapason* [the double octave]. Finally, the ratio between 8 and 9 produces the *epogdous* [the sesquioctaval proportion] from which comes the tone. But they call the sound less intense than a tone a half-tone.[24] Therefore all these proportions we have described as absolutely necessary to the art of music come from the numbers that are described in figuring the soul. These numbers signify that the soul's natural composition and its natural motion and action alike are the most harmonious and the most numbered of all. And one even finds thinkers who use the same proportions, or almost so, to measure the magnitudes too of the celestial spheres and the intervals between them, and the motions, habits, and aspects of the planets; and who order the vital spirit by using a like tempering of its qualities.[25]

I am leaving aside, and with reason, many contentions that 14 many men engage at this point, whether frivolously or curiously, concerning the shaping powers of numbers and of figures. This is the very summit of the Pythagorean and Platonic mystery. I am setting aside the fact that frequently their practice is to call understanding "unity" because it comes from simple intuition; to call knowledge "duality" because it proves a conclusion from a premise; to call opinion "trinity" because it introduces with a certain ambiguity the opposite of the conclusion; and to call sense "quaternity" because it seems to be chiefly concerned with objects compounded from the four elements.[26] I am also setting aside the fact that they [the Pythagoreans and Platonists] call the soul a chariot because the motions it effects are circular, and that in it they posit: first, a straight line in a way insofar as it moves and looks to bodies; then a lower circle like the rotation of the planets when it returns to itself; and also a higher circle like the rotation of the fixed stars insofar as it is converted to higher things. They also assign it two

fixarum, quatenus ad superiora convertitur. Alas duas, scilicet instinctum intellectus ad ipsum verum atque voluntatis ad ipsum
bonum; aurigam mentem; caput aurigae, divinam unitatem mente
superiorem; equos superiores, scilicet idem et statum; equos infe-
riores, scilicet alterum atque motum; item equum bonum atque
malum, scilicet irascendi et concupiscendi naturam. Ira[25] enim
propinquior rationi quam libido esse videtur.

15      Denique, ut summatim dicam, hac ratione Pythagorici et Platonici omnes rationales animas, tum nostras tum nostra superiores,
paene similiter esse compositas arbitrantur. Unde sequi existimant, ut et caelestes animae in volvendis sphaeris inaestimabilem
pariant melodiam, et nostrae huiusmodi concentibus mirifice de-
lectentur. Verum inter caelestes atque nostras quasi longe distantes
tres gradus medios interponunt medio modo compositos, qui nostras cum divinis quodammodo vinciant, atque hos gradus secundum essentiae, vitae, intellegentiae proportionem procedere opinantur. Angelicas enim animas ab intelligibili mundo proxime
emicantes, intelligibile lumen sequentibus infundere, per modum
essentiae permanentes;[26] deinde daemonicas animas per modum
interminabilis vitae atque processus, postremo heroicas secundum
mentis conversionisque modum. Mitto quod angelicas secundum
intellectualem virtutem a deo procedere arbitrantur; daemonicas
secundum opificiam atque providentem, ideoque fabricare mundana; heroicas secundum conversivam praecipue facultatem, idcirco purgandarum animarum officio fungi; has omnes harmonice
temperatas et harmonica facere et harmonicis mirabiliter oblectari.
Sed de his animarum generibus convenientius in sequentibus per-
tractabimus.

wings, the instinct of the intellect for Truth itself and of the will for the Good itself; a charioteer, namely the mind; the charioteer's head which is a divine unity higher than the mind; higher horses, namely identity and rest; lower horses, namely otherness and motion; and a good and bad horse, namely the nature of wrathful passion and of appetitive desire.[27] For wrath seems closer to reason than desire.

To sum up, this is why all the Pythagoreans and Platonists 15 think the rational souls, our own and those superior to our soul, are similarly compounded or almost so. Hence they conclude that celestial souls, in turning the spheres, give birth to an inestimable melody, and that our souls are marvelously delighted by such harmonies.[28] But between the celestial souls and our souls, far apart so to speak as they are, they interpose three intermediary grades compounded as a middle way so that they may link our souls in some manner with the divine souls. They suppose that these three grades proceed according to the proportion of essence, life, and understanding thus: a) angelic souls, blazing out from the intelligible world and being so close to it, pour out the intelligible light into all subsequent things by way of essence and they remain at rest; b) demonic souls do so by way of limitless life and of procession; and c) heroic souls finally do so by way of mind and of conversion. I leave aside their view that angelic souls proceed from God by way of intellectual power; that demonic souls proceed by way of their power to fashion and provide and so to craft the things of the world; that heroic souls proceed by way principally of their power to convert and so to perform the office of purging souls; and that all these souls are harmoniously tempered and produce things in harmony, and are wonderfully delighted by such things. We will treat more fittingly of the classes of these souls in what follows.

: III :

*Species et circuitus animarum secundum duas similiter*
*academias ultimas.*

1 Quatuor sunt animarum genera. Sunt animae divinae, id est animae sphaerarum, mundi atque siderum, quae ideo divinae dicuntur, quoniam et deo proximae sunt et communem mundi providentiam agunt in regione perpetua. Sunt animae profanae, id est
animae bestiarum propriae, omnis divinitatis expertes. Sed has in
praesentia dimittamus. Sunt inter haec extrema media duo, animae scilicet semper deum sequentes, quales sunt animae daemonum heroumque sublimium, quae licet proprie divinae non appel-
lentur, numquam tamen a deo discedunt.

2 In primo et hoc animarum genere sic principia disposita sunt,
ut illic quidem essentia, hic vero, ut ita loquar, identitas cetera
principia quodammodo superet. Sub iis[27] sunt animae, quae quandoque sequuntur deum, quandoque relinquunt. In his principium,
quod ipsum alterum appellatur, alia quodammodo superare videtur. Tales sunt inferiorum daemonum heroumque animae, sed
manifestius hominum animae, quae cum sint mentium omnium
infimae, non eam vim habent, per quam possint duo admodum di-
versa perfecte simul implere, id est per humanam rationem intueri
divina ac terrena corpora gubernare. Utrumque tamen agere eas
oportet, postquam natae sunt ad utrumque. Quare vicissim fa-
ciunt, quod eodem tempore nequeunt. Utuntur autem vicissitu-

: III :

*The species and circuits of souls, again according to the last
two academies.*

There are four genera of souls. There are divine souls — those of   1
the spheres of the world and of the stars — who are called divine
because they are closest to God and enact in [their] perpetual region the world's universal providence. There are profane souls, the
souls proper to beasts entirely devoid of divinity. But let us dismiss these for the present. Between these extremes are two means.
[First] are the souls who always follow God, of which kind are the
souls of the eminent demons and heroes, souls who are not properly called divine yet who never depart from God.[29]

In these two species of souls the [universal] principles are so   2
disposed that in the case of the demons essence rules in a way over
the other principles, but in the case of the heroes, identity (if I
may use the term[30]). Under these are the souls who sometimes follow God and sometimes abandon Him. In these the principle
called otherness seems in a way to rule over the other principles.
Of such a kind are the souls of the lower demons and heroes, and
more obviously of men who, being the lowest of all minds, do not
have the power to be able to perform two completely different
functions perfectly at the same time, namely, to use the human
reason to gaze upon things divine and to govern earthly bodies.
But souls must do both since they are born to do both. Wherefore what they cannot do simultaneously they do in alternation.
They deploy alternation, however, principally in three ways. First,
they cross over from the intelligible world to the sensible and the
reverse. In the intelligible world, furthermore, they accomplish
different species of contemplation in turn; and in the sensible region they pass from one species of living to another. Plato quite

dine tribus praecipue modis. Primo quidem ab intellegibili mundo ad sensibilem atque converso se transferunt. Praeterea in ipso intellegibili varias vicissim contemplationis species peragunt. Rursus in sensibili regione diversas vivendi species mutant. Quas quidem vicissitudines Plato tum saepe alibi, tum in *Phaedro* praecipue describit, atque ibi manifestius, ubi animas, inquit, alias aliorum deorum in caelo comites esse atque in contemplandis ideis similem pro viribus cum deo[28] suo discursionem mente peragere, tum super caelum circa divina, tum in caelo circa caelestia, tum sub caelo circa naturalia gradatim consideranda. Et quatenus deos imitari possunt, eatenus apud superos permanere. Item cum multiplices a causis ad effectus atque vicissim circuitus repetant, ait animum, qui intuitus est ideam, quae caput circuitus est, in circuitu illo, qui per ipsam proprie ideam continuatur, non cadere, sed tunc labi cum malus equus, id est concupiscendi vis, incitata per vim generandi, iam suo quodam tempore invalescentem a contemplando divertit ad generandum. Deinde vitas dinumerat novem, non quod tot solum sint, sed quia per septem planetas ignemque et aerem delabuntur. Demum transmigrationes multas per inferiora reditumque ad superiora describit, ubi multa proculdubio poetica sunt potius quam philosophica. Igitur iam ad ordinem magis philosophicum nos conferamus.

3    Profecto Platonici multi putant aliquid esse quod infinitam ex se vitam habet, aliquid quod ex alio, aliquid quod ex neutro. Rursus quod habet ex alio, aut ad summum aut ad imum potius declinare, aut omnino medium possidere. Nempe deum infinitatem vitae manentem ex se ipso penitus possidere; angelum quoque manentem, sed ex deo susceptam; animas deinde divinas nostris su-

often describes these alternations in other texts but chiefly and most clearly in the *Phaedrus*. There he says that various souls accompany various gods in heaven: in contemplating the Ideas, they enact with their mind the same discursive [flight], insofar as they can, with their god, step by step considering things divine above heaven, things celestial in heaven, and things natural under heaven.[31] And insofar as they are able to imitate the gods, they are able to remain among the higher beings. Likewise, since the souls repeat their multiple circuits from causes to effects and the reverse, Plato says that the rational soul, which has intuited the Idea at the head of its circuit, does not lag behind in [making] that circuit, which properly continues through the Idea itself.[32] It only lags behind when the bad horse, that is, the power of appetitive desire, incited through the waxing power of generating (waxing now at this its particular time), turns the soul away from contemplation towards generation.[33] Plato then enumerates nine lives, not because only nine exist, but because souls descend through the seven planets and through [the spheres] of fire and air.[34] At the close he describes the manifold transmigrations through lower things and the return to things higher;[35] and here doubtless a number of his words are poetical rather than philosophical.[36] So let us turn now to the more philosophical order of exposition.

Of course, many Platonists think that there exists: a) something which has infinite life from itself, b) something else which has life from another, and c) yet something else that has it from neither; and they think that what has this life from another either ascends towards the highest or descends towards the lowest or remains entirely in the middle. They certainly suppose a) that God possesses infinity of life utterly from Himself, infinity that is unchanging; b) that the angel too possesses infinite unchanging life but has received it from God; c) that the divine souls, those superior to ours, have infinite life from another but such a life in ongoing motion, moving still in a certain order by proceeding from

periores infinitam quidem aliunde habere vitam, sed currentem; currentem tamen certo quodam ordine a speciebus in species discurrendo, defectus omnis et oblivionis expertem. Animas denique nostras vitam habere similiter infinitam, sed non modo currentem, verum etiam inordinate, atque a meliori habitu in peiorem, vicissimque tum reminiscendo, tum obliviscendo mutabilem. Animas vero infra nostras nullo modo esse vitae infinitae participes. Ubi sectatores Procli suum illud confirmant,[29] scilicet caelestes animas etiam intellegendo discurrere, quia inter deos, qui intelligibilia et semper et manendo suscipiunt, atque particulares animas, quae illa et aliquando suscipiunt et currendo, congrue medium obtineant caelestes sublimesque animae, quae semper intuentur quidem, sed de speciebus in species transeundo. Nos autem alibi sententiam hac in re Plotini narravimus.

4       Proinde sic esse volunt infinitum unum tam virtute[30] quam perseverantia; deinde infinita multa perseverantia potius quam virtute — perseverantia inquam, vel sua omnia simul possidente vel de aliis ad alia succedente, sive id maiori sive minori ordine fiat — denique multa, quae neque virtute sua neque perseverantia aliunde accepta sint infinita. Talem in spiritibus ponunt ordinem. In mundo vero sensibili polus, utcumque potest, primum ordinis illius gradum refert; axis vero secundum; sphaera caelestis tertium; elementalis sphaera quartum; quintum denique, quae ex elementis quatuor componuntur.

5       Sed digressione hac omissa ad nostras animas redeamus. Semper quidem erit hominis anima, quoniam inhiat sempiternis. Semper et fuit, ut aiunt, quoniam haberet quandoque finem, nisi initio careat. Pythagorae anima ante ortum Pythagorae fuit quandoque a

species to species though devoid of all defect and all oblivion; and finally, d) that our souls have a similarly infinite life, but a life that is not only in motion, but in a disorderly motion, tumbling from a better habit into a worse, and changeable in turn, now remembering, now forgetting. The Platonists think that the souls below ours do not participate in any way in infinite life. And here the followers of Proclus confirm his view that even in understanding the celestial souls move discursively,[37] because between the gods, who receive the intelligibles forever but do so by remaining unmoved, and particular souls, who receive those intelligibles at certain times but do so by moving continuously, the middle position should fittingly be occupied by celestial and sublime souls who forever intuit [the intelligibles] but do so by passing from Ideas to Ideas. But we have spoken about Plotinus' view on this matter elsewhere.[38]

So the Platonists want there to be: a) an infinite one, infinite in  4 power and in constancy; b) an infinite many, infinite in their constancy rather than their power, in constancy meaning either possessing all that is their own simultaneously or else passing successively from some things to others, whether this occurs with a greater or a lesser [degree of] order;[39] and c) many things which are infinite in neither their power nor their constancy, having received these from elsewhere. The Platonists establish such an order among the spirits. But in the sensible world, the world's pole refers, insofar as it can, to the first level of the world's order; the axis to the second; the celestial sphere to the third; the elemental sphere to the fourth; and the fifth level finally consists of [all] those objects compounded from the four elements.

But let us abandon this digression and return to our souls.  5 Man's soul will always exist because it covets everlasting things; and it did always exist, so the Platonists say, because, unless it had no beginning, at some time it would have an end. Pythagoras' soul existed at some point free of an earthly body before the birth of Pythagoras, and then when he was born it was enclosed in

terreno corpore libera, post inclusa est nascente Pythagora. Duae hic vitae sunt, una libera, altera corporalis. Vita illa quae fuit libera, finem accepit in vitae corporalis initio. Ergo et initium aliquando prius habuerat. Quod enim cessat, incepit. Itaque non fuit ante Pythagoram semper extra corpus, licet quandoque. Et postquam coepit esse in corpore, non erit in iis[31] corporibus semper, quia quod incipit, desinit. Unde sequitur, ut innumerabiliter ante Pythagoram anima eius in corpore terreno fuerit atque[32] extra, rursusque post Pythagoram extra corpus futura sit vicissim atque in corpore. Et sicut omnes mundi sphaerae per animas suas variant formas ac tandem recursus proprios repetunt, quod in quatuor anni temporibus et quatuor lunae alternis vicibus intuemur, sic animae nostrae, animorum caelestium similes, varias formas corporum induuntur certisque curriculis temporum iisdem quibus antea corporibus involvuntur. Quam παλιγγενεσίαν, id est regenerationem, Zoroaster appellat, de qua multa Mercurius cum filio suo Tatio disputat. Et Plato in libro *De regno* resurrectionem hanc describit futuram in fine mundanae revolutionis, iubente deo ac daemonibus ministrantibus.

6     Quod autem per vitam unam explet mundus, anima nostra per multas exsequitur. *Timaeus* enim Platonis tradit deum, mundi opificem, iecisse in pateram quandam cuncta semina rerum eaque invicem musicis, ut supra diximus, modulis[33] temperavisse. Ex qua temperatione rationales animas tribus creaverit gradibus distributas, ita ut in qualibet anima cuncta inserta sint semina, ut cum sit ex ipsis omnium mixta generibus, omnia per cognationem quandam facile posset agnoscere, movere omnia atque vivificare omniformemque vitam facilius experiri. Quid aliud dei pateram quam

a body. We have in this case two lives: one free, the other corporeal. The life that was free accepted an end in the beginning of [Pythagoras'] corporeal life; so at some point it had a prior beginning too; for what ends has begun. So before Pythagoras this life was not always outside a body, though it was so on occasion. And having begun to exist in a body, it will not always be in these bodies, because what begins ends. It follows that as Pythagoras' soul lived inside and outside an earthly body numberless times before Pythagoras himself, so again it will live alternately outside and inside a body after Pythagoras. And just as all the world's spheres by way of their souls vary their forms but eventually reenact their own returns — we see this in the four seasons of the year and the four alternating phases of the moon — so our souls, like celestial souls, don the various forms of bodies and at the end of fixed cycles of time they are wrapped in the same bodies as before. Zoroaster calls this *palingenesis*, that is, regeneration;[40] and Mercurius has much to say about it with his son Tat.[41] In his book, *The Statesman*, Plato describes this resurrection as something that is going to occur at the end of a cosmic revolution under the commandment of God and with the aid of demons.[42]

But what the world fulfills by way of one life, our soul discharges through many lives. For Plato's *Timaeus* relates that God, the world's maker, threw all the seeds of things into a bowl and tempered them together with musical measures,[43] as we said above. From this tempering He created rational souls and distributed them on three levels such that in each soul were planted all the seeds of things. The result was that, since each soul was mixed from the genera themselves of all things, it could easily recognize them all through a certain kinship with them; and it could move and vivify them, and experience life in all its forms more easily. For what else do we understand by this "bowl" of God than the third essence, the mean between the divine and the corporeal, ablaze with the sparks of things divine and pregnant with the seeds of

6

essentiam tertiam intellegimus, inter divina et corporalia mediam, scintillis divinorum micantem, corporalium seminibus gravidam? Ex hoc fonte tres praecipuae animarum species manaverunt: divinae, deum sequentes semper, aliquando sequentes deum. Primis assignant Pythagorei sapientiam, secundis opinionem rectam, tertiis opinionem ancipitem. Unde colligitur, quod saepe iam diximus, animam nostram esse quodammodo omnia, ideoque omnium viventium progressus in suis visceribus continere. Non tamen omnes explicat sigillatim. Plura enim operantur animae primae quam secundae; hae quoque plura quam tertiae. Quamobrem licet non ad omnes, ad multos tamen vitarum progressus anima hominis instituta videtur. Neque violentia quadam illata extrinsecus neque discursu consilii de vita transfertur in vitam,[34] sed tali quodam naturali instinctu, quali in hac vita suo quaeque tempore prodeunt, dentes, pili, semen et reliqua.

7    Sicut enim in ipsa universi natura, sic in particularium animarum naturis aeterna quadam lege ordinata sunt singula prodeuntque ita in actum, ut et sibi et universae naturae est consentaneum. Certe una quaedam ex cunctis mundani animalis membris fit harmonia, per quam singula singulis et universo undique consonant. Ergo sicut ipsa mundi anima certis temporibus certa producit, sic et particulares animae seminibus insitis tempore certo ad certas vivendi species naturaliter inclinantur atque disponuntur. Ac dum paulatim praeteritae vitae affectus actusque remittitur, vicissim vitae sequentis intenditur, conferente singulis passim universi natura.

8    Meminisse vero oportet,[35] quemadmodum docet liber *De republica* decimus, ⟨quod⟩ animae fato descendunt, id est, quod generationem appetant et tali quodam appetant tempore, ex naturali in-

things corporeal? Three principal species of souls issue from this fountain — the divine species, the species of those who always follow God, and the species of those who sometimes follow Him. To the first the Pythagoreans assign wisdom, to the second right opinion, to the third wavering opinion. From this we conclude, as we have often said already, that our soul is in some manner all things, and so contains in its own womb the life-progresses of all living things. Yet it does not unfold them all individually. For the first [order of] souls unfolds more than the second, and the second more than the third. So the soul of man seems appointed for many if not all the progressions of lives. It is transferred from life to life, impelled not externally by some kind of violence, nor as a result of [its own] deliberation, but by a kind of natural instinct, the sort which in this present life produces teeth, hairs, semen, and the rest, each at its appropriate time.

For as in the nature itself of the universe so in the natures of  7 particular souls individual things are governed by a sort of eternal law, and they proceed into an act such that it is in harmony both with themselves and with universal nature. Certainly, from all the members of the World-Animal emerges one harmony via which individuals are everywhere in consonance with other individuals and with the universe. Therefore, just as the World-Soul itself produces specific things at specific times, so particular souls too by virtue of the seeds implanted in them are naturally inclined and disposed towards specific kinds of living at a specific time. And when the emotions and acts of a past life are gradually remitted, those of the life to follow are in turn intensified, the nature of the universe contributing to individuals everywhere.

We must remember, however, that the souls descend as a result  8 of fate, as the tenth book of the *Republic* teaches us;[44] remember in other words that they desire generation, and desire it at such time when, out of natural instinct, they are joined to the order of the universe. Out of choice, however, they elect one or other particular

stinctu provenit ordini universi coniuncto, sed arbitrio talem vitam eligunt aut talem. Quamvis enim vitam corpoream prius naturaliter concupiverint quam cogitaverint, tamen talem aut talem vitae speciem prius cogitant quam adsciscant. Plurimum vero, inquit, eligere secundum prioris vitae consuetudinem et affectus, qui habitus affectusque ex liberis quondam actibus fuerint procreati. Ideo inquit: 'Culpa eligentis est, non dei. Non vos daemon sortitur, sed vos daemonem.' Virtus enim libera est. Postquam vero quis vitam daemonemque elegerit, virtus electam vitam disponere et componere potest potius quam deponere. Oportet enim curricula certa sortis impleri.

9     Quod autem ibidem scribitur 'mundum inter necessitatis deae genua volvi,' alias exposuimus. 'Necessitas' enim anima mundi ideo dicitur, quoniam fatali eius virtute ducitur universum. 'Inter genua,' inquam, id est, per virtutem eius inferiorem volvendis sphaeris accommodatam, siquidem mente rationeque divinis incumbit. Etsi inferior virtus eius universalis est una, tamen quasi triplex cognominatur. Lachesis, id est sortitia, quia sortes singulis[36] singulas inserit. Clotho, id est revolutrix, quia involutas a principio sortes unicuique suas certis ordinibus temporibusque evolvit. Atropos, id est inconvertibilis, quia in sortibus evolvendis immutabili ratione procedit. Ad has omnes deas Plato asserit ire animam ad inferiora vergentem, eo videlicet ordine ut postquam et sortibus in eam Lachesis incidentibus naturaliter elementalem concupiverit vitam, et propositis multiplicibus vitarum exemplis, pro arbitrio certam vitam eiusque ducem elegerit daemonem, tunc Lachesis electionem

life. For though they naturally [i.e. instinctively] longed for the corporeal life before they thought about it, they nonetheless think about a particular species of life before they opt for it. For the most part, Plato says, they choose it in accordance with the habitual behavior and emotions of their prior life, the habits and emotions that were engendered by the free acts of a former time.[45] Thus Plato declares, "The fault is the chooser's not God's. For the demon is not allotted you: you choose the demon."[46] For virtue is free.[47] But after someone has chosen a life and a demon, [his] virtue is able to arrange and compose the life elected rather than to set it aside.[48] For the courses determined by the lot must be fulfilled.

Elsewhere we have explained Plato's writing in the same passage that "the world revolves between the knees of Necessity."[49] For the World-Soul is called "Necessity" precisely because she leads the universe through her fatal power. "Between her knees" means through her lower power, the power suited to revolving the spheres, since with [her] mind and reason she devotes herself to things divine. Although Necessity's universal lower power is one, it is referred to as if it were threefold: it is called Lachesis, that is, she who appoints the lots, because it introduces individual lots to individuals; Clotho, that is, she who revolves, because it takes the lots that have been rolled up from the beginning and unrolls them for each person at fixed times and in fixed arrangements; and Atropos, that is, she who is irrevocable, because it proceeds with unchanging reason to the unrolling of the lots.[50] Plato declares that the soul inclining to things inferior goes to all three goddesses in the following order. After it has naturally coveted an elemental life that falls to it in Lachesis's lottery and from the many life-options proposed to it has freely selected a particular life and its guardian demon, then Lachesis confirms the choice. With the same demon the soul is thence led to Clotho, to Atropos, and to Necessity.[51] At this point who does not see that the soul, because

confirmet. Inde eodem daemone ad Clotho et Atropon Necessitatemque ducatur. Quis hic non viderit animam ob solam corporis huius affectionem in omnem mox fatorum incidere potestatem? Postremo ad Lethaeum oblivionis flumen, in hoc videlicet corpus, unde divinorum statim obliviscatur. Proinde significat animam, quae plus ex eo flumine biberit, id est quae affectu vehementiore sibi corpus adsciverit, oblivisci magis superiorum atque tardius reminisci; contra vero, quae contra. Sed ad diversas iam vivendi species veniamus.

10    Agit quandoque angelicam vitam in aethere apud eam stellam cui est vel natura vel usu facta propinquior, cumque illa[37] simul in certa[38] universi gubernatione consentit atque concurrit. At[39] potest per omnes sphaeras gradatim sursum deorsumve discurrens certum tempus in qualibet vitam, gubernationem contemplationemque agere illi sphaerae stellaeque congruam. Agit quandoque daemonicam vitam in igne similiter, tum heroicam in aere, humanam in terra atque ferinam. Ac saepe dum hominis vitam ducit, sensim ex eius seminibus in naturalem instinctum et phantasiam vita scaturit equina vel leonina vel similes. Quod significant affectus et mores, qui talium bestiarum proprii nobis suboriuntur. Deposita denique figura hominis, eius bestiae subit corpus, cuius se moribus simillimam praestitit, seu inserat se ferino foetui fiatque propria ferini corporis anima, ut Plotinus, Numenius, Harpocratius, Boethus existimant, seu animae ferinae se ipsam iungat atque ferae sit comes, ut placuit Hermiae Syrianoque et Proculo. Ac postquam de alia bestia migravit in aliam explicuitque[40] omnes progressus illos vitae ferinae, quibus explicandis pronior fuerat, promit iterum

of its affection solely for this body, straightway falls completely into the power of the Fates? Finally it comes to Lethe, the river of oblivion, that is, to this body, whence it immediately forgets things divine.[52] Plato means therefore that the more the soul drinks from that river, that is, the more vehement its desire to appropriate the body for itself, the more it forgets higher things and the longer it takes to remember. And with the contrary, the contrary. But let us now come to the different kinds of living [in these later Platonists].

The soul at some point lives the angelic life in the aether in the company of the star to which it has become very close either by nature or by familiarity; and together with that star it accords with and contributes to the established government of the universe. But it is able, by traveling up and down by degrees through all the spheres, to live the life in any one of them for a certain time, and to enact the governance and contemplation concordant with that sphere and that star. At another time similarly it lives the demonic life in the fire; then the heroic life in the air; and then the human life on the earth along with the life of the beasts. Often when living the life of a man, the life of a horse or a lion or suchlike gradually sprouts from its seeds and enters its natural instinct and phantasy. Signifying this are the emotions and behavior proper to such beasts that arise successively in us. Finally, having laid aside its human shape, the soul submits to the body of the beast which it has made itself most resemble by its behavior, whether it inserts itself into the fetus of the beast and becomes the soul belonging to the beast's body, as Plotinus, Numenius, Harpocratius, and Boethus suppose;[53] or whether it unites itself to the beast's soul and becomes the beast's companion, as Hermias, Syrianus, and Proclus believe.[54] But after it has migrated from one beast to another and unfolded all the life-progresses of the bestial life that it was particularly disposed to unfold, the soul lays out again the progresses of human life, then of heroic life,

10

41

progressus humanos, post heroicos, deinde daemonicos, postremo divinos. Aliae vero alibi plus minusve vivunt, quatenus fato vel fortuna vel electione habituque varie disponuntur.

11      Has transmigrationes restitutionesque Plato annis mille, tribus millibus, decem millibus designavit, disputationis exemplique gratia potius, ut inquit Hermias, quam quod certe dinumerari posse putaret. Horum enim numerorum quilibet non modo plurimus est, sed etiam certa quadam ratione perfectus, ut ostendatur animas ad perfectam purgationem longo quodam, sed certo tempore indigere, et quae vel levius peccaverunt, vel potius philosophatae sunt, eas citius in patriam redituras. Neque tamen intellegendum est animam communiter in eundem omnino hominem numero redituram, nisi fuerit tandem totus mundi cursus impletus, ut scribitur[41] in libro De regno. Quem cursum, ut diximus alias, triginta sex annorum millibus impleri astronomi computant. Interea tamen saepe in idem reverti anima dicitur, in eandem scilicet vitae speciem similemque vivendi modum, a divino videlicet ad divinum, ab humano ad humanum, a bruto similiter ad brutalem, quemadmodum et ipse mundi circuitus saepe interim ad similia redit, donec ad eadem prorsus denique revertatur.

12      Ne quis autem absurdum putet esse animam in tam diversas species se transferre, considerare iubent quam diversos affectus et habitus in hoc etiam corpore saepe animus induat, non in aliis solum, sed in eodem homine, plantae videlicet et bruti hominisve et angeli. Rursus ne quis miretur nos eorum quae in superiori gessimus vita, in hac minime recordari, animadvertere iubent non so-

then of demonic life, and finally of life divine. But some souls live more or less in one place or another as they are variously determined by fate or fortune or choice or habit.

Plato has used [spans of] a thousand, three thousand and [55] ten thousand to signify these transmigrations and reincarnations more for the sake of debate and example, as Hermias says, than from the supposition that they can possibly be numbered for certain.[56] For each of these numbers is not only considerable but also perfect for a specific reason: that it might show that for perfect purgation souls need a considerable but also a fixed length of time, and that those who have sinned just a little, or philosophized rather, will return the more swiftly to their native land. Yet it must not be supposed that the soul in general will return in a numbered span[57] to entirely the same man, unless the whole course of the world has at last been fulfilled, as Plato writes in the *Statesman*.[58] This course, as we declared elsewhere, the astronomers compute as lasting for thirty-six thousand years.[59] Yet in the meanwhile the soul is said to revert to "the same," that is, to the same species of life and to a similar mode of living. In other words, it goes from divine mode to divine mode, from human to human, from brute likewise to brute, just as in the interim the world's circuit itself often returns to similar [positions], until it is restored at last entirely to the same position.

But to prevent anyone thinking it absurd that the soul should [12] transfer itself into so many various species, they [the philosophers of the last two academies] ask that we bear in mind that the rational soul, even in this [human] body, often assumes appetites and habits that are as diverse as possible and co-exist not only in various men but in the same man—assumes, in other words, the appetites and habits of plant and brute or of man and angel. Again, lest anyone should marvel that we cannot recall in this life the things we did in a previous life, they ask us to bring to mind not only how much we have forgotten of our infancy in old age, but

lum, quam multum in senectute infantiae, sed etiam quam facile hodie hesternarum rerum obliviscamur. Haec illi, quibus propheticum illud obiicitur: 'In circuitu impii ambulant.' Quasi dicat illos esse impios iudicandos, qui eiusmodi animarum circuitus introducunt.

: IV :

*Quod Plato rectius exponatur more academiarum
quatuor praecedentium,
praesertim primae et quartae.*

1 Academiae vero quatuor iis antiquiores in hoc ab iis[42] discrepabant[43] inter se congruentes, quod scripta Platonis omnino poetica esse arbitrabantur. Sed inter se differebant, quod Carneades Platonem et putavisse et tractavisse omnia opinabatur Scepticorum more velut ambigua, neque ullum in rebus ullis habuisse delectum. Archesilas autem certum quidem nihil habuisse Platonem, verisimile tamen aliquid et probabile. Xenocrates[44] simul atque Ammonius illum aliqua non modo tamquam verisimilia tenuisse et probabilia, verum etiam tamquam vera certaque affirmavisse, eaque esse paucula quaedam de providentia dei animorumque immortalitate. Nos ergo Xenocratis[45] et Ammonii vestigia sequentes Platonem affirmavisse quaedam de anima non negamus, sed multa, quae de circuitu eius ab ipso tractantur, tamquam poetica, aliter intellegimus quam verba videantur significare. Praesertim cum circuitus huiusmodi haud ipse invenerit, sed narraverit alienos: primum quidem ab Aegyptiis sacerdotibus sub purgandarum animarum figura confictos, deinde ab Orpheo, Empedocle, Heraclito

also how easily today we forget the things of yesterday. Such is the view of these philosophers, to which the prophetic verse runs counter: "The wicked walk in a circle."[60] It is as if the verse were saying that those who introduce soul-circuits of this kind must be condemned as wicked.

: IV :

*That Plato may be better explained in the manner of the first four academies, and especially of the first and fourth.*

But the four academies older than those [of Plotinus and Proclus] 1 differed from them while agreeing among themselves in supposing the writings of Plato entirely poetic. But they mutually disagreed in that Carneades was of the opinion that Plato, in the manner of the Skeptics, had thought and treated of all things as being doubtful, and had not come to any decision on any issue; whereas Archesilas supposed that Plato held nothing for certain but only what was verisimilar or probable.[61] Xenocrates together with Ammonius thought that Plato not only had held some things as being verisimilar and probable but had affirmed other things as being true and certain — and these were just a few truths concerning divine providence and the immortality of souls.[62] So, treading in the footsteps of Xenocrates and Ammonius, we do not deny that Plato had affirmed certainties about the soul, but much that he says about the soul's circuit, being poetic, we take to mean differently than the words appear to signify [literally].[63] And this is especially since he did not invent such circuits himself but described those of others: first those invented by the Egyptian priests under the figure of the purging of souls, and then those intoned in poetic

poeticis dumtaxat carminibus decantatos. Mitto quod Pythagoras animarum transmigrationes consuetis illis semper confabulationibus suis symbolisque inseruit. Quamobrem ita ad academias ultimas respondebimus.

2      Nituntur autem duobus praecipue fundamentis: ratione propria et auctoritate platonica. Quae de rerum generibus musicaque animae compositione exponunt, ac rursum quod in argumentatione assumunt quatuor esse species animarum, admittimus. Rursus, quod anima nostra vix efficere queat utrumque simul, divina scilicet videre et corpora regere, praesertim ineptiora, id quoque damus. Sed non putamus ob hoc necessarium esse eam sursum atque deorsum vices innumerabiles agere, cum satis utrumque officium peragat, si dum vivit in terris, modo corporalia curet, modo se ipsam deumque colat; et cum hinc abierit, facilius vehiculum suum regat intentiusque divinis incumbat. Concedimus insuper animam esse vitarum omnium seminibus gravidam, ideoque posse earum omnium progressiones peragere, eo tamen pacto ut ea semina secundum humanae animae specieique modum in hac ipsa sint anima pullulentque ex illis affectus habitusque ceteris speciebus congrui, numquam tamen fiat vera de specie in speciem transmigratio. Sive enim anima ita comparetur ad corpus, sicut forma propria ad propriam materiam comparatur, sive ut ars propria ad roprium instrumentum, non poterit anima quaelibet corpus quodlibet ingredi. Nam quis audeat dicere lunae formam lapidis formare materiam aut musicam artem figuli instrumenta subire?

3      Merito divinus Iamblichus transmigrationem animae ab homine in bestias reprobavit. Reprobavit Porphyrius etiam circuitum

songs only by Orpheus, Empedocles, and Heraclitus.[64] I leave aside the fact that Pythagoras introduced the transmigrations of souls always into those his customary conversations and symbols.[65] So let us respond to the last [two] academies as follows.

They rest mainly upon twin foundations: upon an argument that is their own and upon Plato's authority. We accept what they set forth concerning the genera of things and the musical composition of the soul, and also their argument's assumption that four species of souls exist. Next, we also grant that our soul is scarcely able to perform both duties together: namely to gaze upon things divine and to rule over bodies, especially bodies less suited [to the soul]. But we do not think that on this account it has to voyage upwards and downwards innumerable times, since it can perform both offices sufficiently well, if, while it lives on earth, it takes care of bodily things at one moment and cultivates itself and God at another; and if, when it hence departs, it rules its vehicle with greater facility and focuses with more intensity upon matters divine. We concede, moreover, that the soul is pregnant with the seeds of every [kind of] life, and so can enact the courses of all these lives, but with this proviso: that in this very soul the seeds exist according to the mode of the human soul and its species, and that from them burgeon the desires and habits consonant with all the other species, and yet that a true transmigration from species to species never occurs. For whether the soul is compared to the body as the proper form is compared to the proper matter, or the proper art to the proper instrument, not just any soul can enter into any body. For who would dare to assert that the form of the moon forms the matter of stone or that the musical art yields to the potter's instruments?

The divine Iamblichus condemned, and justly so, the transmigration of the soul from a man into beasts.[66] Porphyry condemned infinite soul-circuiting too, and conceded that in the human species souls wander only for a fixed number of centuries. He as-

infinitum, atque in specie humana solum certis saeculis pererrare
concessit, ac tandem purgatam hominis animam patri semper haerere caelesti asseveravit, numquam ad huius vitae miseriam[46] redituram, quoniam non posset umquam esse beata, si aut ignoraret se
huc reditura esse, cum esset huc aliquando reversura, aut[47] futura mala praevideret atque metueret. Quod quidem inde confirmatur, quia instabile bonum appetitum implere naturalem nequit, qui aeternum infinitumque proprie et agnoscit et appetit.
Rursus animam infinita potentia, veritate, bonitate fruentem
neque violentia inde divellit, neque fallacia dimovet, neque voluntas ulla divertit. Non voluntas dei, cuius proprium est convertere;
non animae, quae cum nihil eligat umquam nisi ratione boni, non
habet quod extra ipsum eligat, in quo totam boni rationem prorsus agnoscit. Neque mutatio ulla vitae cadit in animam super tempus in aeternitate viventem. Denique dicere animam fine fruentem
inde quandoque seiungi, perinde se habet ac si quis dixerit vel terram ipso centro vel ignem ipsa luna proxime perfruentem vel fer-
rum immensae magnetis moli haerentem inde diverti.

4    His atque similibus, ut arbitror, rationibus commotus Porphyrius erubuit animam centro suo semel infixam temere[48] inde divel-
lere. Proclum quoque Syrianumque et Hermeiam[49] puduit caelestem animam in corpora bestiarum[50] praecipitare, atque ut debita
supplicia immanibus rependerent vitiis, obversari putarunt sacrile-
gas animas inter animas bestiarum, non tamen brutorum corpora
regere, quoniam si bruta evaserit anima, non purgabitur inde, sed
prorsus inficietur.[51] Non enim purgatio fit, nisi ubi regnat quaedam conscientiae reclamatio. Quod praeterea negant animam, nisi

serted that in the end the purged soul of man always clings to its heavenly Father and will never return to the misery of this life, because it could never enjoy happiness if either it did not know it was going to return here (since it was going to have to return here at some point) or if it foresaw and feared future ills.[67] Confirming this is the fact that an inconstant good cannot satisfy the natural appetite which properly recognizes and desires an eternal and infinite good; and again that neither does violence wrench the soul away from enjoying infinite power, truth, and goodness, nor does deception seduce it, and nor does any will separate it — not the will of God whose property is conversion, and not the will of the soul, which, since it never chooses anything except by reason of the good, has nothing to choose outside the good wherein it wholly recognizes the entire rational principle of the good. No alteration of life whatsoever befalls the soul living above time in eternity. Finally, for someone to declare that a soul [already] enjoying its end will be separated from it some day is exactly comparable to saying that earth will be separated from the center of the world, or fire from enjoying its proximity to the moon, or iron from clinging to the mass of a huge magnet.

Persuaded by these and similar reasons, I believe that Porphyry 4 was ashamed rashly to tear away the soul from its center once it had been established there.[68] Proclus and Syrianus[69] and Hermeias too[70] were ashamed to hurl a celestial soul down into the bodies of beasts; and in order to punish monstrous vices with due punishments, they supposed that sacrilegious souls hover over beasts' souls yet do not rule over beasts' bodies, since if a soul has become brutish it will not be purged thereafter but be totally infected. For no purgation occurs except where a sovereign conscience cries out [against the offense]. Elsewhere we have said why we must condemn these Platonists' notion that unless the soul always existed in the past it is not going to exist always in the future;[71] and we will speak of it again. So their arguments do not persuade us to

fuerit semper, non semper esse futuram, quo pacto damnetur, alias diximus et dicemus. Quocirca rationes eorum nobis non persuadent, ut infinitis animarum erroribus ambagibusque et absurdis specierum confusionibus fidem adhibeamus. Sed ne positionem suam auctoritate platonica tueantur, meminisse debemus Platonem pythagoricam sapientiam, quae a Zoroastre manaverat, ab Archyta, Euryto, Philolao didicisse, et cum peragrasset orbem aliasque omnes philosophorum opiniones examinavisset, pythagoricam denique sectam tamquam verisimiliorem prae ceteris elegisse, quam suis litteris illustraret. Propterea Pythagoricos inducit in dialogis suis praecipuis disputantes, Timaeum Locrum, Parmenidem Eleatem[52] atque Zenonem, a quibus Socrates apud Platonem discit, quae in ceteris Platonis dialogis ipse aliis referat.

5     Tria vero prae ceteris signa videntur evidentissima, quibus iudicare possimus eum pythagorica illa nequaquam affirmavisse. Primum, quod eosdem disputantes inducit, qui quondam talia dixerant. Secundum, quod fingit Socratem ambiguum quae audiverat referentem, qui nihil aliud scire se praedicabat quam hoc ipsum quod nihil sciret. Tertium, quod quae de rebus huiusmodi scripserat, non confirmavit in senectute. Siquidem in libris *De legibus*, quos scripsit in senio, in quibus solis ipsa Platonis persona loquitur, nihil asseruit tale. Et in epistola ad regem Dionysium, cum esset admodum senex, inquit nihil se de rebus divinis umquam composuisse neque esse Platonis opus de iis ullum[53] neque umquam fore, quasi non suam mentem aperuerit, sed narraverit alienam. In epistola quoque ad Syracusanos, quam postea scripsit senior, eadem repetivit, ubi adiunxit neminem exstare tunc aut fore in posterum, qui mentem Platonis de huiusmodi rebus intellegat. Merito, quia non scripsit.

put any faith in infinite soul-meanderings and wanderings and in
the absurd confusions of various species.[72] But to guard against
their invoking the authority of Plato for their position,[73] we have
to bear in mind that Plato learned about the Pythagorean wisdom
(which emanated from Zoroaster) from Archytas, Eurytus, and
Philolaus;[74] and that when he had traversed the world and examined all the other opinions held by philosophers, he eventually
chose the Pythagorean school before the rest as being closer to the
truth and the one he would illuminate in his own writings.[75] He
accordingly introduced Pythagoreans as debaters in his principal
dialogues: Timaeus of Locris, Parmenides of Elea, and Zeno,[76]
from whom (in Plato) Socrates learned all that he repeats to others in the rest of Plato's dialogues.

Three pieces of evidence emerge from the rest, however, and    5
seem to be especially prominent, and they enable us to decide that
Plato did not affirm these particular Pythagorean views at all.
First, he introduces those who had formerly affirmed such views as
now debating them. Second, he depicts Socrates as being in doubt
when he reports what he had heard — Socrates who used to pro-
claim that he knew nothing except the fact that he knew nothing.
And third, in old age Plato did not confirm what he had [earlier]
written on such matters. Indeed, in his books on the *Laws*, written
in old age and where alone Plato's persona itself is speaking,[77] he
asserted nothing like this. And in his letter to king Dionysius,
since he was a very old man, he declared that he had never written
anything about matters divine and that no work of Plato existed
on these matters or would ever exist;[78] it is as if he were not revealing his own mind but talking about another mind. In his letter
to the Syracusans too, which he wrote subsequently when he was
even older still, he repeated the same sentiments; and he added
that there was nobody then existing or who would exist in the future who might understand his views on such matters — and justly
so, since he did not write them down.[79]

6    Num ergo nihil de divinis affirmat Plato? Quaedam proculdubio: deum scilicet humana curare atque animae immortali operum praemia reddere vel supplicia. Aliud vero affirmat nihil. Paucula enim haec non in aliis modo dialogis asserit, in quibus aliae personae loquuntur, verum etiam in *Legibus* et[54] *Epistolis*, ubi loquitur ipse. Mundum semper fuisse non asserit, sed ipsum generat in *Timaeo*; generat, inquam, ab initio temporis ordinati, eadem ferme ratione qua primum Moyses, deinde Mercurius, ut exposuerunt Severus, Atticus, Plutarchus et alii multi Platonicorum. Hinc Numenius pythagoricus exclamavit: 'Nihil aliud esse Platonem quam Moysen attica voce loquentem,' quamvis Plotinus, Porphyrius, Iamblichus, Proculus perpetuam mundi generationem ibi a Platone accipi velint. Quod si forte illud ita exponendum est, Timaei pythagorici sententia erit potius quam Platonis, siquidem Plato ipse in *Epinomide* inquit astra aut immortalia fore aut alio[55] longeva ut vita sua illis sufficiat atque longiore non egeant. Id illi consonat in *Timaeo*, videlicet astra per se dissolubilia fore, quia videlicet ab initio composita sunt, nisi componentis voluntate serventur. Rursus in libro sexto *Legum*[56] inquit humanum genus aut fuisse semper aut multis ante saeculis ortum, ubi videtur initium quam aeternitatem eligere maluisse. Aristoteles quoque ubi de quaestionum natura disputat, inquit quaestionem de aeternitate mundi esse neutram, quasi dicat non tam sententiam demonstrabilem quam opinionem quodammodo ad utrumque probabilem. Animas autem Plato in *Legibus* esse ante corpora ita fortasse vult ut naturae dignitati id potius quam tempori tribuatur. Quamquam per ali-

Does Plato affirm nothing then about matters divine? Without 6
a doubt he affirms a few truths: that God cares for human affairs,
and rewards and punishes the immortal soul for its works. But he
maintains nothing else. And these few assertions he gives us not
only in the other dialogues where other characters are speaking
but also in the *Laws* and the *Letters* where he is speaking himself.
He does not declare that the world has always existed, but in the
*Timaeus* he generates it,[80] generates it, I say, from the start of an
appointed [or ordered] time for almost the same reason as first
Moses and then Hermes Trismegistus[81] had [also] generated it.
Severus, Atticus, Plutarch and many other Platonists have explained this[82] — hence Numenius the Pythagorean exclaimed that
Plato was nothing other than Moses speaking Attic Greek[83] — although Plotinus, Porphyry, Iamblichus, and Proclus maintained
that in the *Timaeus* Plato accepts that the generation of the world
is perpetual.[84] If it is perhaps to be so interpreted, then this will be
the view of Timaeus, the Pythagorean,[85] rather than that of Plato,
since in the *Epinomis* Plato says himself that the stars are either going to be immortal or for a different purpose long-lived: that their
[one] life might suffice for them without their needing a longer
one.[86] This accords with the passage in the *Timaeus* that declares
that the stars, because they are compounded from the onset, are in
themselves dissolvable, unless they are saved by the will of the
compounder.[87] Again, in book six of the *Laws*, Plato says that the
human race either always existed or arose many centuries earlier;
and he seems to have preferred opting here for its having a beginning rather than for eternity.[88] Aristotle too, when he is discussing
the nature of questions, says that the question of the world's eternity is moot: it is as if he were voicing not so much a demonstra-
ble view as an opinion that makes either choice in a way plausi-
ble.[89] But in the *Laws* Plato wants souls to be prior to bodies but
only perchance insofar as this is being granted to their natural dig-

quam temporis morulam animas antecedere corpora etiam Christianorum aliqui opinantur.

7    Animas hominum transire in bestias in *Legibus* non confirmat. In nono autem libro inquit secundum fabulas sacerdotum ire eas in alios homines, et in septimo declarat, quomodo exponendum sit, si quando dicantur corporibus aliis se inserere. Ubi tradit eum, qui 'necessarias doctrinas' ignoret,[57] numquam fore 'inter alios homines,' deum aut daemonem aut heroem, quasi per comparationem ad alios homines et haec dicantur et illa, quae nonnumquam de ferinis corporibus fabulatur, quamquam in *Phaedro* non dicit animam hominis in bestiae corpus transire, sed in ferinam vitam, et in *Timaeo* in naturam ferinam, non in corpus ferae. In ultimo *De republica* Thersitae animam non in simiae corpus, sed in simiam. In quibus intellegitur habitus vitaeque potius quam speciei vel corporis permutatio.

8    Praeterea in *Phaedone*, postquam narravit poetarum more transitum animarum in beluas propter supplicia peccatorum, subiunxit non esse prudentis viri talia confirmare, sed id solum asseverari posse prudenter, quod poenas aliquas pendunt flagitiorum. Addit purgatas per legitimam philosophiam animas apud deum in aeternum sine corporibus esse victuras. Quod quidem in *Epinomide* confirmat, dicens pium animum a corpore separatum reliquum tempus in rerum omnium pulcherrimarum contemplatione versari. In *Gorgia* quoque et *Theaeteto* et decimo libro *De iusto* perpetua describit supplicia impiorum ob multa peccata quae expiari

nity rather than to time,[90] though some Christians also think that souls precede bodies for just a short span of time.[91]

In the *Laws* Plato does not assert that men's souls cross over   7 into beasts. But in its ninth book he says that, according to the priests' fables, they do cross over into other men;[92] and in the seventh book he declares how any declaration that they insert themselves into other bodies must be interpreted. For there he says that the person who ignores the "necessary doctrines" will never be "among other men" a god, demon, or hero,[93] as though this were being said by way of comparison with other men. And the same goes for the tales Plato sometimes invents about the bodies of beasts, though in the *Phaedrus* he does not say that a man's soul crosses over into a beast's body but into a beastly life;[94] and in the *Timaeus* he says that it crosses over into a beastly nature but not into a beast's body.[95] In the last book of the *Republic* the soul of Thersites crosses over, not into the body of an ape, but into an ape.[96] In such instances one understands Plato to mean a change of habit and life rather than of species or body.

Moreover, in the *Phaedo*, after he had recounted, in the manner   8 of the poets, the crossing over of souls into beasts as a punishment for their sins,[97] he added that a prudent man should not encourage such stories, but that one can assert with prudence only that men pay certain penalties for their offences.[98] Plato adds that souls purged by way of lawful philosophy are going to live with God for eternity without bodies.[99] He confirms this in the *Epinomis* when he declares that a righteous thinking soul separated from the body will spend the rest of time in the contemplation of the most beautiful of all things.[100] In the *Gorgias* too and the *Theaetetus* and in the tenth book of *On Justice* [i.e. the *Republic*], Plato describes the punishments of the unrighteous for the many sins that they cannot expiate.[101] He also asserts [in the former] that such punishments have been instituted for the sake of justice and as an example rather than a cure;[102] and [in the latter] he condemns those

non possint, taliaque supplicia iustitiae exemplique potius quam curationis gratia fuisse asserit instituta, ubi reprobat errores illos inexplicabiles animarum. Per haec patet Platonem Christianorum more sempiternum bonum malumve significavisse. Quod vero purgatorium appellant Christiani, ibi Platonem intellexisse, ubi purgaturus animam saepius per inferiora revolvit, videlicet non tam per corpora quam per vitas et commercia bestiarum; denique purgatam caelo restituit. In libro nono *De iusto* figurat hominis animam hunc in modum: est aliqua congeries capitum plurium beluarum quasi in globum coacta ferinum. Ex hac multiplici capitum ferinorum congerie pullulat quasi stipes aliquis ex radicibus, qui stipes hinc leo est, inde draco. Huic stipiti homo aliquis superponitur[58] clavam manu tenens, qua bestias verberat saevientes. Demum corporis humani pellis omnia illa circumdat, per quam animal unum videatur esse, quod est multiplex animal. Congeriem plurium bestiarum esse vult insatiabilem concupiscentiae partem, stipitem leone et dracone compositum iracundiae vim. Quae leo dicitur, cum suffragatur rationi, draco cum refragatur. Homo est ratio.

9      Post haec iubet Plato, ut interiorem illum hominem nutriamus potius quam bestias illas, ne propter famem, deficiente homine, solae in nobis supersint bestiae. Per haec admonemur ut transitum animarum accipiamus non in varias species, sed in habitus. Erit itaque arbor apud Platonem qui nutritioni deditus die nocteque torpebit; milvus qui raptu vivet per concupiscentiam; leo qui egregie militabit; draco qui crudeliter in genus hominum saeviet; homo qui ratione civili vivet; heros qui naturalia perscrutabitur; daemon qui mathematica; angelus qui divina. Talis enim

labyrinthine wanderings of souls.[103] It is obvious from this that Plato, in the manner of Christians, has signified everlasting good and evil. What Christians call Purgatory, however, Plato understood to mean the place where the person awaiting purgation takes [his] soul and time and again leads it on a circle through lower things, that is, through not so much the bodies as the lives of beasts and their dealings. [104] Finally after purgation he restores it to heaven.[105] In the ninth book of *On Justice* Plato depicts man's soul in the following way. It is an assemblage of many heads of monsters arranged in a sort of ring of wild beasts; and from this manifold conglomeration of monstrous heads there bursts, from roots as it were, a sort of tree-trunk, a lion on one side, a dragon on the other.[106] On top of this trunk is a man holding a knotty cudgel in his hand, which he uses to thrash the raging beasts.[107] Finally the skin of a human body envelops all these beasts and makes what is a manifold animal look like just one animal. Plato wants the conglomeration of many beasts to be the insatiable part of concupiscence and the trunk compounded from a lion and dragon to be the force of irascibility,[108] a force that is called a lion when it supports the reason but a dragon when it rebels against it. The man is the reason.

After this Plato tells us to nurture the inner man rather than   9 the beasts, lest, if this man grow weak from hunger, the beasts alone survive in us.[109] We are thereby warned to interpret the crossing over of souls as being not into various species but into [various] habits.[110] So in Plato there is going to be: a tree which, given over to nourishing will remain rooted day and night without motion; a kite[111] which will live by seizing hold of things through desire; a lion which will wage war with noble ire; a dragon which will cruelly torment mankind; a man who will live the life of sociable reason; a hero who will examine things in nature; a demon who will study mathematics; and an angel who will contemplate

fit animus, qualem induitur habitum. Talis, inquam, in corpore, talis et extra corpus.

10 Eadem in *Phaedro* Socrates comprobat dicens: 'Ego itaque considero, utrum ipse sim bestia Thyphone multiplicior, sive divinius animal.' Et postea in libro eodem in anima aurigam ponit et geminos equos, bonum atque malum, rationem scilicet irascendique et concupiscendi potentiam. Ubi apparet in ipsis animae viribus et hominem et beluas esse. Eodem modo Parmenides pythagoreus in libro de natura animam figuraverat. Timaeus quoque pythagoreus nobilissimus migrationem in bestias inquit induci falso ad terrorem hominum impiorum. Sed rem omnem ita Pythagoras ipse significavit:

Ἢν δ' ἀπολείψας σῶμα ἐς αἰθέρ' ἐλεύθερον ἔλθῃς
Ἔσσεαι ἀθάνατος θεός, ἄμβροτος οὐκ ἔτι θνητός.

Id est: 'Si deposito corpore liberum ascenderis aetherem, eris immortalis deus, immortalis, non ultra mortalis.' Quasi dicat ita deus immortalis efficieris, ut omnino futurus sis procul a morte, nunquam amplius ad mortalia reversurus. Orpheus quoque in ipso Mercurii terrestris hymno de Mercurio inquit:

Κωκύτου ναίων ἀνυπόστροφον οἶμον ἀνάγκης.

Id est: 'Cocyti habitans irremeabilem viam necessitatis.' In iis verbis poenas apud inferos ponit aeternas regressumque illum multiplicem a vita in vitam penitus aufert.

11 Sed neque etiam omnes Aegyptii sacerdotes transitus animarum de specie in speciem fieri revera existimant. Immo vero de ferino vel heroico animae habitu intellegi volunt, quando hominem fieri bestiam aut heroem asserunt, quoniam apud eos homo solus est animus. Quod aperuit Mercurius, Aegyptiorum pontifex maximus, qui cum talem quandam migrationem ritu poetico descripsisset, adiunxit legem divinam non permittere migrationem animorum nostrorum in corpora beluaram. Poenas quoque sempiternas

matters divine. For the rational soul becomes the habit it dons; for whatever it is in the body such it will be outside the body.

Socrates introduces the same notion in the *Phaedrus* when he 10 says, "I will therefore consider whether I am a beast more manifold than Typhon or an animal more divine."[112] And later in the same book he postulates in the soul a charioteer and twin horses, a good and a bad, that is, the reason and the powers of wrathful passion and of appetitive desire;[113] and from this it appears that in the soul's very powers beasts exist and a man exists. Parmenides, the Pythagorean, depicts the soul in the same way in his book on nature.[114] Timaeus too, a particularly distinguished Pythagorean, says that transmigration into beasts is introduced (but falsely) in order to terrify unrighteous men.[115] But Pythagoras himself signified all this when he declared, "If you ascend into the boundless aether, having left the body behind, you will be an immortal god, immortal and mortal no more."[116] It is as if he were saying that you will so fashion yourself into an immortal god that you will become totally removed from death and never more return to mortal things. Orpheus too, in his hymn to the terrestrial Mercury, says of Mercury: "He dwells on the way of necessity, the way of Cocytus from which there is no return."[117] With these words Orpheus affirms the eternity of punishment among those in the lower world and eliminates entirely that manifold returning from life to life.

Not even all the Egyptian priests, however, suppose that the 11 migration of souls from species to species really occurs. Rather, when they assert that a man becomes a beast or a hero, they intend it to be understood that a habit of soul becomes bestial or heroic, because with them a man is the rational soul alone. Mercurius [Trismegistus], the greatest high-priest of the Egyptians, revealed this. Since he had described such a migration of the soul poetically, he added that the divine law does not allow our souls to migrate into the bodies of beasts.[118] He also assigns ev-

tribuit impiis animis in mundi huius infimis elementis, atque manifeste asserit impiorum animas aeterno supplicio per immortalem
sententiam subiugari. Agit quoque deo gratias, quod bonos viros
aeternitati consecraverit. Item[59] dicit mentem usque adeo coniungi
deo ut numquam ulterius implicetur erroribus. Denique Zoroaster, priscae illius inventor theologiae, sic inquit:

Σὸν γὰρ ἀγγεῖον θῆρες χθονὸς οἰκήσουσιν.

Id est: 'Tuum vas bestiae terrae habitant.' Quod si intra nos
bestiae sunt, intra quoque, non extra, de homine in bestiam ac de
bestia transimus in bestiam.

12    Neque desunt qui transmigrationem in bestias sic exponant ut
animarum, quae brutis similem duxerunt vitam, aliae inter alias
bestiarum turbas versentur. Quod quidem Platoni admodum consentaneum Olympiodorus iudicat, propterea quod Plato animas
purgatissimas inter deos versari censueri; impuras autem saepe inter sepulcra revolvi, quarum umbris perterreri aliquando soleamus,[60] quippe cum corporei nonnihil circa se, sicut et in se traxerint. Quo fieri Plato vult, ut videri quandoque possint.

13    Simile huic est, quod scribit iunior Plinius, infamem Athenis
fuisse domum, in qua et strepitus audiebatur et simulacrum horridi senis aspiciebatur, atque Athenodorum Tarsensem philosophum conducta domo vidisse simulacrum illud, eoque duce comperisse in area domus sub terra ossa inserta catenis. Ea sicut mos
erat sepelisse. Domum deinde illam eo strepitu liberatam. Subdit
se pluribus haec affirmantibus credere. Nihil igitur mirum est impuras animas, si inter haec, similiter quoque inter bruta versari.

14    Ex omnibus iis concludimus Platonem ea solum de rebus divinis affirmavisse, quae in *Epistolis* ac *Legibus* comprobavit. In iis au-

erlasting punishments in this world's lowest elements to impious souls; and he clearly asserts that the souls of impious men are subjected to eternal punishment by way of an eternal sentence.[119] He also thanks God for having consecrated good men to eternity.[120] Again, Mercurius says that the mind is joined to God to such an extent that it is never further entangled in errors.[121] Finally, Zoroaster, the inventor of that ancient theology, declares, "The beasts of the earth inhabit the vessel of your [body]."[122] But if the beasts are within us, then we cross over from man to beast and from beast to beast inside ourselves too, not outside.

There are those too who interpret transmigration into beasts to   12 mean that of the souls who have led a beast-like life various ones dwell among various herds of beasts. Olympiodorus maintains that this is fully consonant with Plato's meaning in that Plato believed that souls who have been completely purged dwell among the gods, whereas impure souls often haunt graves; and that we are customarily terrified on occasions by their shadows, since, just as they drag something of the corporeal around themselves, so do they drag it into themselves.[123] This is why Plato supposes that they can be seen at times.[124]

What Pliny the Younger writes is similar to this.[125] He says   13 that there was an infamous house in Athens; and in it one heard a clanking din and saw the specter of a frightening old man. Having rented the house, Athenodorus of Tarsus, the philosopher, saw the specter, and was led by it to discover, in a courtyard of the house, some bones shackled in chains under the earth. As was the custom he gave them proper burial. Thereafter the home was free of that din. He adds that he believed the story himself since many had affirmed it was true. If impure souls are found in these circumstances, it is not surprising therefore that they are also likewise found among brutes.

We conclude from all this evidence that Plato only affirmed   14 facts about matters divine that he sanctioned in the *Letters* and the

tem circuitus animarum infiniti non approbantur atque ea, quae solum in ceteris tamquam priscorum inventa recensuit, probabilia potius habuisse quam certa. Ac si quis ea etiam Platonem affirmavisse contenderit, nos quoque affirmare forsitan disputationis gratia concedemus, verum longe aliter quam verba designent, exponenda esse censebimus, quemadmodum declaratum est paulo ante tum Platonis verbis tum theologorum veterum testimoniis.

*Laws.* But in these works the infinite circuits of souls are not approved and the things that he reviewed only in the remaining dialogues as inventions of the ancients he held as being probable rather than certain. And if anyone contends that Plato also affirmed them, we too will concede that perhaps for the sake of discussion he did affirm them. Nonetheless, we shall maintain the opinion that they have to be explained in a sense far different from their literal one, as we declared a little earlier with reference both to Plato's words and to the testimonies of the ancient theologians.

# LIBER DUODEVICESIMUS[1]

: I :

*Quod Plato non prohibet fidem adhibere theologiae*
*Hebraeorum, Christianorum Arabumque communi,*
*scilicet mundum fuisse creatum.*[2]

1　Plato igitur nihil prohibere videtur fidem adhibere theologiae Hebraeorum, Christianorum Arabumque communi, coepisse mundum quandoque, angelos ab initio creatos, animas[3] hominum im-
mortales creari quotidie. Ad haec cogimur auctoritate divina; ad
haec rationibus huiusmodi ducimur.

2　　Mundi moles per se esse non potest, ita ut non pendeat
aliunde, sed in esse se suo stabiliat, alioquin se ipsam quodammodo faceret. Facere autem aliquid non ad corpus pertinet, quod,
quicquid agere videtur, per virtutem quandam exsequitur incorpoream in subiecto iacentem, immo ad essentiam ipsam spectat, penitus incorpoream, in se ipsa manentem virtutisque illius originem. Praeterea corporea moles se ipsam continere non potest,
siquidem continere nisi aliquid agendo nequit, praesertim cum
continere sine unione non valeat. Unire autem non ad naturam divisibilem, quae et ipsa indiget unione, sed ad vim tandem penitus
individuam spectare videtur. Rursus moles eadem per se operari
moverique non potest, quia si nequit sibi esse dare, multo minus
praestare poterit actionem. Ac vicissim si posset se ipsam agere,
posset etiam agere per se ipsam. Quod autem per se operari non
valeat, hinc etiam patet quod se movere non potest, ut in libro

# BOOK XVIII

## : I :

*That Plato does not forbid us putting our trust in the theology*
*that is common to the Hebrews, Christians, and Arabs,*
*namely that the world was created.*

It seems, therefore, that Plato does not forbid us putting our trust  1
in the theology common to the Hebrews, Christians, and Arabs,
the theology that the world began at a certain moment, that angels
were created from the beginning, and that men's souls are daily
created immortal. We are compelled to acknowledge these truths
by divine authority, and we are led to them for the following reasons.

The world's mass cannot exist of itself such that it does not de-  2
pend on another and establish itself in its own being; otherwise it
would in a way make itself. But to make something does not pertain to body, which does whatever it seems to do [only] through
an incorporeal power lying in it as substrate; rather it pertains to
essence itself, which is entirely incorporeal, abides in itself, and is
the origin of that power. A corporeal mass moreover cannot contain itself, since it cannot contain except by doing something, especially since it cannot contain without union. But to unite seems
to pertain, not to the divisible nature that is itself also in need of
union, but to a power finally that is entirely undivided. Again, the
same mass cannot act and be moved through itself, because, if it
cannot give itself being, still less can it provide action. Alternatively, if it can act upon itself it can also act through itself. But the
fact that it cannot act through itself makes it obvious too that it
cannot move itself, as we proved in the sixth book.[1] Elsewhere we

sexto probavimus. Ostendimus insuper alibi perpetuo ordinatissimoque mundi motui virtute infinita opus esse, quam finita determinataque natura corporis ex se habere non potest. Ideoque[4] mundus tamquam ex se erraticus dissolubilisque aliunde indissolubilem ordinem mutuatur. Sed undenam mutuatur?

3    Profecto si mundus neque per se subsistere, neque se continere, neque per se agere moverive[5] potest, necessario a causa per se existente seque continente dependet; causa, inquam, prorsus indivisibili,[6] ne illa similiter vel sit per aliud, scilicet per partes partiumve congregatorem, vel contineatur ab alio, scilicet ab unitate partes invicem connectente, vel sit insufficiens, cum partibus egeat, vel admixtum habeat non esse, cum compositum ex partibus nulla sit partium. Proinde cum mundus ex dissimilibus sit compositus, oportet compositionis huiusmodi causam perscrutari. Non enim se ipsum componit corpus, quod neque actionis neque unionis principium est. Neque dicendum est partes mundi suo quodam motu in compositionem huiusmodi confluxisse; non enim corpora per se moventur. Neque tamquam ad id et aliunde compulsas et invicem compellentes. Quid enim est quod impellit? Et quid impellit primo? Rursus nefas est impulsionibus carentibus ordine ordinem committere tam mirandum. Quonam pacto ex inordinatis inornatisque ordo tantus et ornatus efficitur, quippe cum soleat semper agens causa effectu esse praestantior. Praeterea si mundi partes esse compositionis huius materiales dixeris causas, de causa efficiente quaeremus. Sin autem efficientes, iterum perquiremus quonam pacto ex rebus ratione carentibus rationale opus efficiatur.

showed, moreover, that an infinite power is required for the perpetual and supremely ordered motion of the world,[2] a power that the finite and determined nature of body cannot possess of itself. And so the world, being in itself erratic and dissoluble, borrows an indissoluble order from another source. But from where does it borrow it?

If the world can neither subsist through itself nor contain itself 3 nor act or be moved through itself, it necessarily depends on a cause that does exist through itself and does contain itself. This cause is entirely indivisible, otherwise either it similarly exists through another, that is, exists through parts or through something assembling parts; or it is contained by another, that is, by the unity connecting the parts in turn; or else it is insufficient, since it needs parts; or it has non-being mixed in with it, since a compound made from parts is not itself one of those parts. Therefore, since the world is compounded from things unlike, we must examine the cause of such compounding. For body does not compound itself, since it is the principle neither of action nor of union. We cannot say that the world's parts have flowed together into this compound by their own particular motion, for bodies are not moved through themselves; nor can we say that the parts have been forced as it were from another source into this compound and are in turn forcing themselves. For what is it that impels them? And what first impels them? Again, it is sacrilegious to assign such a marvelous order to the impulses of things lacking order. For how can such an order and design be made from things lacking order and design, seeing that the agent cause is usually always more outstanding than the effect. Besides, if you assert that the world's parts are the material causes of this compound, we will enquire about the efficient cause. But if the parts are not the efficient causes, we will ask yet again how a rational work can be made out of things lacking reason. So, if the world is compounded

Quapropter si mundus neque ex se, neque casu compositus est, certe compositionis causam habet certam.

4     Neque afferat quispiam solam habere finalem causam. Habet enim eam, cum ad bonum tamquam ad finem recte feratur; cum vero ad id frustra non moveatur, aliquid certe boni ab illo consequitur. Accipit autem secundum essentiam, quandoquidem secundum essentiam appetit atque movetur. Igitur ab eodem accipit esse, a quo essentialem accipit bonitatem. Itaque causa illa tam efficiens est quam finis. Est et exemplar. Si enim mundus certa ratione fertur ad bonum, certe deus illum certa ratione tamquam exemplari ad bonum [illum][7] continue dirigit. At vero cum ad finem ducere bonumque petere sit voluntatis officium, nimirum deus voluntate movet mundum, quem similiter et voluntate composuit.

5     Idem ita insuper confirmatur. Quod fortuitum et contingens dicitur solet eo quod ordinatum est[8] determinatisve constat causis, posterius esse. Igitur non potest ordo mundi priore casu aliquo contigisse. Ac si multas mundanorum effectuum causas aliquis afferat, nisi omnes sub una conciliet, non poterit quam ob causam mundus, licet ex diversis constet, sit et unus et unitus afferre, et qua ratione unum totum sit melius partibus multis, nisi unam inveniat causam et communem et praestantiorem causis multis, cuius virtute omnes in unum congrediantur. Quamobrem una est universi unionisque ipsius causa, ad quam coordinata sunt omnia. Si haec esset rationis expers, homines qui ratione utuntur seque ipsos cognoscunt prima causa praestantiores essent atque opus humanum opere divino perfectius redderetur. Igitur deus infinitam

neither from itself nor by chance, certainly it has a definite cause for [its] being compounded.

Nor should someone argue that it has a final cause only. Certainly it has one, since it is rightly borne towards the good as to its end; but since it cannot be moved towards the good in vain, it certainly takes something of the good from the good. But it accepts the good in accord with its essence, since it desires and is moved in accord with its essence. Therefore it receives its being from the same source it receives essential goodness. So that cause [i.e. the good] is the efficient cause even as it is the end. It is also the exemplar. For, if the world is borne towards the good for a definite reason, certainly God directs it as by an exemplar continually and for a definite reason towards the good. But since to lead to the end and to seek the good is the office of the will, certainly God moves the world by [His] will, the world He has likewise framed by [His] will.

The same argument is also confirmed by the following. What is said to be fortuitous and contingent is customarily posterior to that which has been ordered or is established from determined causes. So the world's order cannot have been contingent on some prior chance. And were someone to introduce many causes of the world's effects, he could not explain, unless he were to unite them all under one cause, why the world, though constituted from diverse parts, is both one and united. Nor could he explain, unless he were to find a cause that is both common to and more outstanding than the many causes, a cause whose power unites them all, why the one whole is better than the many parts. So the cause of this universe and of this union is one, and all things are coordinated to it. If this cause were without reason, men who do use reason and who know themselves would be more outstanding than the prime cause, and a human product would appear to be more perfect than a work divine. So God knows by way of reason that His infinite goodness is multipliable through all things. Hence

bonitatem suam rationaliter novit per omnia propagabilem, unde placuit sua sibi bonitas per singula propaganda, quippe cum boni proprium sit ut placeat, ac summi boni ut summopere placeat. Quo quidem rationalis voluntatis affectu rationaliter atque optime omnia tum procreata sunt, tum continue disponuntur.

6  Ratione voluntateque divina disponi mundum in oraculis Chaldaeorum, quae recitat Proclus, iis verbis significatur. 'Intellectus patris emanans perfecto consilio ideas omniformes intellegit, quae quidem ab uno fonte omnes prodierunt. A patre enim erat voluntasque finisque. Distributae vero sunt intellectuali quodam igne, atque in alias quasdam intellectuales deinde divisae. Rex enim multiformi mundo intellectualem figuram indeficientem praeposuit, cuius secundus mundus est vestigium, properans una cum forma, et mundus apparens omniformibus dotatus ideis. Fons unus, ex quo erumpunt divisae aliae innumerabiles, circa mundi corpora producentes, quae circuitu quodam rite assimilatae ferantur, undique conversae. Sed alibi aliae intellegentiae a fonte paterno, tamquam ab igne scintillae pervigili, circa primordiales ideas. Prima enim a patre idea effluxit atque fons voluntarius.' Hactenus oraculum, in quo de Patre, Filio, Spiritu, ideis, angelis, dispositione voluntaria mundi mentio fit. Sed nos iam ad institutum ordinem revertamur.

7  Elementa et plantae quicquid agunt necessaria quadam naturae suae operantur affectione. Ea una est dumtaxat. Unum igitur quiddam quaelibet operantur. Bruta praeterea operantur per appetitum, qui prout modis per sensum variis lacessitur, aggreditur varia, et sicut elementa et plantae innata necessitate agunt, ita bruta necessitate operantur illata. Rationalis anima per voluntatem agit quae quidem ad opus movetur, non a rerum formis, ut appetitus,

multiplying His goodness through individuals has been pleasing to Him, since to please is the property of the good, and to please to the highest degree, of the highest good. By the desire of [God's] rational will all things are both procreated and continually arranged in a rational way and in the best way.

That the world has been arranged by the divine reason and will  6 is signified in the oracles of the Chaldaeans (which Proclus cites) with these words: "The intellect of the Father emanating as it does from perfect counsel understands the omniform ideas, which all issue from one fountain; for the will and the end are from the Father. But He has distributed them with a certain intellectual fire and then divided them into various particular intellectual [ideas]. For the King has instituted an intellectual, never failing figure [or model] prior to the multiform world, and the second world is a mere trace of it hurrying along after that form; and He has endowed this apparent world with the omniform ideas. The fountain is one and from it the various divided [ideas] burst forth beyond number, rippling out around the world's bodies, which, having been duly made to resemble [the ideas] and everywhere turned back towards them, are borne around in a circuit. But elsewhere other intelligences from the paternal fountain, like sparks from an ever-watchful fire, are borne around the primordial ideas. For the prime idea flowed from the Father and [is] the fountain of His will."³ Thus far runs the oracle wherein mention is made of the Father, the Son, the Spirit, ideas, angels and the voluntary disposition of the world. But let us now return to our established plan.

Whatever the elements and plants do they do by a necessary in-  7 clination of their own nature; and this inclination is singular, so they all do one something. The beasts operate through the appetite besides, which, being provoked in various ways through sensation, undertakes various things; and just as the elements and the plants act by an inborn necessity, so do the brutes act by an im-

sed a notionibus et consiliis intellectus. Haec libera operatio est merito perfectiori conveniens animali. Talis quaedam prae ceteris esse debet operatio dei. Quapropter Plato in *Timaeo* inquit voluntatem dei beneficam originem rerum certissimam extitisse. Mercurius quoque mundum divina voluntate constare, quam cuncti comitentur effectus. Orpheus ubi de summo Iove loquitur, sic inquit:

Πάντα γὰρ κρύψας, αὖθις φάος ἐς πολυγηθές
Ἐξ ἱερῆς κραδίης ἀνονέγκατο μίμερα ῥέξων.

Id est: 'Cum abscondisset omnia, deinceps in lumen gratum emisit, ex sacro corde operans cogitata et mirabilia.' In iis verbis Orpheus aperte declarat mundum a voluntate divina initium temporis habuisse.

8    Natura et appetitio numquam opus aliquod novum aggrediuntur, nisi quando natura varie afficitur, et appetitio varie lacessitur. Intellectus autem atque voluntas etiam in homine novum opus incohant saepe absque propria novitate. Mane statuit Plato vespere accersire Xenocratem.[9] Stat futurae vocationis firma sententia, donec ea hora Xenocratem vocet. Mutatio quidem fit non in mente et voluntate, sed ore Platonis membrisque Xenocratis. Erat semper in mundi architecto machina mundana praescripta, ac momentum incohationis eius in architecti voluntate signatum. Eo ipso momento quod praesignaverat, incohata est machina, nulla intercedente dei mutatione. Compleverat ab aevo deus substantialem mundum intra se totum. Permisit umbratilem mundum inde tunc emanare, quando fuit melius. Melius fuit, quando statuit bonitatis

posed necessity. The rational soul acts through the will that is moved to do something, not by the forms of things as the appetite is moved, but by the notions and judgments of the intellect. This free activity is justly appropriate to a more perfect animal; and such an activity before all others has to be God's. Wherefore in the *Timaeus* Plato says that God's beneficent will was the most certain origin of things;[4] and Mercurius [Trismegistus] also [says] that the world is made by the divine will and that all effects accompany this will.[5] When he speaks of highest Jupiter, Orpheus writes, "Though he had hidden all things, he finally released them into the light that gladdens us, out of his sacred heart performing the marvelous things he had thought about."[6] In these words Orpheus openly declares that the world had a temporal beginning by divine will.

Nature and desire never undertake some new work except   8 when nature is variously affected and desire variously stimulated. But even in a man the intellect and the will often begin some new work without novelty being their property. In the morning Plato decided to send for Xenocrates in the evening. The decision to summon him in the future stays firm until the hour he summons Xenocrates. A change occurs not in the mind or the will but in Plato's mouth and Xenocrates' limbs. The world machine had always been inscribed beforehand in the architect of the world, and the moment of its inchoation was signified in the architect's will. At the very moment God had signified earlier the machine began, without God changing in the interim. God had perfected the substantial world wholly in Himself from eternity. He then permitted the shadowy world to emanate from it when it was better to do so. It was better when the will of the divine goodness decided it was so, and through this will all things are good. We wish for things (if only we did) because they are good. But these things are good for the reason that God wills them. And they are only good in the manner and at the moment that corresponds to how He wishes

divinae voluntas, per quam bona sunt omnia. Nos siquidem res, quia bonae sunt, volumus. Hae vero ideo bonae sunt, quia vult eas deus. Et quo pacto esse et quando vult fieri, eo solum pacto et momento sunt bonae. Similiter ideo res intellegimus vere, quoniam ita ut revera sunt intellegimus. Contra vero ita revera sunt ideo, quoniam eas ita deus intellegit. Sic ergo a divina intellegentia rerum veritas, a divina voluntate rerum bonitas proficiscitur. Ubi causa prima rerum, ibi ratio rerum summa. Quapropter ita rationaliter debebant fieri ut intellegebat deus atque videbat. Temporaliter, id est ab initio temporis, emanare ab ipso debere deus intellegebat atque volebat hanc umbram, cuius natura in motu temporeque versatur. Et umbrae mundanae motus ab initio temporali ad finem produci debebat et debet, cuius tempus momentis singulis in principio simul est atque fine.

9     Neque perquirendum est cur illo momento potius quam priori inceperit inde hic mundus effluere,[10] nam si mille annis ante incepisset, etiam quaeremus cur non prius. Initium tamen aliquando habere debebat. Adde quod phantasiae est ista fallacia. Non sunt ante primum mundi momentum ulla temporis momenta, quibus ante creari debuerit. Quicquid cogitatur ante mundum, unicum et stabile est aeternitatis punctum. Omnis momentorum temporalium discursio[11] cum mundo coepit, mundo currente. Similiter neque investigandum est, quamobrem hic potius quam illic situs sit mundus. Phantasiae est ista fallacia. Non est corporalis locus extra mundum. Tempus totum cursum totum mundi metitur; totus corporalis locus mundi amplitudine prorsus impletur. Atque, ut *Timaeus* Platonis ostendit, par tempus est cursui, locus aequalis est amplitudini. Fallitur qui corporeum locum cogitat extra mundum; fallitur qui ante mundum tempora fingit; falletur et qui cre-

them to be so and when He wishes them to become so. Similarly, we truly understand things only because we understand them as they truly are. Contrariwise, they truly are the way they are only because God understands them thus. So the truth of things comes from the divine understanding, the goodness of things from the divine will. Where you have the first cause of things, there you have their highest rational principle. So things had to come to be just as God understood and saw them, namely in a rational manner. God understood that they had to emanate from Himself in a temporal manner, that is, from the beginning of time; and He willed this shadow whose nature is situated in motion and time. And the motion of the world-shadow had to, and it still has to, be extended from the beginning of time to the end; and its time in the beginning and end alike consists of single moments.

There is no point asking why this world began to flow forth at 9 the moment it did rather than at an earlier moment, for had it begun a thousand years beforehand we would still ask why not earlier. But it had to have a beginning at some time. Moreover this is a trick of the phantasy. Prior to the world's first moment there were no other prior moments of time in which it should have been created. Whatever one thinks about as being before the world is a unique and unchanging point of eternity. The course of temporal moments all began with the world—when the world began its course. Likewise there is no point enquiring why the world is situated here rather than there. This [too] is a trick of the phantasy; for there is no corporeal location outside the world. The whole of time measures the whole course of the world; the whole of corporeal space is filled totally by the amplitude of the world. As Plato's *Timaeus* shows, time is equal to that course, space equal to that amplitude.[7] The person who thinks about corporeal space outside of the world is deceived; and he who imagines moments of time prior to the world is deceived. And he who believes that something can be added to, or subtracted from, divine perfection (de-

diderit divinae perfectioni accedere aliquid vel decedere, manante illinc[12] mundo vel non manante. Qui multo minus est ad deum quam ad corpus sit corporis umbra; corpori autem ex umbra neque accedit aliquid umquam neque decedit.

10    Profecto spiritalis ille mundus, mundi huius exemplar primumque dei opus, vita aequalis est architecto. Fuit semper cum illo eritque semper. Mundus autem corporalis, quod secundum est opus dei, discedit iam ab opifice ex parte una, quia non fuit semper. Retinet alteram, quia sit semper futurus. Composita vero corpora, quae tertia dei opera sunt, omnem partem aeternitatis[13] amittunt. Rationabile est mundum deo non aequari secundum vitam, postquam secundum substantiam non aequatur, neque esse undique infinitum, ut divinae cedat infinitati. Decet etiam sicut res omnes duos habent actus, internum scilicet atque externum, et ille est vita aequalis agenti, hic vero posterior, ita ipsum quoque rerum opificem foetum vita aequalem intra se continere, partum vero extra se posteriorem producere, ut non minus aeternitas quam perfectiones aliae deficiat in effectu. Atque hic mundus sicut a deo infinito finitus virtute magnitudineque producitur, sic verisimile videtur, ut ab aeterno deo fiat novus et initio circumscriptus. Et sicut mundo assignatur certus situs, quia ita hic est ut non per immensum sit spatium, ita illi quasi certum assignetur tempus, quia ita in hoc est tempore, ut non ante fuerit per immensum. Ac si deus universi substantiam infinitis perfectionis excedit gradibus, multo magis universi durationem infinitis gradibus durationis excedat.

11    Praestantior enim in re qualibet est substantia quam duratio. Quisquis autem considerat partes mundi quae sunt infra lunam,

pending on whether the world does or does not emanate from it) he too will be deceived. For the world is much less to God than the body's shadow to the body; and yet nothing is ever added to the body from [its] shadow or subtracted from it.

Certainly, that spiritual world, the model of this [corporeal] 10 world and the first work of God, has the same [eternal] life as the architect. It has always been with Him and will always be so. But the corporeal world, which is the second work of God, has already departed from its Maker in one regard, for it has not always been. It holds on to Him in another regard for it will always be. But composite bodies, which are the third works of God, lose hold of eternity in both regards. There is good reason for the world not to be equal to God in terms of its life, since it is not equal to Him in terms of its substance; and for it not to be in every respect infinite that it may yield to the divine infinity. Just as all things have two acts, an internal and an external one, and the former is equal to the life of the agent, but the latter is subsequent to it, so is it proper that the very Craftsman of things should contain within Himself a fetus that in terms of life is equal [to Him], but produce later an offspring outside Himself, so that eternity might be no less wanting than other perfections in effecting something. Just as this world is made finite in power and magnitude by an infinite God, so it seems probable it can be made anew and circumscribed with a beginning by an eternal God. And just as a certain spatial position is assigned to the world—for the world is such that it does not occupy a measureless space—so a sort of fixed time can be assigned to it, because it exists in this [fixed] time and has thus not existed earlier through a measureless time. And if God exceeds the substance of the universe in infinite degrees of perfection, still more must He exceed the universe's duration in infinite degrees of duration.

For in any object the substance is much superior to its duration. 11 Whoever considers: a) that the world's parts which are under the

de hoc esse in illud mutari atque e converso, ac partes eiusdem
quae super lunam sunt, de esse tali in esse tale transire vicissim, et
quia mutantur ubique, ideo indigas imperfectasque esse, rursusque
universum ipsum ex subiecto aliquo formaque constare, et subiectum, quia naturaliter antecedit formam, posse et subire formam
talem et non subire; item constare mundum non modo ex partibus
quantitatis, sed ex partibus etiam inter se pugnantibus; denique
universum corpus nullo modo per se esse, sed omnino per aliud,
quia per omnem causam, scilicet efficientem, finem, formam, materiam, ideoque secundum se penitus vacillare—quisquis,[14] inquam, quatuor haec considerat, is plane coniicere potest universam
mundi molem natura sua fore de esse in non esse mutabilem. Talis
non foret, nisi de non esse quandoque transisset in esse.

12      Hinc ferme Democritii, Cyrenaici, Stoici, Cynici fateri coacti
sunt mundum initium temporis habuisse. Aegyptii primum
mundi diem ita illuxisse aiunt, ut Aries in[15] medio esset caelo,
Cancer exoriretur, Luna in Cancro, Sol in Leone, Mercurius in
Virgine, Venus in Libra, in Scorpio Mars, Iupiter in Sagittario,
Saturnus in Capricorno, singulosque planetas eorum signorum
dominos esse aiunt, in quibus, dum nasceretur mundus, fuisse
creduntur. Chaldaei, nascente[16] mundo, Solem in Ariete fuisse
putant. Utrique mundum natum existimant fuisse aliquando, et
Arietem, sive quod in eo Sol esset, sive quod ipse medium percur-
reret caelum, signorum caput appellant. Ideo ab ingressu solis in
Arietem praecipue totius anni fortunam astronomi iudicant, quasi

moon are changed from this being into that being and back again, and the same world's parts which are above the moon in turn traverse from one kind of being to another, and because they are everywhere changed are thus wanting and imperfect; b) that the universe is constituted from a substrate and a form, and that the substrate, since it naturally precedes the form, is able both to submit and not to submit to such a form; c) that the world is constituted not only from quantity's parts but from parts too that are fighting among themselves; and finally d) that the universal body does not exist in any way through itself but entirely through another because it exists through every cause (that is, through the efficient cause, the end, the form, and matter) and so vacillates utterly with respect to itself—whoever, I say, thinks about these four considerations is clearly able to conjecture that of its own nature the universal mass of the world is going to be changeable and pass from being into non-being. It would not be such unless it had already passed at some time from non-being into being.

Hence the Democriteans, the Cyrenaics, the Stoics, and the Cynics were compelled to admit that the world had a temporal beginning. The Egyptians say that the world's first day dawned such that Aries was in mid-heaven, Cancer was rising, the Moon was in Cancer, the Sun in Leo, Mercury in Virgo, Venus in Libra, Mars in Scorpio, Jupiter in Sagittarius, and Saturn in Capricorn; and they declare that the individual planets were lords of their signs, the signs in which they were believed to have been situated when the world was born.[8] The Chaldaeans think that when the world was born the Sun was in Aries. Both they and the Egyptians suppose that the world was born at some point in time; and both call Aries the head of the [zodiacal] signs, either because the Sun was in it or because it was itself coursing through mid-heaven. Thus the astronomers judge the fortune of the whole year principally from the entrance of the Sun into Aries, as if virtually all things depended on it. I skip over the fact that the Egyptians assigned

12

inde paene omnia pendeant. Mitto quod Aegyptii solum Leonem Soli, solum Lunae Cancrum assignaverunt. Reliquis vero planetis, praeter illa signa quibus tunc inhaerebant, reliqua quinque sic adiunxerunt, ut a fine prioris ordinis ordo secundus inciperet. Sic enim Aquarius, qui Capricorno succedit, Saturno, qui ultimus fuerat, traditur, Pisces deinde Iovi, qui Saturno proximus fuerat, Marti Aries, Veneri Taurus, Gemini vero Mercurio. Sed his[17] omissis ad propositum revertamur.

13    Proclus demonstrat mundum, quoniam extensam et compositam habet essentiam, ideoque ex se distractam atque dissipabilem, idcirco solum per individuam quandam virtutem a divina unitate infusam connecti. Rursus quia naturali appetitu semper ad bonum ordinate movetur, ideo naturam talis appetitus motusque originem a divina mente bonitateque accepisse. Hanc vero virtutem, per quam connectitur atque movetur, oportere infinitam esse, per quam absque fine connecti moverique possit. Quam ex se, cum sit finitus, habere non valeat, sed ab infinitate divina semper accipiat, haud simul totam (non enim ⟨ita⟩ capit), sed pro sua potius temporali natura, scilicet quasi guttatim momentis singulis hauriat. Hanc ostendit non aliter quam momenta defluere subito, rursusque cum momentis momentaneam similiter hauriri, semperque hoc pacto, ut narravimus alias, mundum corporalem fluere fierique, sed esse revera numquam, quasi umbram eminentis arboris in torrente, quae et cum videatur arbor, non est arbor, et cum diu eadem appareat permanere, tamen continue renovatis undis continue renovatur. Cuinam igitur mirum videri debeat, mundum ab initio ex non esse processisse semel in esse, cum apud quosdam

Leo alone to the Sun and Cancer alone to the Moon.[9] They gave the other planets, however, besides the signs in which they were then inhering, the five extra signs such that their second ordering would begin from the end of the first order. Thus Aquarius which succeeds Capricorn is allotted to Saturn who was last [in the planetary order], Pisces to Jupiter who was next to Saturn, Aries to Mars, Taurus to Venus, and Gemini to Mercury.[10] But leaving all this [astronomy] aside, let us return to our theme.

Proclus demonstrates that the world, since it has an extended, composite essence, and thus an essence separated from itself and dispersible, is therefore connected only through an undivided power poured into it by the divine unity.[11] Again, because the world is moved by a natural desire and in an orderly way always towards the good, it has received the nature of such a desire and the origin of this motion from the divine mind and from goodness. But Proclus shows that this power via which the world is connected and moved (and via which it can be connected and moved without end) must be infinite. The world cannot attain this power from itself since it is finite: it always receives it from the divine infinity, not all of it simultaneously (for it does not receive in this manner), but rather according to its temporal nature: it swallows it drop by drop as it were in individual moments. He shows that this power flows quickly on as moments do, and again that with the moments it is likewise taken in as itself momentary. And in this way, as we have described it elsewhere,[12] the corporeal world forever flows away and becomes, but never truly is. It is like a shadow or image of a towering tree in a rapid stream: though it seems to be the tree, it is not the tree, and though it appears to stay the same for a long time, yet it is continually renewed as the racing ripples are born again. Should it come therefore as a surprise to anyone that the world from the beginning proceeded first from non-being into being, since according to some it is so shadowy and unstable that in single moments it passes from being into

adeo umbratilis instabilisque sit ut momentis singulis ab esse in non esse vicissimque pertranseat? Sed haec Proclus ipse viderit.

14    Plato in libro de mundi generatione ostendit mundum divinae bonitatis gratia fuisse creatum. Non autem ad hoc est opus huiusmodi constitutum, ut deum, qui ipsa bonitas est, faciat meliorem, sed ut divinam referat bonitatem, sicut neque parentes ob aliam causam filios generant quam ut eorum imago videatur in filiis. Praecipue vero mundus refert dei opificis bonitatem, si non modo quam munifica sit, sed etiam quam excellens ostendat. Quam munifica sit ostendit, prout semper a deo servatur incolumis, qui sibi ipsi relictus dissolveretur, ut in *Timaeo* inquit Plato; quam excellens testatur, prout esse coepit aliquando. Per quam incohationem clare perspicitur quod mundus non a se ipso, sed a deo est; quod infinito intervallo deus excedit mundum, qui in infinitum erat, ut ita dixerim, ante mundum; quod infinita virtute mundum produxit ex nihilo; quod libertate voluntatis agit, non necessitate naturae. Talem mundanae generationis originem planius Trismegistus Mercurius docuit. Neque mirum videri debet hunc talia cognovisse, si homo idem Mercurius fuit atque Moyses, quod Artapanus historicus coniecturis multis ostendit.

: II :

*Angelos et animos non semper fuisse.*

1    Ordinem in corporibus posuimus, ponamus ordinem in spiritibus. Est spiritus ille supremus, qui fuit semper et erit. Is[18] est deus.

non-being and back again? But let Proclus himself look to these matters.

In his book on the generation of the world, Plato shows that the world was created by the grace of divine goodness.[13] But this work [of the world] was not constituted for the purpose of making God, who is goodness itself, better; but so that it might declare the divine goodness, just as parents beget children for no other reason than that their image might be seen in their children. But the world especially declares the goodness of God as creator if it shows not only how generous that goodness is but how excellent. It shows how generous that goodness is in that it is always kept safe by God, whereas left to itself it would be dissolved, as Plato says in the *Timaeus*;[14] and it testifies how excellent that goodness is in that it commenced existing at some point. Because of this commencing it is quite obvious: a) that the world comes not from itself but from God; b) that God exceeds the world by an infinite interval—God who existed to infinity, one might say, before the world; c) that He produced the world from nothing by His infinite power; and d) that He moves it of His own free will, not from some necessity of nature. Mercurius Trismegistus has expounded this same origin of the world's generation even more plainly.[15] It should not seem surprising to us that Mercurius knew such things if he was the same man as Moses (as the historian Artapanus uses a number of conjectures to show).[16]

: II :

*Angels and rational souls have not always existed.*

We have established an order among bodies; let us now establish an order among spiritual beings. There is the supreme spirit who

Sunt et spiritus infimi bestiarum, qui nec semper fuere, nec erunt. Medii sint oportet duo quidam spiritus inter extrema adeo discrepantia, qui partem primi illius spiritus habeant, partem spirituum infimorum. Quo igitur pacto hos medios componemus? Numquid dicemus eos fuisse semper, sed quandoque desinere? Minime. Quod enim fuit semper, id per infinitam virtutem vixit in infinitum; infinita virtus numquam minuitur. Quare si fuerunt semper, semper et erunt, atque pares in duratione sunt deo, non medii spiritus. Ergo ut in perseverantia medii sint, oportet eos coepisse quandoque, desinere numquam. Qui etsi ex nihilo facti sunt, non tamen vertentur in nihilum. Ipsum enim quod dicimus nihilum in eorum creatione neque materia neque effector ipsorum est ex quibus fiant, sed terminus forsitan unde fiant. Neque etiam terminus est revera, sed dicitur. Non ergo coguntur ipsius nihili sequi naturam, per quam in nihilum revertantur, quam quidem naturam ante reiecerant, cum primum in esse prodirent. Immo naturam illam suae causae servant, unde essentiam acceperunt, ut per eandem infinitam virtutem in ipso esse serventur, procul a nihilo, per quam ex nihilo emerserunt in esse, posthabito nihilo.

2     Haud absurdum est quod ab infinito principio atque infinito fine, id est deo, proxime procreatur, cogitare finem non habiturum, cum multa etiam, quae ab initio ac termino quodam finito procedunt, rite considerentur absque fine procedere. Sic enim ab unitate numerus, sic a puncto mathematica linea, sic a praesenti momento futurum tempus absque fine, nihilo prohibente, progredi cogitatur. Aliquid vero creatum fore semper, praesertim animam,[19] non religio solum, sed etiam Avicenna et Alganteles tamquam philosophi

always was and will be, that is, God. There are the lowest spirits of the beasts too who never always existed and never will. Between such distant extremes there must be two [kinds of] intermediate spirits who possess part of the first [the supreme] spirit and part of the lowest spirits. So how shall we compose these intermediate spirits? Shall we assert that they have always existed but at some time will cease to exist? Absolutely not. For what has always existed has existed to infinity by way of infinite power; and infinite power never diminishes. So if these spirits have always existed, and will always exist and be equal in duration with God, they are not intermediate spirits. Thus in order to be intermediate in duration, they must begin at some point and never cease: even if they have been made from nothing, they will nonetheless not be turned into nothing. For in their creation what we call nothingness is neither the matter nor the creator of the things out of which they are made, but perhaps the terminus from which they arise. And it is not even a real terminus: it is just called so. Hence the spirits are not forced to follow the nature of nothingness itself, the nature through which they would be turned into nothing again and which they had earlier rejected as soon as they issued into being. Rather they preserve the very nature of their own cause from which they have received essence, so that through this same infinite power they are preserved in being itself and are far removed from nothingness. Thanks to this infinite power they have emerged from nothingness into being, having left nothingness behind.

It is not absurd to suppose that what is directly created by the   2 infinite beginning and by the infinite end, that is, by God, will not have an end, since even many things that proceed from a beginning and from a finite terminus may rightly be considered to proceed endlessly. For number is thought to proceed in this way from unity, a mathematical line from a point, and future time from the present moment, and they do so endlessly if nothing prevents them. Not only religion indeed, but Avicenna and Algazel too as

probant. Itaque angeli unum quidem[20] medium obtinent inter deum et beluas.

3 Alterum medium statim post angelos sortitae sunt hominum animae, quae cum angelo conveniunt quod semper erunt, differunt quod non fuerunt saltem per omne tempus, ut angeli, qui ab initio rerum orti naturali ordine ante caeli cursum, cuius comes est tempus. Licet non fuerint per omnem aeternitatem, tamen per omne fuere tempus. Animae nostrae post temporis ortum natae cedunt angelis, neque tamen[21] sunt temporales. Nam deus per id ipsum aeternitatis suae punctum, quod semper est idem, et universum supereminet complectiturque temporis ambitum in quo angelos procreavit, animas quoque hominum procreat. Igitur supra temporis passiones fiunt animae, quamvis fiant post temporis ortum. Animae vero brutorum et post ortum temporis et sub temporis passionibus generantur, quia non fiunt a deo per aeternitatem dei proxime, sed per caelorum conversiones animarumque virtutes, quo fit ut non vivant semper. Nam et mutationi temporis sunt obnoxiae, quae per caeli motum sunt factae sub tempore. Et si quid habent praeclari, id totum defluit iugiter ab ipso tertiae essentiae fonte, cuius ipsae non rivuli sunt, sed umbrae. Idcirco Platonici eas esse putant idola quaedam animae mundi vel animae sphaerae illius quam habitant, mediasque inter essentiam tertiam disponunt et corporum qualitates, ad hanc tamen essentiam reducunt eas ut umbras. Hinc Plotinus inquit: quemadmodum ab uno vultu multae per specula multa diffunduntur imagines, sic ab anima sphaerae in corpora brutorum multa animae unius simulacra multa. Corpora, inquam, brutorum, quibus humanae non in-

philosophers[17] prove that something created, especially a soul, will be forever. The angels therefore hold one of the mean positions between God and the beasts.

Men's souls are allotted the other mean immediately after the angels: they share with the angel the fact they will always exist but they differ from the angel in that they have not existed at least through all time like the angels, who emerged in the natural order from the very beginning of things before the circling of the heavens, the companion of which is time. Although the angels have not existed through all eternity, they have existed through all time. Our souls were born after the birth of time and yield to the angels, yet they are not temporal entities. For God takes the very point of His eternity—a point which is always the same and surpasses and embraces the whole circling of time wherein He has created the angels—and creates the souls of men too. Thus the souls are made above the effects of time even though they are made after the birth of time. The souls of beasts are generated after the birth of time and are subject to temporal effects, because they are not made by God through His eternity and without mediation, but through the revolutions of the heavens and the powers of souls; consequently they cannot live forever. For things that have been made subject to time through heaven's motion are also subject to the mutability of time. And whatever excellence they have, it flows continually and wholly from the fountain itself of the third essence [i.e. of Soul] of which they are not the rivulets but the shadows. Hence the Platonists suppose that the beast-souls are particular images of the World-Soul or of the soul of the sphere which they inhabit; and they insert [them as] means between the third essence and the qualities of bodies, while subordinating them as shadows to this essence. So Plotinus says, "Just as from one countenance many images are scattered through many mirrors, so from the soul of a sphere many images of that one soul are scattered onto many beasts' bodies,"[18] beasts' bodies, I say, in which human

sunt animae. Ubi enim hae sunt, ibi potentia irrationalis rationalem animae nostrae substantiam sequitur velut umbra.

<br>

: III :

*Animae creantur quotidie.*

1    Verum cur novae quotidie animae creantur a deo? An non poterat
deus, mundo constructo, creare simul animas cunctas, quemadmodum cunctos in mundi exordio angelos procreavit? Non decuit.
Nam si diu a vinculis corporum solutae vixissent, sincere iudica-
vissent quanto pretiosior sit vita soluta quam alia, nec ingredi umquam corpora voluissent. Videlicet quatenus intellectuales sunt,
neque deus vel angelus volunt liberam voluntatem animae cogere.
Non enim aliter mens quam persuasione movetur. Immo neque
etiam singula quaeque corpora anima cognovisset, quae posset eligere, cum desit illi ante sensus cognitio singulorum. Itaque careret
divinis sacerdotibus sacrisque hymnis pars haec media templi divini. Oportet tamen in singulis huius templi circulis proprios duci
choros sacerdotum deo canentium.

2    Consonat praeterea rationi, ut sicut sphaerarum animi sive angeli non fuerant per moras aliquas temporum ante sphaeras proprias procreati, sic neque animae nostrae ante corpora propria.
Item anima est forma actusque corporis. Actus autem quamvis in
universo secundum naturae ordinem prior quam potentia sit, in
eodem tamen subiecto secundum tempus est posterior, quoniam a
potentia in actum motus efficitur. Quapropter prius fuit semen
quod est potentia vivum quam anima quae vitalis est actus. Ad

souls are not present. For where human souls are the irrational power follows our soul's rational substance like a shadow.

<br>

## : III :

### *Souls are created daily.*

Why are new souls created daily by God? Could not God, having  1
constructed the world, create all the souls at the same time, just as He created all the angels at the world's beginning? It was not appropriate. For had the souls lived freed from the chains of bodies for a long time, they would in all honesty have judged how much more precious this freed life was than any other, and would never have wanted to enter bodies. Insofar as souls are intellectual, neither God nor an angel wishes to compel the soul's free will; for the mind is not moved otherwise than by persuasion. Or rather the soul does not even know about the various individual bodies it could choose, since prior to sensation it lacks any knowledge of individuals. Therefore this middle part of the temple divine would lack divine priests and be without divine hymns. And yet the individual circles of this temple deserve to be occupied by their own priestly choirs singing hymns to God.

Moreover, it accords with reason that just as angels or the ratio-  2
nal souls of spheres were not created[19] during individual moments of time before their own spheres, so our souls were not created before their own bodies. Again, soul is the form and act of body. But although in the universe and according to the order of nature act is prior to potentiality, yet in one and the same subject and according to time act is posterior to it, since motion is brought about from potentiality into act. Hence the seed that is living in potentiality is prior to the soul that is living act. It is natural to each form, fur-

haec cuique formae naturale hoc est, ut materiae propriae uniatur, alioquin quod ex materia formaque componitur esset congeries aliqua praeter naturam. Prius autem rei cuique tribuitur quod ipsi convenit secundum naturam, quam quod praeter naturam. Quod enim secundum naturam convenit, per se inest[22] cuique; quod praeter naturam advenit ex aliquo contingente. Animae igitur, qua ratione anima est, prius convenit ut coniuncta corpori sit quam separata. Quomodo igitur vixit ante corpus?

3    Adde quod si superior mens quaelibet, ut quidam putant, et una est in specie una et immortalis, forma vero quaelibet corporalis et multiplex fit in eadem specie et mortalis, hominis anima, quae illis mentibus succedit, praecedit has formas, sic utrarumque particeps erit, ut sit vel unica anima in una hominum specie atque mortalis, vel immortalis et multiplex. Primum fieri nequit. Si enim anima unica totius speciei animarum gerat vicem, innumerabiles animas, quae fieri sub illa specie possunt, suis viribus complectetur. Sic immensae quodammodo virtutis erit et immortalis, praesertim quia rerum species sempiternae sunt, et quod totam capit speciem est sempiternum. Rursus quia nullam haberet cum his corporeis rebus communionem, esset procul admodum ab interitu. Immo si talis esset, meram speciei suae servaret simplicitatem. Ea species est a caduco corpore segregata. Igitur in puritate propria remaneret a corporibus mortalibus aliena, neque praestaret his vitam. Ex iis constat hominis animam non posse esse unicam in cunctis hominibus, rursus non posse esse unicam simul atque mortalem. Itaque erit immortalis et multiplex. Immortalitate imitabitur mentes, multitudine formas penitus corporales.

4    Erit forte id rerum ordini consentaneum, ut primum gradum teneant ideales ipsae rerum species, secundum vero quae species

thermore, that it be united to its own matter; otherwise what results from compounding matter and form would be an unnatural clump. But to each thing is first given what naturally agrees with it and then what is unnatural to it. For what naturally accords with it is intrinsic to it per se; but what happens to it unnaturally results from something extrinsic. Therefore, by very reason of its being soul, it is proper that soul be bound to body before being separated from it. How has it lived therefore before body?

Moreover, if any higher mind, as some believe,[20] is one in one species and immortal, but any corporeal form is made multiple in the same species and mortal too, [then] man's soul, which succeeds minds [but] precedes forms, will so participate in both that it is either the unique soul in the one human species and yet mortal, or it is immortal and multiple [in that species]. The first option is impossible. For if one soul were to play the role of the whole species of souls, it would embrace with its own powers the innumerable souls that are able to exist under the one species. Thus it would be in a way both of measureless power and immortal, especially since the sundry species of things are everlasting and what contains the whole species is everlasting. Again, because it would have nothing in common with corporeal things here, it would be totally divorced from death; or rather if it were unique it would preserve the pure simplicity of its species. This species is separated from the fallen body. So it would remain in its own purity divorced from mortal bodies; and it would not give them life. It follows then that man's soul cannot be one in all men; and it cannot be one and mortal simultaneously. So man's soul will be immortal and multiple. In its immortality it will imitate minds; in its multiplicity it will imitate wholly corporeal forms.

It will accord perchance with the universal order that the ideal species of things should occupy the first rank, and the things that receive these species, the second. And of the things that receive, the first set belongs to those who, according to the capacity of each

capiunt. Atque ex iis quae capiunt, primum quae totam pro facultate creaturae suam capiunt speciem atque semper; secundum vero quae non totam, sed tamen semper; tertium quae neque totam neque semper. Quemadmodum in summo ponimus exemplar luminum, id est solem, in secundo stellas, quarum quaelibet totum inde suum semperque accipit lumen, in tertio lunam, quae semper quidem accipit, sed non totum (et si pati videtur eclipsim, tamen subito recipit), similiter aerem et aquam; in quarto illa ex elementis composita, quae perspicua quodammodo et nitida sunt: talia cupiunt[23] quidem, sed neque semper neque totum, ut opposita praetermittam, quae nullo modo in se lumen admittunt.

5    At una haec animae species unde multiplicem accipit numerum? Forte non ex eo quod imitatur mentes. Ex eo igitur quod formas imitatur corporeas. Quales hae sunt? Incipiunt cum corpore et cum corpore desinunt. Anima nostra si talis sit omnino, ut incipiat simul et desinat, non imitatur eas, sed generis est eiusdem atque illae.[24] Si neutrum horum habet,[25] non imitatur, non congruit, non haeret illis, non vivificat. Ergo habebit alterutrum: vel incipiet cum corpore tantum, vel tantum cum corpore desinet. Desinere non potest cum corpore mens, quae[26] ad immortalem veritatem bonitatemque dirigitur tamquam finem; agit enim omnia huius gratia. Sicut autem de rerum initio habemus ab efficiente causa coniecturam, sic de rerum perseverantia coniecturam sumere solemus a fine. Si igitur mens ad sempiternum finem proprie naturali quadam cognatione dirigitur, sempiternae perseverantiae est capax. Proprius enim finis proprio respondet agenti; perseverantia rei ad finem directae inter utrumque tenet medium. Mens igitur,

creature, receive the whole of their species and receive it forever; but the second set belongs to those who do not receive the whole species but do receive it forever; and the third set, to those who neither receive the whole nor receive it forever. Similarly, we put the exemplar of lights, that is the sun, at the zenith; in second place, the stars, each of which receives from it the whole of its light and receives it forever; and in third place, the moon, which receives light forever indeed but not the whole of it (and even if it seems to endure an eclipse yet it reacquires the light immediately) — and the like goes for air and water. In fourth place we put things compounded from the elements that are in some manner perspicuous and bright: such things desire [the light] but not the whole of it and not forever (and let me leave aside their complete opposites which never admit light into themselves).

But this one species of soul receives its multiplicity from where?　5 Not perchance from the fact that it imitates minds. From the fact then that it imitates corporeal forms. What are these like? They commence with body and they end with body. If our soul is entirely such that it begins and ends likewise, it does not imitate these forms, but it is of the same class as them. But if it has neither [beginning nor end], it does not imitate the forms, and it does not accord with, does not adhere to, and does not vivify them. Therefore our soul will have one of two alternatives: either it will only begin with the body, or it will only end with the body. The mind, which is directed towards immortal truth and goodness as its end, cannot end with the body; for it does all for truth's sake. But just as we arrive at a conjecture concerning the beginning of things from the efficient cause, so we customarily derive a conjecture about the lasting nature of things from the end [cause]. So if the mind is properly directed to an everlasting end by a natural affinity with it, it is capable of lasting everlastingly. For the appropriate end corresponds to the appropriate agent [i.e. the mind]. The lasting of something directed to an end is the mean between

cum proprium finem habeat sempiternum, habet quoque agens proprium sempiternum atque idcirco utrinque vitam perseverantiamque perpetuam. Si non desinit cum corpore, incipit saltem cum corpore.

6    Multiplex profecto fit anima hominis in multis corporibus. Quod quidem significatur ex opinionibus hominum affectibusque contrariis. Talis vero non fit ex specie sua, per quam est una, sed, ut quidam putant, quodammodo ex corporibus, immo ex deo animarum corporumque conciliatore. Non quia in corpore sit divisa; non quia ex materia sit ut corpus; non quia nascatur ex corpore. Unde igitur, nisi quia divina voluntate comes fit corporis? Quando deus simul initium praebet utrisque, non tamen praebet principium idem; igitur neque naturam eandem, neque exitum similem, sed initium, ut diximus, idem, unde et numerum tradit eundem.

7    Hinc affectus animae ad naturam corporis augetur, quia corporis initium comitatur, atque in huius creatione mutatio, quae una videtur, est triplex. Mutatio quidem animae ex nihilo ad esse per deum solum facta creatio est; mutatio vero corporis non viventis ad vitam ipsam ab anima capiendam formatio quidem corporis; animalis autem generatio nuncupatur. Creationis terminus ad quem dirigitur anima in se ipsa est, divinae solum aeternitati respondens, quae terminus est a quo creatio provenit. Formationis autem terminus ad quem fit est anima, non tam in se ipsa perma-

them both. So the mind, since it has its own everlasting end, also has its own everlasting agent, and therefore on both accounts has perpetual and lasting life. If it does not cease with the body, at least it begins with the body.

Certainly, man's soul is made multiple in many bodies; the con- 6 trary opinions and emotional dispositions of men testify to this. But such a multiple condition does not derive from its species through which it is one: it comes in a way, so some suppose, from bodies, or rather from God (the reconciler of souls and bodies). It does not come because the soul is divided in the body, nor because it is from matter like the body, nor because it is born from the body. Whence then if not because it is made by the divine will the companion of the body? When God gives a beginning to both soul and body at the same time, nevertheless He does not give them the same principle [of being], nor accordingly the same nature, nor a like end, but just the same beginning, as we said, whence He bestows the same number [or principle of individuation].

Hence the soul's desire for the nature of the body is increased 7 because it accompanies the body's beginning; and in the creation of this [new entity] the mutation, which appears to be single, is in fact triple. The mutation of the soul from nothing into being (a changing effected through God alone) is creation; but the mutation of a non-living body in order to receive life itself from the soul is that body's formation; with an animate being, however, the mutation is called generation. Creation's terminus towards which it is directed is the soul in itself, the soul responding only to the divine eternity, which is the terminus from which creation issues. But formation's terminus towards which it is directed is the soul abiding not so much in itself as in the body; while the terminus from which it issues seems to be nature. Finally generation's terminus towards which it is directed is an ensouled being compounded from soul and body; while the terminus from which it issues is

nens quam in corpore; terminus vero a quo fit videtur esse natura. Denique generationis terminus ad quem est animal ex anima corporeque compositum; terminus autem a quo ferme similiter est natura — natura, inquam, non particularis tantum, sed etiam universalis, in cuius virtute particularis corpus ad animam praeparat. Universalis vero natura virtus quaedam dicitur sive instrumentum animae mundi. Ideo Plato in *Philebo* dixit: 'Si mundus anima careret, undenam nos haberemus?' Non quia ab anima mundi sit anima in se ipsa, sed quia per eius operam sit in corpore. Animas enim nostras ab eodem deo et ex eodem fonte, quo et superiores omnes fieri Timaeus ostendit. Hinc illud quoque ostenditur quod Timaeus inquit, rationalem videlicet animam a solo deo esse, irrationalem vero vitam sub ea corpori mancipatam a diis caelestibus, deo iubente, pendere, quia scilicet et corpus ad ipsam praeparant, et animam nostram ad eam corpori infundendam corroborant. Sed haec tamquam hic supervacua dimittamus.

8 Sint igitur, dicet aliquis, animae multae, incipiant etiam cum corporibus. Hoc aures non offendit, hic tamen unus restat scrupulus. Quonam pacto conveniat deo singulis momentis ad libidinem concumbentium animas singulas procreare? Non malum est concubitus, quoniam ad bonum est naturaliter institutus, sed defectus moderationis in animis concumbentium. Non fit ex privatione moderationis, sed ex concubitu corporis generatio. Huic generationi deus distribuit animas, non ad libidinem coeuntium, sed ad praescriptam providentiae legem, quae et numerum et tempora concumbentium ab initio rerum videt in aevo.

9 In aevo iamdudum concipit animas. Cur ergo deus animas parit quotidie? Quia non simul, sed per successionem erant cor-

likewise nature, or almost so, nature meaning here not only a particular nature but also universal nature in whose power a particular nature prepares a body for a soul. But universal nature is called a particular power or instrument of the World-Soul. Thus in the *Philebus* Plato declared, "If the world were to lack a soul, whence would we have [souls] ourselves?"[21] It is not because the soul in itself is from the World-Soul, but because it is in the body through the work of the Soul. For Timaeus shows that our souls come from the same God and the same fountain whence all higher things derive.[22] Hence the evidence too, as Timaeus says, that while the rational soul comes from God alone, the irrational life, which is chained to the body under it, depends on the celestial gods under God's command: they prepare the body for this life and strengthen our soul for the purpose of pouring it into the body. But let us dismiss these matters here as being beside the point.

So let there be many souls, someone will say, and let them even 8 begin with bodies. This does not sound objectionable, yet one scruple remains here. How is it proper for God in single moments to create single souls according to the desire of the partners coupling? What is evil is not sexual union, since it was naturally instituted for the good, but rather the defect of moderation in the souls of those coupling. The generation of the body comes, not from the absence of moderation, but from [sexual] union. For this generation, God distributes souls not according to the desire of those uniting but according to the prescribed law of providence, which from the very beginning of things sees in eternity both the frequency and the times of sexual union.

In eternity long ago God conceives souls. So why does God 9 produce souls day by day? It is because bodies had to be generated successively, not together. Moreover, God continually illuminates

pora generanda. Adde quod continue illuminat angelos, et sicut numquam desistit mentes superiores formare, ita numquam cessat mentes infimas procreare. Perpetua illic formatio fit, hic perpetua procreatio. Procreatio, inquam, tamdiu assidua quamdiu sol, dei vicarius, continue superiora illuminat corpora et continue generat infima.

10     Decet immensam dei potentiam ita semper sese potentem ostendere mentium oculis, ut videant deum in infimo gradu mentium propter ultimum mundi locum continue aliquid ex nihilo procreantem; ut hoc effectu continuo infinitam[27] omnino dei potentiam clarius agnoscant in infinitum creationis actum infinite, si placuerit, peragentem; venerentur eam illuminantem in caelis; admirentur, ut ita loquar, in terra creantem. Excellentior sane operatio est creatio quam illustratio; illa igitur magis quam haec convenit deo. Haec continua fit a deo; illa igitur pro dei arbitrio fit continua. Caelos movent ministri dei. Hoc motu sequentia generantur, dum species quaelibet rerum in terris aliquid agit et in agendo ministra fit caeli. An deus ipse solus agit nihil, quamdiu cetera omnia aliquid operantur? Absit ut primus actus agat nihil, agentibus aliis.

11     At inquies eum agere satis, dum agentia non deserit reliqua, sed vim illis operandi suppeditat. Non satis est istud. Nempe hinc propria causarum aliarum sequuntur opera, atque imagines illarum fiunt in mundo, non dei. Cur nolit et deus assidue opera propria propriasque imagines facere, plurima semper sine medio procreando? Igitur cum creatio propria dei operatio sit, generatio

the angels, and just as He never stops forming the higher minds, so He never stops creating the lowest minds. With the higher minds His forming is perpetual, with the lowest His creating is perpetual. His creating is as constant as the sun, the vicar of God, which continually illuminates the higher bodies and continually generates the lowest.

Properly, God's measureless power always reveals itself to the 10 eyes of minds as being so potent: a) that they may see God continually creating something out of nothing in the lowest rank of minds on account of its being the world's lowest place; b) that they may recognize more clearly in this continual creating God's utterly infinite power engaging infinitely — if He so wills — in the infinite act of creation; c) that they may venerate this power in the heavens as the illuminating power; and d) that they may marvel at it so to speak on earth as the creating power. Creation is undoubtedly a more excellent activity than illumination; and thus the former befits God more than the latter. Continual illumination proceeds from God; hence creation is continuous too if God so decides. God's ministers move the heavens; and by this motion subsequent things are generated while each species of things on earth does something and in so doing becomes a minister of heaven. Does God Himself alone do nothing when all other things do something? When other things act, it is inappropriate for the first act to enact nothing.

You will say that He does enough, however, when He does not 11 abandon all the other agents but supplies them with the power to operate. But that is not enough. From Him follow certainly the proper works of other causes; and the images of them, not of God, are made in the world. Why doesn't God too wish to make His own works and their appropriate images continually, the majority always by creating without an intermediary? Therefore, since creation is the proper work of God, but external generation is the

autem externa operatio propria aliorum, non cessabit deus creare aliquid, quamdiu alia non cessabunt aliquid generare.

12     Centrum mundi verum deus est, ut in libro *De amore* disseruimus, quia unus, simplex, stabilis est et in omnibus, atque alia quaelibet omnino plura, composita, mobilia, circa ipsum per naturalem ipsius appetitum perpetuo revolvuntur. Ita centrum deus est omnium, quia sic est in omnibus, ut cuique rei interior sit, quam ipsamet sibi. Est etiam circumferentia mundi, quia extra cuncta existens ita supereminet universa, ut cuiusque rei summum apicem dignitate excellat immensa. Item quanto est omnium, si dictu fas est, minimus quantitate, tanto virtute est maximus omnium. Ut est centrum quidem, est in omnibus; ut circumferentia vero, est extra omnia. In omnibus, inquam, non inclusus, quia est et[28] circumferentia; extra omnia quoque non exclusus, quia est et centrum. Quid ergo deus est? Ut ita dixerim, circulus spiritalis, cuius centrum est ubique circumferentia nusquam. At enim si centrum id divinum in aliqua mundi parte imaginariam aliquam aut perspicuam operationis sedem habeat, potissimum in rerum medio dominatur, tamquam rex in medio civitatis, cor ferme in medio corporis, sol in medio planetarum. In sole igitur, id est in tertia mediaque rerum essentia deus posuit tabernaculum suum — tabernaculum, inquam, virtutis suae frequentius demonstrandae. Quae sedes familiaris est deo, non tam quod species animae est quam quod divinae civitatis est medium, aerarium publicum et consona urbanarum partium moderatio.

13     Animam hominis esse rerum medium saepe iam declaravimus. In hac igitur regione praecipua dei operatio frequentius praevalebit. Talis creatio est. Creat igitur assidue animas hominum. Profecto quia stabile centrum est, creat continue. Quia circumferentia

proper work of others, God is not going to stop creating something as long as others are not going to stop generating something.

The world's true center is God as we discussed in the book *On Love*, because He is one, simple, unchanging, and in all things, whereas all other things are wholly many, composite, mobile, and through their natural desire for Him they revolve around Him perpetually.[23] Thus God is the center of all, because He is so in all things that He is more internal to each thing than it is to itself. He is also the world's circumference because, in existing outside all things, He so transcends all things that His dignity immeasurably excels the highest summit of each thing. Again, He is greatest of all in power to the extent He is least of all in quantity, if this is a permissible way of putting it. As He is the center, He is in all, but as the circumference, He is outside all: in all, but not included because He is also the circumference; outside all too but not excluded because He is also the center. So what is God? One might call Him a spiritual circle whose center is everywhere, whose circumference is nowhere.[24] But if this divine center were to have some imaginary or clearly evident seat of operation in some part of the world, it would chiefly reign in the midst of things as a king in the midst of a city, the heart in the midst almost of the body, the sun in the midst of the planets. So in the sun, that is, in the third and middle essence of things, God has placed His tabernacle,[25] a tabernacle for manifesting His power more often. This seat is home to God not so much because the soul's species [or beauty] is there as because the center of the divine city is there, its public treasury, the harmonious government of its civic parts.

We have already declared and repeatedly too that man's soul is the universal mean. So in this [mean] region God's principal activity will prevail more often. This activity is creation. Hence God continually creates men's souls. Certainly because He is the unmoving center, He creates [them] continually; and because He is the circumference that encircles the world's circumference, He creates

est quae mundi ambit circumferentiam, creat eas, ut Platonici dicerent, quodammodo in circumferentia mundi. Rursus quia centrum, ideo est summa rerum. Quia summa, ideo singula fundit, tum sigillatim singula semel ab initio rerum, tum cuncta summatim quotidie, prout creando animam, quae rerum medium est, effundit e sinu proprio universa quae summatim confunduntur in medio.

: IV :

*Unde anima descendit in corpus?*

1   Undenam descendit in corpus anima? Revera cum deus extra locum adsit omni loco, et anima non claudatur loco momentoque[29] et creetur et adsit, neque dicendum proprie est[30] eam descendere, neque unde descendat est quaerendum. Sic enim ab ipso deo manans adest corpori, ut ita dixerim, sicut a solis lumine radius oculo. Sed delectat interdum una cum priscis confabulari. Igitur si Zoroastri et Mercurio credimus, ex amplo demittitur ambitu mundi atque, ut illorum sententiam ordine referam, infima mens supremo corpori primum adhaeret, neque haeret solummodo, sed infunditur, quo tamquam medio crassioribus corporibus copulatur. Spiritus simplex immortalisque non aliter composito mortalique corpori quam per corpus simplex et immortale coniungitur. Neque id quidem iniuria, quoniam anima per suam essentiam corpori praestat vitam. Essentia eius vita est sempiterna. Sempiterna vita, cui primum haeret, haeret in sempiternum, praesertim quoniam essentia animae immutabilis est, quo fit ut immutabiliter

them, as the Platonists would say, in a way in the world's circumference. Again, because He is the center, He is the sum of all things; and because the sum, He produces individuals in abundance, both individuals individually just once at the very beginning of things, and all things collectively day by day, just as in creating the soul, which is the universal mean, He brings forth from His own bosom the universe of things which are collectively mingled in that mean.

## : IV :

### *From where does the soul descend into the body?*

From where does the soul descend into the body? Truly, since God ₁ is present in every place but is outside place, and the soul is not enclosed by place and is created and appears in a moment, properly we should neither say that it descends nor inquire whence it descends. For emanating from God Himself the soul is present to the body, so to speak, as a ray is present to the eye from the sun's light. Now and then, however, it is pleasant to converse with the ancients. Thus, if we believe Zoroaster and Mercurius [Trismegistus],²⁶ the lowest mind is sent down from the vast circumference of the world and—if I may relate their view in the right order—clings first to the highest body; and not only does it cling to it, it is poured into it; and with this highest body as a mean it is then joined to grosser bodies. The only way a simple and immortal spirit is joined to a composite and mortal body is through a simple and immortal body; not unjustly so, since through its own essence a soul gives life to a body. Its essence is everlasting life. Everlasting life clings for eternity to the thing it clings to first, especially since the soul's essence itself is immutable.

proximum sibi corpus vivificet, siquidem perpetuae vitae proprius
actus est vivificatio sempiterna.

2 Tale quiddam opinari poterit aliquis Aristotelem cogitavisse in
secundo *De generatione animalium*[31] libro, ubi cum probavisset intellectualem animam esse a corpore separabilem, propterea quod
cum operatione sua non communicat operatio corporalis, paulo
post subdidit huic animae convenire corpus aliquod, quod sit a ge-
niturae corpore separabile. Ex quo etiam apparet, quod contra
Averroem in superioribus quaerebamus, scilicet intellectualem animam esse formam corpus vivificantem. Praesertim quia, cum Aristoteles ibidem probavisset ex tribus animabus, scilicet vegetali sen-
suali intellectuali, hanc solam esse et ab extrinseco et a corpore
separabilem, quia huius tantum operatio per se absque instrumento possit expleri, subiunxit has omnes, scilicet tres animas pariter esse in semine secundum potentiam. At vero, si quis haec
consideret diligenter, inveniet non posse potentiam ullam his esse
communem per quam corpus pari ad tres animas modo in potentia sit, nisi facultatem quandam qua[32] ab intellectuali anima similiter atque ab[33] aliis vitam motumque accipiat. Sed iam ad corpus
animae proximum redeamus.

3 Hoc vocant Magi vehiculum animae, aethereum scilicet corpus-
culum acceptum ab aethere, immortale animae indumentum, naturali quidem figura rotundum propter aetheris regionem, sed in
humanam effigiem sese transferens quando corpus humanum ingreditur atque in priorem se restituens cum egreditur. Quod ob
eam causam Magi necessarium arbitrantur, quoniam angeli tales
sunt ut et virtute separabiles et actu separati sint a corporibus, irrationales animae neque virtute separabiles neque actu; ex quo sequitur rationales animas tamquam medias tales esse debere, ut vir-

Consequently it immutably vivifies the body closest to it, since the proper act of perpetual life is to give life everlasting.

Someone could argue that Aristotle had this in mind in the second book of his treatise *On the Generation of Animals*, where, having proved that the intellectual soul is separable from the body on the grounds that corporeal operation has nothing in common with the soul's [intellectual] operation,[27] he added shortly thereafter that [only] some body which is separable from the body of a generated being is appropriate for this soul.[28] From this emerges too the proof against Averroes we were looking for in earlier [chapters],[29] namely that the intellectual soul is the form giving life to the body. This is especially because Aristotle had proved in the same treatise that of the three souls, the vegetative, the sensitive, and the intellectual, only the intellectual is separable both from anything extrinsic to itself and from body, because its operation alone can be discharged of its own accord and without an instrument. Given this, Aristotle added that all these souls — the three that is — are in the seed (semen) and equally so in terms of potency.[30] But were someone to consider these matters carefully, he would discover that no potency which enables the body to be in equal potency with regard to the three souls can be common to the souls, unless it is some power by which the body may accept life and motion from the intellectual soul just as it may accept them from the other [two souls]. But let us return to the body next to the soul.

The Magi call this body the vehicle of the soul,[31] that is, the little aethereal body received from the aether, the soul's immortal garment; it is round in its natural shape because of the [rotundity of] the aether's region, but it transforms itself into our [angular] human shape when it enters the human body, and restores itself to its former shape when it departs from it. The Magi think it necessary for the following reason. Because the angels are such that they are separable in power from bodies and have been separated in act, whereas irrational souls are separable neither in power nor in act,

tute quidem semper separabiles sint, quia si illis subtrahantur corpora, non peribunt, actu autem sint semper coniunctae, quia familiare corpus nanciscuntur ex aethere, quod servent per immortalitatem propriam immortale. Quod Plato currum tum deorum tum animarum vocat in *Phaedro*, vehiculum in *Timaeo*, quo utantur animae sphaerarum caelestesque purissimo, daemonum animae minus puro, nostrae quoque minus propter terreni corporis mixtionem. Quam ob causam ita praecipit Zoroaster:

Μὴ πνεῦμα μολύνῃς μηδὲ βαθύνῃς τὸ ἐπίπεδον.

Id est: 'Ne foedes spiritum, neque in profundum exaugeas quod est planum.'

4    Spiritum planumque appellat ipsum vehiculum, non quia corpus non sit atque profundum, sed quia propter tenuissimam et splendidam puritatem sit quasi non corpus. Praecipit ergo ne propter nimium corporis elementalis affectum cogas ipsum etiam post hanc vitam sordidum atque grave superfore caliginis elementalis adiunctione, quam animae umbram prisci theologi nuncuparunt. Neque tamen volunt rationalem animae partem proxime haerere vehiculo, sed rationalem ipsam animam, quantum et rationalis est et comes caelestium animarum, edere actum vivificum in vehiculum, quod animae idolum saepe iam appellavimus. Quam speciem animae mortalem in libro *De mundi generatione* Plato nuncupat, non quia moriatur aliquando, sed quia subtracto vehiculo rueret, ut quidam putant. Sicut enim lunae splendor in nube promit ex se ipso pallorem, sic anima in corpore caelesti emittit idolum, quasi [stella] crinita comam. Quod evanesceret, si evanesceret corpus illud, sicut pallor exstinguitur, nubibus dissipatis. Quia tamen numquam vehiculum subtrahetur, Zoroaster inquit:

Ἔστι καὶ εἰδώλῳ μερὶς εἰς τόπον ἀμφιφάοντα.

it follows that rational souls as intermediaries must be such that they are always separable in power (since if bodies are withdrawn from them they are not going to perish), but are always joined in act (because they acquire their [truly] familiar body from the aether and keep it immortal through their own immortality). In the *Phaedrus* Plato calls this aethereal body the chariot at one time of the gods, at another of souls.[32] In the *Timaeus* he calls it the vehicle[33] that the souls of the spheres and heavenly souls can ride in its utmost purity, the souls of demons can ride when it is less pure, and our souls can barely ride because of the mixture of earthy body. For this reason Zoroaster exhorts us: "Do not sully the spirit; do not extend what is planar into depth."[34]

He calls the vehicle spirit and plane, not because it is not a    4
body and not three-dimensional, but because it is almost not a body given its extreme tenuity and radiant purity. So Zoroaster is telling us: Do not compel the vehicle, on account of the elemental body's excessive desire, even after this life to remain as a vehicle made squalid and heavy by the addition of the elemental murk, which the ancient theologians called the soul's shadow.[35] And yet these theologians do not want the soul's rational part to be what most clings to this vehicle. Rather they want the rational soul itself, insofar as it is rational and the companion of the celestial souls, to impart a life-giving act to the vehicle (which we have often now called the idolum of the soul[36]). In his book *On the Generation of the World*, Plato calls this species [or form] of the soul the mortal species,[37] not because it can die at some point itself but because, if the vehicle were withdrawn, it would tumble, some think, to its ruin. For just as the splendor of the moon projects a paleness out of itself onto a cloud, so the soul sends out its idolum onto its celestial body like a comet its tail. The idolum would vanish, if the [celestial] body vanished, just as the paleness is lost when the clouds have dissipated. Yet because the vehicle will never be withdrawn, Zoroaster declares, "There is a place for the idolum too in

Id est: 'Est idolo quoque locus in regione perspicua.' Quia scilicet cum vehiculo simul et anima rationali recurret in caelum.

5 Plotinus autem ipsum esse putat simpliciter[34] immortale, etiam si ipsi vehiculum subtrahatur, similiterque ait solis lumen in aere, immo praesens aeri, haud exstinctum iri, etiam si aer tollatur e medio. Ex solo enim sole pendere tamquam perennem ipsius actum, neque esse passionem aeris qualitatemque aeri propriam, siquidem momento adest atque abest, neque ipsius quicquam, sublato sole, restat in aere. Neque solum adest aeri, sed similiter omni perspicuo, etiam si contrariae inter se naturae perspicua sint, quasi non a certa natura subiecti dependeat. Neque aliquo modo a perspicuo, qua ratione perspicuum est, dependet, sed tantum illi adest, quia non impeditur illi adesse, sicut adesse opaco impediri videtur. Sol enim hunc actum emittit semper, non dimittit, non immittit. Sorte vero contingit subesse quod capiat, immo quod capere videatur. Actus hic solem vicissim perpetuo comitatur. Similiter se habet et vultus ad speculum et ad corpus anima. Haec Plotinus.

6 Inesse[35] autem idolo huic opinantur phantasiam quandam irrationalem atque confusam; sensus praeterea tales, ut per totum vehiculum videatur pariter atque audiatur, quibus sensibus proprie homines quam paucissimi utantur et raro. Sentiri vero per illos saepe concentus caelorum mirabiles vocesque et corpora daemonum, quotiens aliquis ad tempus, terreno corpore derelicto, sese in corpus suum caeleste receperit. Ideo Tatius, Mercurii filius, cum

the region of clarity."[38] This is because it will return to heaven with its vehicle at the same time as the rational soul.

But Plotinus thinks that the idolum is unconditionally immortal even if the vehicle is taken away from it.[39] Similarly, he says, the sun's light, which is in the air or rather present to the air, will not be extinguished even if the air is taken from its midst. For the light depends on the sun alone as its eternal act: it is not a passion of the air or a quality proper to the air, since it is present and absent in a moment; and when the sun is borne away, none of it remains in the air. It is present not only to the air, but to anything that is similarly transparent, even if transparent things are of a contrary nature among themselves: it is as though the light does not depend on the fixed nature of a subject. Nor does it depend in any way on a transparent subject by reason of its being transparent. It is present to such a subject only because its being present is not impeded by it, just as [contrariwise] its being present obviously is impeded by an opaque subject. For the sun always emits this act [of light]: it does not send it away from or into something.[40] But it is just chance that what receives that act, or rather appears to receive it, happens to be below. By contrast the act itself perpetually accompanies the sun. The face has a similar relationship to the mirror and the soul to the body. All this is from Plotinus.

The philosophers are of the opinion, however, that a certain irrational and troubled phantasy is present in this idolum; and that the senses are present too such that seeing and hearing alike occur through the whole vehicle, senses properly speaking which very few men use and then only rarely. And they think, as often as someone gathers himself again into his celestial body, having cast aside for a time his earthly body, that he will often perceive through those senses the marvelous harmonies of the heavens and the voices and bodies of demons. Hence Tatius, the son of Mercurius [Trismegistus], after he had been purged by his father's

esset paternis sacris expiationibusque purgatus, illico exclamavit esse se tunc in corpus immortale translatum ac intueri mirabilia et audire. Quod et ipse Mercurius narrat sibi quoque paulo ante in abstractione animi contigisse. Olympiodorus quoque platonicus tradit Apollonium Theaneum hac ratione solitum ex urbe Roma, que fiebant in Aegypto, prospicere.

7     Mitto quod Platonici multi putant animam tribus uti vehiculis: primo quidem immateriali et simplici, id est caelesti, secundo materiali et simplici, id est aereo, tertio materiali atque composito, id est ex elementis quatuor constituto; et primo quidem dare vitam irrationalem, sed immortalem; secundo vero vitam irrationalem, sed longaevam, quae videlicet composito corpore aliquando dissoluto ad certum tempus supersit in simplici corpore; tertio denique vitam et irrationalem et una cum dissoluto corpore dissolvendam. Praeterea in prima vita communicata vehiculo sensum esse communem atque impatibilem; in secunda patibilem et communem, id est per vehiculum universum sensum pariter universum; denique in tertia sensum divisum pariter atque patibilem.

: V :

*Qua parte caeli animae creantur*
*quave descendunt?*

1   Qua parte caeli animae procreantur? Quamquam stultum est quaerere situm in his, quae situ aliquo non clauduntur, et sicut

rites and sacrifices, instantly exclaimed that he had then been translated into an immortal body and seen and heard marvels.[41] And Mercurius himself says that he too had happened to fall a little earlier into an abstraction of soul.[42] Olympiodorus too, the Platonist, reports that Apollonius of Tyana was in the habit for this same reason of seeing, from the city of Rome, all that was happening in Egypt.[43]

I leave aside the fact that many Platonists think the soul uses 7 three vehicles:[44] first the immaterial and simple, that is the celestial vehicle; second the material and simple, that is the airy vehicle; and third the material and composite, that is the vehicle compounded from the four elements. To the first the soul gives an irrational but immortal life, to the second an irrational but long-lasting life (one that survives for a certain time in the simple body after the composite body has at some point dissolved); and to the third finally it gives an irrational life that must dissolve along with the body's dissolution. The Platonists suppose, furthermore, that in the first life communicated to the vehicle the sense is common and impassible; that in the second life it is passible and common (that is, the sense is equally whole through the whole vehicle); and that in the third life the sense is alike divided and passible.

: V :

*In what part of heaven are souls created*
*and from what part do they descend?*

In what part of heaven are souls created? Although it is foolish to 1 enquire after a place in the case of these souls which are not confined to any place — and just as wherever the sun shines, a ray is emitted, so wherever God is present, the rational soul is sent

ubicumque sol fulget, ibi mittitur radius, sic ubicumque deus adest, mittitur animus, delectat tamen cum antiquis interdum poetice ludere. Igitur alias, inquit Timaeus, apud alias stellas a mundi opifice seminari, quarum fiant in vita comites animae. Quod ita Platonici intellegi volunt, ut non singulae animae, sed animarum legiones singulis stellis accommodentur. Addit deum animas suis imposuisse vehiculis ac universi naturam legesque fatales edocuisse.

2      Qua parte caeli descendunt? Cancro praecipue, ut aiunt Platonici, vicissimque per Capricornum, Cancro oppositum, ascendere putant, atque hinc illam hominum, hanc deorum portam appellant. Nemo vero adeo falli debet[36] ut descensum ascensumve hic accipiat secundum situm. Sed quia luna, Cancri domina, generationi proxima est, Saturnus vero, dominus Capricorni, remotissimus, ideo per Cancrum, id est lunarem vegetalemque instinctum, descendere animas dicunt, per Capricornum vero, id est per saturnium intellectualemque instinctum, ascendere. Saturnum enim prisci mentem vocant, qua sola superiora petuntur. Accedit ad haec quod Capricorni Saturnique sicca virtus, dum spiritus ad intima contrahit atque colligit, ad contemplandum assidue provocat, lunaris autem humor spargit atque dilatat et animum circa sensibilia distrahit. In ipso autem descensu animus accipit, et a Saturni numine per se, et a Saturni lumine per corpus aethereum atque idolum adminicula quaedam sive incitamenta ad contemplationem aptius exsequendam. Ab Iovis numine atque lumine similiter ad vitae civilis gubernationem. A Marte similiter ad magnanimitatem propter iniurias propulsandas. A Sole ad phantasiae et sensuum claritatem. A Venere ad caritatem. A Mercurio ad interpretatio-

forth—yet it is delightful to play poetically for a while with the ancients. Thus Timaeus says that various souls are sowed by the world's craftsman in various stars, and that during their life souls become companions of these stars.[45] The Platonists take this to mean that not just individual souls but legions of souls are distributed among individual stars.[46] Timaeus adds that God has placed the souls in their vehicles and taught them the nature of the universe along with the laws of fate.[47]

From what part of heaven do they descend? Principally from 2 Cancer, according to the Platonists, and they suppose they ascend in turn through Capricorn, [the sign] opposite to Cancer; hence they call the first the gateway of men, the second the gateway of the gods.[48] But nobody should be deceived to the point of accepting the descent and ascent here as referring to a place. Because the Moon, the mistress of Cancer, is closest to generation, however, while Saturn, the lord of Capricorn, is most remote, they say that souls descend through Cancer, that is, through the instinct that is lunar and vegetative, but ascend through Capricorn, that is, through the instinct that is saturnian and intellectual. For the ancients call Saturn the mind by which alone we seek higher things. Moreover, the dry power of Capricorn and of Saturn, while it internally contracts and collects the spirits, stimulates us ceaselessly to contemplation, whereas the wetness of the Moon disperses and dilates [the spirits] and distracts the rational soul with sensibles. In the descent, however, the rational soul receives, both from the divinity of Saturn through itself and from the light of Saturn through its ethereal body and idolum, certain aids or inducements to better prepare it for contemplation. Similarly, from the divinity and light of Jupiter, it receives inducements to the governing of civil life; from Mars likewise, to the magnanimity that wards off injustices; from the Sun, to the clarity of the phantasy and the senses; from Venus, to charity;[49] from Mercury, to interpretation and eloquence; and from the Moon, to generation.[50] And though

nem atque eloquentiam. A Luna ad generandum. Et quamvis inde[37] singula dentur bona, possunt tamen in mixtione terrena ad malum degenerare.

3    Descensus huiusmodi ita ferme subito potest fieri, ut radii descensus a sole, qui quamvis subito demittatur[38] in terram, variis tamen in ipso casu nubium vestitur coloribus. Nonnulli vero putant animas in qualibet sphaera ad certum tempus vitam agere sphaerae illi convenientem. Sortiri enim a sphaeris singulis vehicula propria, ac tandem post multa saecula ad elementa descendere atque in igni et aere daemonicam, in terra humanam brutalemve vitam agere; item similibus gradibus tandem ad superna redire. Haec illi.

4    Nos autem in omnibus quae scribimus, eatenus affirmari a nobis aliisque volumus, quatenus Christianorum theologorum concilio videatur.

: VI :

*Quando infunditur anima corpori et quo,*
*dum in corpore vivit,*[39] *ducitur?*

1   Quando infunditur anima corpori? Postquam in alvo mulieris ipsum semen, quod a toto viri corpore ante defluxerat traxeratque secum formatricem vim ab anima viri, per hanc ipsam vim diebus circiter quinque et quadraginta sic est affectum, ut sex primis diebus lac evaserit, novem sequentibus sanguis, duodecim aliis caro, decem et octo reliquis fuerit figuratum, tunc anima creatur atque infunditur.

2   Qui animas ante ingressum vixisse putant, eas daemonem vitae ducem naturaliter elegisse dicunt in ipso descensus initio prius-

individual goods are bestowed from these sources, nonetheless in the earthly mixture they can degenerate and become evil.

Such a descent can happen as suddenly almost as the descent of 3 a ray from the sun, which, though it is suddenly dispatched to earth, in that descent is clothed nonetheless in the various colors of clouds. But some people think that the souls in every sphere live for a certain time a life appropriate to that sphere.[51] For they are allotted appropriate vehicles from the individual spheres, and after many centuries they descend at length towards the elements and pass in the fire and air a demonic life, and on earth a human and bestial life; and then they return at length by similar degrees towards things supernal. Such are the ancients' views.

In everything we pen, however, we want to affirm, and others to 4 affirm, only what may appear acceptable to a council[52] of Christian theologians.

## : VI :

*When is the soul poured into the body and by whom*
*[or what] is it led while it lives in the body?*

When is the soul poured into the body? It is only after the seed in 1 the woman's womb — the seed which had earlier flowed out of the man's whole body bearing with it the formative power from the man's soul — has been so affected through this formative power for some forty-five days that for the first six days it has emerged as milk, for the next nine days as blood, for twelve days more as flesh, and has been shaped for the eighteen remaining days. It is then that the soul is created and poured in.

Those who think that souls have lived before this entry [into 2 the body] declare that they naturally selected their life's demon-

quam corpus ingrederentur. Alii vero, postquam electione uti coe-
perint[40] eligendo mores, interim daemonem vitae ducem latenter
eligere. Saepe etiam eundem daemonem a pluribus eligi; posse
enim animas multas genio uno, id est uno ingenii duce daemone
uti. Qui ante eligere opinantur ex illa potissimum turba[41] daemonum accipere volunt, quae[42] eidem accommodetur stellae, cui et
anima ab ipso mundi opifice fuerit assignata. Tot enim esse daemonum heroumque legiones, quot stellae sunt numero. Atque ex
tali quadam turba illum sortiri prae ceteris, qui cum illa electa vita
maxime convenit et figura caeli, quae eo ipso electionis descensus
momento componitur, maximamque his de causis in hominum in-
geniis fortunisque differentiam provenire.

3     Qui vero post ortum pro diversitate morum diversos animas
adipisci genios aiunt, permutari quoque duces eiusmodi conce-
dunt, moribus permutatis, plusque consilio tribuere quam vel fato
vel fortunae videntur.

4     Verum utcumque sit, perpetua indigemus custodia numinum.
Quod quidem Plato cum in *Symposio, Protagora, Politico, Critia* dicat,
sic probat in *Legibus,* videlicet quoniam inter falsa bona et innumerabilia mala versamur, unde perpetua fallacia et perturbatio nascitur, ideoque tamquam oves mira divinorum pastorum custodia
semper egemus. Addit, cum nos proprium quidem vitium perdat,
propria vero virtus velut exigua servare non possit, ideo sola supe-
rorum virtute custodum, quorum virtutis imago quaedam exigua
sit nostra virtus, nos posse servari, praesertim cum, sicut alibi di-

guide at the very beginning of the descent, before they entered the body.[53] But others think that only after they have begun to exercise choice by selecting a moral way of life, do they choose in the meantime, though in secret, that life's demon-guide; and they suppose too that the same demon is often chosen by the majority — for many souls can use one genius, that is, one demon, as the guide of their innate intelligence. Those who think the souls choose [the demon] earlier than this claim that they accept it from the crowd of demons chiefly which is attached to the same star, the star to which a soul too has been assigned by the world's artificer Himself. For there are as many legions of demons and heroes as there are stars. And from such a huge crowd, they claim, the demon is allotted before all others who is most in harmony with that chosen life and with the configuration of the heavens as it pertains at the very moment of the choice of the descent; and they argue that the greatest difference in men's mental capacities and fortunes derives from these causes.

Those who say that souls acquire their different genii after 3 the beginning and according to the diversity of their moral habits also concede, however, that such guides change when their habits change; and they seem to attribute more to deliberation than to fate or fortune.

Whatever the truth, we need spiritual beings to watch over us 4 perpetually. Though Plato asserts this in the *Symposium*, *Protagoras*, *Statesman*, and *Critias*,[54] he proves it in the *Laws*[55] on the grounds that, since we are hemmed in between false goods and innumerable evils that give rise to perpetual deception and perturbation, we always need divine shepherds to watch over us in a marvelous way like sheep. He adds that since our own vice destroys us, but our own virtue cannot save us, being too frail, we can be saved only by the virtue of higher guardians (of whose virtue our virtue is but a frail image); and especially since, as he says elsewhere and as Hermias explains,[56] the malefic daemons constantly and to the

cit, Hermia exponente, malefici daemones assidue nos pro viribus ad inferiora detorqueant. Sed alii sunt custodes illi qui nos eligunt, alii daemones quos nos eligimus.

## : VII :

*Qua parte corporis anima ingreditur, qua egreditur,*
*et quo duce progreditur?*

1 Anima qua parte corporis ingreditur, qua egreditur? Anima quae est medium rerum iussu dei, qui est mundi centrum, in punctum cordis medium, quod est centrum corporis, primum infunditur. Inde per universa sui corporis membra se fundit, quando currum suum naturali iungit calori; per calorem spiritui corporis; per hunc spiritum immergit humoribus; membris inserit per humores. Denique per morbum solutis his[43] mediis, statim cum suo illo curru se, ut ita dixerim, colligit refluitque in cor, unde primum effluxerat. Cordis extincto calore, quod proprium erat illius vehiculi susceptaculum,[44] cor deserit tandem suo illam vehiculo comitante, sicut oculo clauso lumen solis, quod illi influxerat, effluit integrum suo ipsum comitante calore. Atque, ut probat Plotinus, non exstinguitur, sed solem suum perpetuo sequitur. Mitto in praesentia quod egredientes animas genii daemonesque sui ad communem iudicem omnes ducunt; sed lata sententia priores abeunt daemones malasque violentus et malus daemon trahit, bonas autem deus tranquille perducit. Haec in *Phaedone*.

best of their ability deflect us towards lower things. However, those guardians who choose us are one group, the daemons whom we choose are another.

: VII :

*By what part of the body does the soul enter and by what part does it leave, and with what guide does it proceed?*

By what part of the body does the soul enter and by what part 1 does it leave? The soul that is the universal mean first enters by the command of God, who is the world's center, into the heart's mid-point, which is the body's center. From there it diffuses itself through all the members of its body when it joins its chariot to the natural heat, and through the heat to the body's spirit. Through this spirit the soul plunges into the humors, and through the humors it inserts itself into the members. At the end, when these intermediaries have been dissolved through disease, it immediately gathers itself together, as it were, along with its chariot and flows back into the heart whence it had first issued. When the heat of the heart is extinguished, which is what properly sustains the soul's chariot, the soul, with its vehicle accompanying it, at length deserts the heart. Similarly when the eye is shut the sun's light, which had flowed into the eye, continues to pour forth in its totality and with its heat accompanying it. And, as Plotinus proves, the light is not extinguished but follows its sun perpetually.[57] I leave aside for the present the fact that their genii and daemons lead all the exiting souls to the common judge; but after the verdict has been pronounced, the earlier daemons depart, and a violent and evil daemon drags off the wicked souls, while God Himself in tranquility leads away the good souls. All this is in the *Phaedo*.[58]

: VIII :

*De statu animae purae,*
*praecipue secundum Platonicos.*[45]

1   Ubinam est anima pura decedens, corpore mortuo? Ubi est lumen solis[46] purum, oculo clauso. At lumen in solem reflectitur. In aetherem quoque reflectitur animae currus aethereus, onere terreno deposito. Ad aetherem aspirat anima nata quondam in aethere, ut inquit Pythagoras, praecipue si vivendi et cogitandi habitum aethereis mentibus similem mente conceperit. Ita enim animus habitu movetur et agit, sicut natura formis. Quod quidem patet in his qui postquam artis habitum contraxerunt, sine consilio et attentione, ut natura solet, quasi naturaliter operantur. Remanere vero in anima separata habitus tum morum tum disciplinarum, tam bonos quam malos, Plato in *Phaedone Gorgiaque*[47] asserit; et ratio illa probat qua dicitur habitum ita in naturam converti, ut talis ab illo, qualis a natura proveniat inclinatio, quod maxime impletur in animis ab hac mutabilitate seiunctis.

2   Sed cur animae quoque elementorum earumque currus ad caelestem habitationem non annituntur? Quoniam (ut platonicorum potius quam mea opinione respondeam) officium illis a deo assignatum est, ut ibi sint semper. Animae cedunt voluntati divinae; currus quoque cedunt desiderio animarum. Animae illae ex hoc officio praestantius officium non amittunt. Currus orbicularem

: VIII :

*On the changeless state of the pure soul,*
*especially according to the Platonists.*

Where is the pure soul when it departs with the death of the    1
body? Where is the pure light of the sun when the eye is closed?
But light is reflected back to the sun. The aethereal chariot of the
soul is turned back to the aether too, once the earthly burden has
been laid aside. The soul once born in the aether yearns for the
aether, as Pythagoras says,[59] especially if it has conceived in its
mind a habit of living and of thinking that resembles that of
aethereal minds. Thus the rational soul is moved and acts by its
habit just as nature is by forms. This is manifest in the case of
those who, having contracted the habit of a particular art or skill,
operate naturally almost without deliberation or attention as nature usually does. But Plato affirms in the *Phaedo* and *Gorgias* that
the habits of behavior and of the disciplinary skills, good and
bad alike, remain in the separated soul;[60] and the particular proof
is where the habit is said to be so converted into nature that
the same kind of inclination issues from it as it does from nature.
This happens most fully in souls separated from this [earthly]
mutability.

But why don't the souls of the elements too and their chariots    2
strive to reach the celestial home? If I may respond with the opinion of the Platonists rather than my own,[61] it is because the office
assigned them by God is to remain always where they are; and the
elements' souls obey the divine will, while the chariots obey the
souls' desire. Those souls do not lose a more outstanding office because of this assigned office. The chariots preserve an unimpeded
orbital motion around their souls. And just as it is natural there
for the heavens to be turned around their souls, so is it natural

motum circa suas animas servant non impeditum. Et sicut caelis naturale est illic circa suas animas verti, ita hic[48] his vehiculis circa suas. At anima nostra, rite functa hic munere sibi ad tempus iniuncto, aetheris eam plagam sibi prae ceteris eligit cui nascendo fuerat assignata, ad illud confugit astrum atque numen, ut Plato inquit, cui vivendo se similem reddidit. Sed haec[49] illi viderint. Proinde sicut in terris considerando a singulis ad communes naturalium species, a speciebus ad rationes divinas, tamquam naturalium causas procedebat, sic in caelo vicissim a rationibus divinis, id est ideis, ad species naturales perfecte, ab his ad singula quodammodo se convertit. Ac quam diligenter hic inspiciebat singula, tam ibi eadem prospicit neglegenter. Rursus quam obscure divina prospiciebat, tam perspicue ibi perspicit eadem. Et quae hic singulatim per instrumenta in externo videbat lumine, illic secundum speciem per se in lumine videt intrinseco.

3      Profecto quantum olim convertebatur ad sensum, tantum convertitur tunc ad mentem, cuius oculo divinum fulget lumen. Quod quidem etsi intrinsecum mentibus dici potest, tamen multo magis ab ipso deo quam infusus oculo radius a sole pendet semper atque servatur plenusque formarum adest, sicuti colorum solis lumen. Formasque ipsas et cuncta per formas eatenus ostendit mentibus, quatenus in ipsum purae ardentesque convertuntur. Tot vero saltem iis omnino conversis patefacit, quot rerum species facit in

here for these chariots to be turned around their souls. But when our soul has for a time rightly performed the task imposed upon it here, it chooses for itself before all else the region of the aether to which it was assigned at birth; and it takes refuge in that star and divinity which, as Plato says, it tried to resemble in its life.[62] But let the Platonists concern themselves with these matters. Consequently, just as in considering things on earth [our soul] was wont to proceed from individuals to the common species of natural things, and proceed from the species to the divine rational principles as the causes of these natural things, so in heaven on the contrary, it starts off from the divine rational principles, the Ideas, and in a way turns itself back perfectly towards the natural species, and thence to individuals. And as diligently as it used to examine individuals here, so as negligently does it look upon them there; and as obscurely as it used to look upon divine things here, so as lucidly does it gaze upon them there. And what it used to see here individually and through the instruments [of the senses] and in an external light, it sees there in terms of a species and through itself and in an internal light.

Certainly, to the extent it was once converted to the sense, our soul is then converted to the mind in whose eye blazes the light divine. Though one can say that this light is internal to minds, yet it depends much more on God Himself than the ray flooding the eye depends forever on the sun; and it is preserved and its presence is full of forms, just as the sun's light is full of colors. To the extent pure and ardent minds are converted to Him, God shows the forms, and all things by way of the forms, to minds. As many species as He makes in the world, that many at least does He reveal to those who have been converted entirely to Him. For it would be improper to form the mind less than the matter of the world, or to give the mind less than it naturally desires. But the mind desires to understand the order of the universe in which it is itself included; it has long sought for it in wonder, and it has itself

mundo. Non enim decet minus formare mentem quam mundi materiam, neque minus tribuere menti quam naturaliter appetat. Optat autem ordinem universi comprehendere, quo et ipsa comprehensa est, quem diuturna iam admiratione quaesivit, in quo et ipsa providentiae cuiusdam sortitur officium. Singula vero et infima tantum in lumine prospicit, sive praeterita illa fuerint sive praesentia sive futura, quantum ad illa vel providentia quadam vel affectu dirigitur. Sane quemadmodum senes puerorum ludos, philosophi studia plebeorum, vigilantes somnia dormientium aut neglegunt aut rident, nisi aliter nonnumquam necessitas postulaverit, ita et multo magis segregatae mentes nostra haec singula et contingentia neglegunt, nisi quantum ab ipso omnium patre (cuius natura providentia ipsa est, cuius agere est providere, cuius officium est omnibus providere), providentia illis quaedam fuerit demandata. Tales Plotinus animas tum ex antiquorum sententia tum ex propria ratione probat curare suos et saepe publice vaticiniis ceterisque beneficiis generi humano prodesse. Sed cum harum providentia voluntati divinae consentiat, non perturbatione ex rebus nostris ulla tanguntur, sed facile haec et tranquille gubernant.

4   Sed ne quis diffidat animam separatam ad tantum posse lumen attolli, propterea quod eam in corpore videamus tanta caligine circumfusam, comparare Platonici iubent intellectum quidem visui, intellegibile vero visibili. Visus numquam lucem ipsam in ipso sole plenissimam comprehendit; illa enim huius semper excedit proportionem. Interdum etiam neque lumen in coloribus impeditus cataracta videt. Aliquando vapore quodam obfusus vel rubro vel croceo, et obscure et aliter quam sit iudicat. Alias autem vel propter contractionem ad interiorem imaginationem externa non vide-

been allotted in that order the office of being a kind of providence. But it sees individuals and the lowest things in the light (whether they were past or are present or are to come) insofar as it is directed towards them either by a certain providence or by desire. Of course, just as old men either neglect or scorn the games of children, and philosophers, the concerns of common people, and waking people, the dreams of those who are asleep — unless necessity demands otherwise on certain occasions — so *a fortiori* separated minds neglect our individual and contingent concerns except insofar as a certain providence has been entrusted to them by the universal Father Himself, whose nature is very providence, whose activity is to provide, whose office is to provide for all things. Plotinus proves, from the opinion of the ancients and from his own reasoning, that such [separated] souls take care of their own and often manifestly provide the human race with prophecies and other benefits.[63] But since their providence conforms to the divine will, they are not perturbed by anything stemming from our affairs, but rather govern these affairs with ease and with tranquility.

Lest someone doubt that the separated soul is able to be raised to   4
such splendor on the grounds that we see the soul in the body enveloped in such deep gloom, the Platonists instruct us to compare the intellect to the sight, and the intelligible to the visible.[64] The sight never takes in the light at its very brightest in the sun; for such light always exceeds the like capacity of the eye. Now and then, prevented by a cataract, the eye does not even see the light in colors. Sometimes, shrouded in a red or yellow vapor, the eye sees obscurely and makes false judgments. At other times, however, because it is concentrating on the inner imagination, it does not appear to see external things; or else, because it is distracted simultaneously by [two] objects far distant from each other, it scarcely

tur aspicere, vel propter distractionem simul ad obiecta inter se
longe distantia vix cernit alterutrum, ac si paulo attentius ad alterum vergit, interim remissius vel nullo modo vergit ad alterum. Similiter intellectus humanus immensam ipsam divini luminis pleni-
tudinem in absoluta dei natura exuberantem numquam penitus
comprehendit, quippe cum illa nimium capacitatem exsuperet.

5 Praeterea idem dei lumen vel in rerum creatarum ideis quasi determinatum vel in angelis iam contractum clare perspicere quidem
potest aliquando, videlicet cum ferme ita fuerit a corporis contagione semotus, ut illa. Elementali vero, ut nunc, coniunctus corpori quasi cataracta quadam adeo eius ad illa proportio impeditur,
ut ideales rationes angelicasque substantias longe admodum a materia segregatas omnino comprehendere nequeat. Proinde quotiens
pro viribus quasdam earum proprietates excogitat, totiens, quia
phantasiae coniunctus est, nimirum phantasiae simulacris quasi
vaporibus nebulisque eas adeo prospicit involutas ut vel obscure
admodum vel aliter quam sint videre cogatur. Postremo etiam si
parumper, quoad potest, phantasiae discutiat nubes, interea tamen
quia et ad difficile regendi corporis ministerium est contractus, et
ad sensibilium imaginum occursum continue impendentem simul
atque ad intellegibilium intuitum est distractus, idcirco supernos
influxus vix quidem suscipit et quasi nec prospicit atque, ut Platonici opinantur, tamquam per repentinam quandam coruscationem
subito vanescentem. Quamobrem nemini mirum videri debet,

sees one or the other. And if it inclines more attentively to the one, it turns meanwhile to the other more negligently or not at all. Similarly, the human intellect never entirely understands the immense fullness of the divine light brimming over in God's absolute nature, since that nature far exceeds its own capacity.

Moreover, at some point the human intellect is able to see this same light of God clearly after it has either been determined as it were in the Ideas of created things, or been contracted already in the angels; at the point, that is, when the intellect has been as separated almost from the body's contagion as the Ideas and the angels are separated. But at present, bound as the intellect is to the elemental body as to a sort of cataract, the [original] proportion between itself and the Ideas and angels is so obstructed that it cannot fully understand the ideal rational principles and the angelic substances at the furthest remove from matter. As a result, as often as the intellect thinks to the best of its ability about their various properties, then just as often, because it has been joined to the phantasy, it sees them shrouded in the images of the phantasy as in vapors and clouds; and so much so, that it is compelled to see them either very obscurely or quite other than they really are. Finally, even if, insofar as it can, this intellect for a little while dispels the clouds of the phantasy, yet in the meantime, because it is assigned the difficult task of ruling the body, it is drawn distractedly both towards the continually threatening encounter with sensible images and simultaneously towards the contemplation of intelligibles. So it scarcely receives the influences from on high and it virtually never sees them; and if it does so, as the Platonists suppose, it is just by way of a sudden spark that vanishes as suddenly.[65] Hence it ought to surprise no one that here [on earth] we do not perceive the clarity of things divine, nor do we ever taste, or barely so, the sweetness which such things have for us up there. Because of formless matter, which is entirely foreign both to the mind and to things divine, the mind cannot savor the truth and

quod hic neque claritatem divinorum percipiamus neque suavitatem ipsam, quae illic gustatur ex illis, ipsi umquam vel paulum degustemus. Nempe mens ob informem materiam, et a mente et a divinis alienissimam, non aliter quam lingua propter pituitam paralitica divinorum saporum veritatem voluptatemque gustare non potest. Sed tunc demum salutarem nectarei liquoris recipiet gustum, cum Lethaei fluminis lethales humores penitus expurgaverit, atque insuper divinum fontem non naturali tantum siti, quae ex se ipsa molesta est, appetierit, sed etiam quodam moralis piaeque sitis habitu ipsum prae ceteris, immo solum elegerit appetendum. Quo autem gustu saporibus his vescatur alibi disputavimus.

6    Huc tendit platonicum illud in *Phaedro*, animas quae ex Lethaea emerserint aqua altius evolare, ibique primo[50] caelestem una cum diis caelestibus, deinde supercaelestem cum supercaelestibus circuitum agere, eo scilicet[51] ordine ut aliae cum aliis ibi numinibus circumvagentur circuitusque huiusmodi alternis vicibus repetant. Hoc autem nihil aliud sibi vult, quam solutas ab elementalibus corporibus animas in caelestibus iam vehiculis in figuram propriam, circularem scilicet restitutis caelestem colere regionem, atque alias una cum stellis caelicolisque aliis, quibus vel natura vel habitu magis familiares sunt, tum in certa quadam mundi gubernatione congruere, tum per rerum species similiter ratione discurrere. Rursus cum diis supercaelestibus, id est angelis, in ipso idearum intuitu et quasi quodam circuitu subito consentire et una cum utrisque feliciter utrumque peragere.

7    Addit eisdem una cum superis illic alimentis, scilicet ambrosia et nectare vesci. Ambrosiam quidem esse censet perspicuum suavemque veritatis intuitum, nectar vero excellentem facillimamque providentiam. Hic panditur et vetus illud arcanum a Platone in li-

pleasure of tastes divine in any way other than a tongue does that has lost its taste from a bad cold. But it will eventually recover a healthy taste for nectar-sweet liquid only when it has wholly purged away the lethal waters of the river Lethe; and when, moreover, it has not only desired the divine fountain with a natural thirst which in itself is troublesome, but also chosen it, with a moral and religious thirst that is [now] a habit, as the fountain that must be desired before all others, nay desired alone. With what relish it enjoys these [sweet] savors we have examined elsewhere.[66]

This is what the Platonic passage in the *Phaedrus* is about: the 6 souls which emerge from the water of Lethe fly ever higher and there they perform first the celestial circuit with the celestial gods, then the supercelestial circuit with the supercelestial gods; and they do so in a [set] order such that particular souls go round with particular divinities, and they repeat these circuits in alternation.[67] But this means nothing other than that souls, liberated from the elemental bodies and restored now to their own shape, that is, to their circular shape in their celestial vehicles, dwell in the celestial region; and that various souls are joined with the stars and other heavenly dwellers to which they are more akin either by nature or by habit. They work in harmony with them in governing the world in a certain way; and they discourse with their reason similarly through the species of things. It also means that the souls are in harmony with the supercelestial gods, that is, with the angels, both in the very contemplation of the Ideas and in performing a circuit that is as it were an instant one. Together with the celestial and the supercelestial beings they enact both circuits in happiness.

Plato adds that the souls are nourished there with the same 7 foods as the gods, namely with ambrosia and nectar.[68] He considers ambrosia to be the clear, delightful gazing at the truth, and nectar to be providence in its supreme goodness and effectiveness. Here is unfolded that ancient mystery celebrated by Plato in the

bro *De regno* prae ceteris celebratum, praesentem mundi circuitum ab oriente ad occidentem esse Iovium atque fatalem; verum fore quandoque alterum huic oppositum sub Saturno ab Occidente vicissim ad Orientem, in quo sponte nascentur homines atque a senio procedent in iuventutem, alimentaque illis ultro aeterno sub vere ad votum suppeditabuntur. Iovem, ut arbitror, animam mundi vocat, cuius lege fatali manifestus hic manifesti mundi ordo disponitur. Praeterea vitam animorum in corporibus elementalibus Ioviam esse vult, sensibus actionique deditam, Saturnum vero supremum inter angelos intellectum, cuius radiis illustrentur ultra angelos animae accendanturque et ad intellectualem vitam continue pro viribus erigantur. Quae quotiens ad vitam eiusmodi convertuntur, eatenus sub regno Saturnio[52] dicuntur vivere quatenus intellegentia vivunt. Proinde in ea vita ideo sponte dicuntur regenerari, quia electione propria in melius reformantur. Rursus in dies reiuvenescere, id est, in dies, si modo ibi dies dinumerantur,[53] magis magisque florescere. Hoc[54] illud Apostoli Pauli: 'Homo interior renovatur in dies.' Denique illis alimenta sponte affatim sub perpetuo vere suppeditari, quia non per sensus operosamque disciplinam, sed per lumen intimum summaque cum vitae tranquillitate atque voluptate miris veritatis ipsius spectaculis perfruuntur. Eiusmodi vitae odor quidem mente pro viribus separata sentitur, sapor vero mente penitus separata gustatur.

8     Addit his in *Symposio* purgatas animas, quae divinam prae ceteris pulchritudinem amaverunt, tandem in ipsum divinae pulchritudinis pelagus sese prorsus immergere divinosque ibi liquores non tantum bibere, sed etiam in alios iam ex se ipsis effundere. Summum vero beatitudinis concludit in *Epinomide*, ubi ait animum

*Statesman* before all others: that the present circuit of the world from east to west is the fatal jovian circuit, but that at some time in the future there will be another circuit opposed to this under Saturn that will go from west back again to the east. In it men will be born of their own accord and proceed from old age to youth; and foods will be spontaneously furnished them at will in an eternal spring.[69] He calls Jupiter, I think, the World-Soul, by whose fatal law this manifest order of the manifest world is disposed. Besides, he wants the life of souls in elemental bodies to be the jovian life, one devoted to the senses and to action, but Saturn to be the supreme intellect among the angels, by whose rays souls are illuminated over and above the angels and set on fire and wafted continually, according to their capacities, up to the intellectual life. As often as souls are turned back towards such a life, and to the extent they live by understanding, they are said correspondingly to live under the rule of Saturn. In that life consequently they are said to be regenerated of their own accord, because they are reformed for the better by their own choice. And they are daily renewed; that is, daily (if days can be numbered there) they blossom more and more. This is what that saying of the apostle Paul refers to: "The inner man is renewed day by day."[70] Finally foods arise of their own accord and are supplied to souls in abundance in a perpetual spring, because they enjoy the wonderful spectacles of Truth itself[71]—enjoy not through the senses and through laborious training, but through an inner light and with life's deepest tranquility and loftiest pleasure. The fragrance of such a life is perceived by a mind that has been separated insofar as it can be; but its flavor is tasted by a mind that has been absolutely separated.

In the *Symposium* Plato adds that the purged souls, who have 8 loved the divine beauty preeminently, eventually immerse themselves utterly in the very sea of the divine beauty,[72] and not only quaff down there the draughts divine but also pour these draughts out of themselves now into other souls.[73] But in the *Epinomis* he

purgatissimum, omni tum mutabilitate firmata tum multiplicitate collecta, sese in propriam unitatem intellectu superiorem omnino conferre, perque hanc in unitatem divinam intellegibili mundo superiorem iam transferre, deoque potius vivere quam se ipso, cui certe mira quadam super intellegentiam ratione sit coniunctus. Hunc vero nodum effici Plato vult divina quadam luce, quae quidem non aliter in mente refulgeat, quam si amore dei prorsus accensa transformetur in deum. Quo fit ut divinum amorem in *Phaedro* omnibus divini furoris gradibus animique bonis longissime praeposuerit. Hic vero potissimum platonica latent mysteria, paucis quae subdam a nobis breviter comprehensa.

9    Nempe segregatae mentes cum primum in se convertuntur, per radium naturalem sibique proprium (tamquam animalia, quae nocte vident) pauca quaedam et illa quidem[55] quasi sub nube vident, quatenus scilicet earum natura sub determinata specie rerumque formulis quasi informibus repraesentat. Deinde vero per radium proprium in lumen commune cunctis mentium sublimium speciebus sese convertentes, iam per ipsum quasi per diurnum lumen perspicue cuncta ab ipso luminis huius auctore creata conspiciunt. Lucem vero ipsam, luminis huius originem, quam naturaliter appetunt, ideoque nec frustra desiderant, assequi suspiciendo non possunt, quoniam et per externum a deo lumen, quatenus externum est, lucem deo intimam omnino penetrare et amplissimum dei angustissimo suo comprehendere nequeunt, siquidem lumen ipsum, quamvis in deo amplum, tamen in mentibus evadit angustum.

10    Verum lucem, licet obscure prospectam,[56] tamen ardenter amando ipsius interim calore penitus accenduntur atque accensae,

concludes with the summit of beauty, when he says that the utterly purged soul—with all mutability rendered constant and all multiplicity collected as one—gathers itself entirely into its own unity, which is higher than the intellect.[74] Through this unity it now transfers itself into the unity divine which is higher than the intelligible world; and rather than in itself, it lives in God to whom it is surely joined by a wonderful principle that surpasses understanding. Plato holds this knot to be the effect of a sort of divine light, which blazes in the mind exactly as if, having been completely set on fire by the love of God, it were being transformed into God. The result is that in the *Phaedrus* Plato has set divine love before all the other degrees of divine frenzy and far exceeding the goods of the rational soul.[75] Here in particular the Platonic mysteries lie concealed, and, in a few words I am about to add, this is how in brief we understand them.

Separated minds, as soon as they return to themselves, see a few things through the natural ray proper to them (as animals that see at night), and these indeed as if they were under a cloud, to the extent, in other words, that their nature represents such things under a determined species and under the formless formulas as it were of things. Then turning themselves back via their own ray towards the light common to all the species of higher minds, the minds now clearly perceive—through the light of day as it were—all those things created by the Author Himself of this light. But the origin of this light, light itself, which the minds desire naturally and do not therefore desire in vain, they cannot attain by gazing upwards, because they can neither entirely penetrate the light that is internal to God through the light external to God (insofar as it is external), nor understand the most ample light of God by their own most narrow light, since the light, though unconfined in God, becomes confined nonetheless in minds.[76]

In loving this light ardently, even though it is obscurely foreseen, the souls are meanwhile utterly inflamed by its heat, and

quod amoris est proprium, transformantur in lucem. Qua denique roboratae ob amorem iam consequuntur quod per aspectum vix eminus sequi potuerant, ut lux iam ipsa amore facillime fiant, quam prosequi oculis ante moliebantur. Tanta vis est amoris, tanta facilitas, tanta felicitas, immo vero, ut rectius loquar, tanta vis est lucis amatae. Mens enim amando lucem non tam sese accendit et transfert, quam a luce blande alliciente, vehementer percutiente, penitus penetrante et accenditur et transfertur et lucet. Cum vero tota perceptionis fruitionisque efficacia quae in sensibus est externis, sit et multo magis in phantasia rursusque longe potentior sit in mente, expedita praesertim, ac praeterea sensibilium rerum oblectamentorumque rationes exactissimae[57] sint in deo, sequitur ut mens, dum expedita potitur deo, summa quaeque et sincerissima omnium oblectamenta sensuum suo quodam miroque modo plenissime sentiat. Neque solum imaginaria circa deum delectatione, quasi videndo audiendoque et odorando (haec enim implere non potest), sed etiam substantiali quadam, gustui tactuique persimili, voluptate permulceatur. Gustum vero tactumve, inquam, non contigui cuiusdam, ut fit in sensibus, sed penetrantis penitus atque penetrati. Penetrati, inquam, a toto immensoque bono, totum secum immensumque gaudium inferente.

### Novem gradus in patria

11 Proinde novem beatorum gradus non solum apud Christianos, sed etiam apud Platonicos tum in angelis tum in animis disponuntur, ob eam, ut arbitror, rationem, quod novem praecipue modis divina

having been set aflame—this being the property of love—they are transformed into light. Finally, strengthened by light and because of love, they now attain what through looking they had scarcely been able to attain from afar, so that with greatest ease they now become through love the very light they were striving to pursue beforehand with their eyes. So immense is the power of love, so immense its facility and felicity, or rather, to speak more correctly, so immense is the power of the beloved light! For in loving the light, the mind does not so much set itself on fire and transport itself, as it is taken by the light which gently seduces it, vehemently assaults it, and totally penetrates it: it is inflamed, it is transported, it is radiant with light. But since the full effectiveness of perception and of enjoyment which exists in the external senses exists even more in the phantasy, and is far more powerful again in the mind (especially when the mind has been freed); and since, moreover, the rational principles of sensible things and of pleasures exist with the utmost exactitude in God—then it follows that the mind, when it achieves God after its liberation, senses in its own marvelous way and to the utmost degree the supreme, the most authentic pleasures of all the senses. In the presence of God, the mind's delight is not only via the imagination, as in seeing, hearing, and smelling (for these cannot satisfy), but it is charmed by a substantial pleasure, one much like the pleasure of taste and of touch. But it is the taste and touch, not of something just next to us as happens in the senses, but of what is penetrating deep within and of what is penetrated—penetrated, I say, by the whole, the measureless good which brings with it the whole, the measureless joy.

### The nine degrees in the father-land

Not only among Christians,[77] therefore, but among Platonists 11 too[78] the orders of the blessed among the angels and souls are arranged as nine for the very reason, I believe, that divine contem-

illic perficitur contemplatio. Sane quemadmodum nos ex rerum potentia, ordine, commoditate potentiam, sapientiam, bonitatem dei qua possumus sagacitate venamur, sic illi vicissim ex divina bonitate, potentia, sapientia, tamquam ex finali efficiente exemplari causa universi, haec tria similiter in rebus agnoscunt, ea videlicet ratione, ut alii divinam bonitatem potissimum in se ipsa considerent, alii ad res ipsas praecipue referant, alii praecipue res ad ipsam velut ad finem, singuli tamen cuncta contueantur. Sic ergo triplex divinae bonitatis impletur intuitus, per quem tres primi beatorum ordines distinguuntur. Tribus quoque modis similiter potentia totidemque sapientia cogitatur. Hinc[58] sex insuper ordines beatorum connumerantur. His novem felicium gradibus apud Platonicos octo caelorum plagae ac nona super caelum excogitata regio congrue accommodari videntur; apud Orphicos autem octo caeli atque sub luna aethereus ignis; apud Christianos circuli sub empyreo novem. Quilibet enim ad illam potissimum regionem habitu quodam simili, quasi naturali levitate, feruntur, cuius habitatoribus angelis sese in vita praecipue similes reddiderunt. Similiter quoque Christiani reprobos animos in novem reproborum daemonum gradus quibus se vivendo fecere similes ipsa similitudine, quasi pondere naturali, putant praecipitari. Sed de his alias.

12    Quod vero novem sint in beatitudine gradus, haec quoque, ut arbitror, ratio comprobat. Nempe divinam potentiam timemus, sapientiam quaerimus, diligimus bonitatem. Solus quidem bonitatis amor animam transformat in deum. Idcirco amor absque inquisi-

plation is perfected there principally in nine ways. Just as we hunt after God's power, wisdom, and goodness with whatever cunning we can, following the power, order, and usefulness of things, so in turn the blessed similarly recognize as coming from the divine goodness, power, and wisdom (as from the final, efficient, and exemplary cause of the universe) the same three attributes in things. And it is for the very reason that some [among the blessed] may consider the divine goodness chiefly in itself, others relate [it] chiefly to things themselves, and still others relate things chiefly to it as to their end; and yet singly they may contemplate all [that is good].[79] So the threefold contemplation of divine goodness is thus fulfilled, and through this contemplation the three prime orders of the blessed are distinguished. Similarly, [divine] power is considered in three ways too and likewise [divine] wisdom. Hence we can count six more orders of the blessed. Matched harmoniously, it seems, to these nine degrees of the blessed according to the Platonists, are the eight heavenly regions and the ninth region thought to be above the heavens.[80] But according to the Orphics it is the eight heavens and the sublunar aethereal fire;[81] and according to the Christians it is the nine circles below the empyrean.[82] For all the blessed are borne by a like habit, as by a natural levity, chiefly towards that region whose inhabitants are the very angels whom the souls have made themselves resemble most in life. Similarly, Christians too think that reprobate souls are cast down among the nine degrees of reprobate demons whom the souls have made themselves resemble in life,[83] cast down by this resemblance to the demons as by a natural weight. But of these matters elsewhere.

That there are nine degrees in blessedness is established I think 12 also by this proof. We certainly fear the divine power, we seek the divine wisdom, and we love the divine goodness. The love alone of goodness transforms the soul into God. So love restores the soul to its native land without its seeking or fearing. The contrary is

tione atque timore animam patriae reddit; contra vero nequaquam. Sed iam gradus ipsos, quibus in caelum ascenditur, ordine disponamus. In primo sint, qui potissimum bonitatem amant, deinde potentiam timent, postremo sapientiam quaerunt. In secundo, qui in primis diligunt bonitatem, circa vero reliqua duo se pariter habent. In tertio, qui similiter erga bonum in primis afficiuntur, deinde sapientiam perscrutantur, postremo timent potentiam. In quarto, qui circa tria aeque se habent. In quinto, qui bonum primo[59] amant, deinde potentiam extimescunt. In sexto, qui similiter bonum diligunt, sequenti vero gradu appetunt sapientiam. In septimo, qui absolute bonum et simpliciter amant. In octavo, quos potentia primum, secundo bonitas, tertio sapientia movet. In nono, apud quos sapientia primo, secundo bonitas, tertio potentia[60] potest.

13     Mysterium eiusmodi in Evangelio ibi significatum arbitror, ubi divinum oraculum sectatores suos novies beatos appellat, propterea quod novem gradibus meritorum duce deo caeli novem ad novem contemplationis ordines beate petuntur. Sed ecce iam beata Evangelii sancti commemoratio nos admonere videtur, ut philosophicis dimissis ambagibus breviori tramite beatitudinem ea quaeramus via, qua Christiani ducunt theologi ac Thomas Aquinas in primis, Christianae splendor theologiae.

*De statu animae purae,*
*praecipue secundum Christianos theologos*

14     Creata mens quaelibet respiciendo vel in suam essentiam (quae ibi differt ab esse et in certa specie est a deo infinite distante), vel in lumen sibimet proprium, vel in quodvis lumen in ea determina-

not true. But let us now arrange in order the nine degrees by which one ascends the heavens. In first place let us put those who love the [divine] goodness most, then fear the power, and finally seek the wisdom; in second, those who love the goodness, but who respond equally to [God's] other two attributes; in third, those who likewise primarily love the goodness, then seek the wisdom, and finally fear the power; in fourth, those who are equally disposed to all three; in fifth, those who first love the goodness, then fear the power; in sixth, those who likewise love the goodness, but subsequently desire the wisdom; in seventh, those who love the goodness absolutely and simply; in eighth, those whom the power moves first, the goodness second, and the wisdom third; and in ninth place, those whom the wisdom rules first, the goodness second, and the power third.

I think that such a mystery is signified in the Gospel when the 13 oracle divine [i.e. Christ] nine times calls His followers blessed,[84] precisely because it is by nine degrees of merits, with God as guide, and with regard to the nine orders of contemplation that the nine heavens are blessedly sought after. But lo, the blessed recollection of the holy Gospel already seems to admonish us to dismiss philosophical meanderings and to seek out blessedness by a shorter path, the path along which Christian theologians conduct us and primarily Thomas Aquinas, the splendor of Christian theology.

> *On the changeless state of the pure soul,*
> *especially according to Christian theologians*

Every created mind, in looking either to its own essence (which 14 differs then from its being and which is in a fixed species infinitely distant from God), or to the light proper to itself, or to any light as it is determined in it [the species?], is unable to understand the divine substance, which, since it is infinite, certainly cannot be represented (in terms of what it is) through something finite. Only

tum, substantiam divinam intellegere nequit, quae cum infinita sit, certe quid ipsa sit per finitum aliquid repraesentari non potest. Solum vero, per ea quae diximus, mentes et deum esse cognoscunt, et quid non sit potius quam quid sit, et qua ratione vel ipse ad alia vel alia referantur ad ipsum.

15     Id Plato in *Parmenide* probat. Idem Dionysius Areopagita in *Mystica Theologia* comprobat, concludens mentes in summo naturalis cognitionis gradu coniungi deo velut ignoto, quasi oculum sub solis lumine caligantem. In eiusmodi vero cognitione naturale desiderium non impletur. Quicquid enim in specie quadam est imperfectum, speciei ipsius optat perfectionem. Talis autem cognitio in ipsa cognitionis specie imperfecta censetur. Solemus enim in nullo cognitionis modo quiescere, priusquam quid sit res ipsa secundum substantiam cognoverimus. Praeterea rationi naturalis est continua per rationes discursio, quousque ad summam perveniat rationem, quae quoniam infinita sit, ideo sola rationis discursum ex se absque fine frustra pervagaturum sistere possit. Siquidem ultra finitum quodlibet mens semper aliquid ulterius machinatur. Quod quidem in numeris et lineis et figuris proportionibusque apparet. Quo fit ut in sola dei substantia, quae sola infinita est, conquiescere valeat.

16     Idque inde provenire censendum quod naturalis tum intellegentiae perspicacia tum voluntatis ardor radius quidam est ab ipsa divina luce proxime per ipsius lumen infusus in eandemque[61] resilit naturaliter, neque moveri cessat, priusquam in suum se solem denique restituerit. Proinde quo quid naturali est fini propinquius, eo vehementius adventat ad finem. Quod in elementorum motibus est manifestum. Segregatae vero mentes per naturalem cognitionem propinquiores deo evadunt quam coniunctae. Igitur cum nostrae naturalis cognitionis suae terminis contentae non sint,

through the ways we have described, however, do minds know that God exists and know what He is not rather than what He is, and by what rational principle He is related to others or others are related to Him.

In the *Parmenides* Plato proves this.[85] Dionysius the Areopagite  15 also proves this in the *Mystical Theology* when he concludes that minds in the highest degree of natural cognition are joined to God as if to something unknown, like an eye blindly squinting in the radiance of the sun.[86] The desire is not fulfilled in this natural cognition. For whatever is imperfect in a particular species chooses the perfection of the species. But in the species itself of cognition such a natural cognition is deemed imperfect. For we customarily come to rest in no one mode of knowing until we know what the thing itself is in terms of [its] substance.[87] Continually discoursing through rational principles, moreover, is natural to reason until it arrives at the highest principle, which, since it is infinite, alone can stop the discoursing of reason from of itself wandering endlessly and in vain, since beyond something finite the mind always devises something still further. This is obvious in the case of numbers, lines, [geometrical] figures, and proportions. Consequently reason is able to rest in God's substance alone, which alone is infinite.[88]

We must suppose that this results from the fact that the natural  16 insightfulness of the understanding and the natural ardor of the will are a sort of ray infused in us directly from the divine light itself (*lux*) via its radiance (*lumen*); and this ray naturally leaps back to the same light: it does not stop being moved before it has finally restored itself to its own sun. Consequently, the closer something is to its natural end, the more vehemently it advances towards that end. This is obvious in the motions of the elements. But through natural cognition separated minds come closer to God than minds joined [to the elements]. So, since our minds are not satisfied with the limits of their natural cognition, certainly those separated minds are even less satisfied.[89] But since the desire of any natural

certe multo minus illae. Quoniam vero naturalis speciei cuiuslibet appetitus ab universali natura directus omnino inanis esse non debet, oportet mentes omnes posse divinam videre substantiam, sine qua nihil perfecte vident. At cum videre illam in specie aliqua creata non possint, opus tamen sit forma per quam videant—forma, inquam, divinae substantiae propria, qua illam non imaginarie, sed proprie cernant—necesse est eas divinae substantiae adeo copulari ut ipsam iam inspiciant per se ipsam. Simile quiddam apparet in visu, qui colores quidem per ipsorum imagines sub lumine cernit, lumen vero per aliud praecipue quam per lumen videre non potest.

17    Sed ne quis absurdum putet deum intellectui coniungere velut formam, meminisse oportet perfectionem mentis consistere circa verum. Verum autem et ens et intellegibile idem. Quicquid autem[62] in hoc ipso genere ex essentia atque esse componitur, tamquam ens verumque potius quam tamquam esse veritasve se habet, neque potest aliorum in eodem genere esse forma, cum iam forma in se sua ad suam quasi materiam sit contracta. Itaque nulla creata mens mentium reliquarum forma fieri potest, immo solus deus ad genus mentium ubique se habet ut forma, qui solus est ipsum esse et simplicissima veritas; ut forma,[63] inquam, non tamquam pars compositi, sed operandi principium, quo mens potius ut deus iam quam ut mens operetur, sicut ignitum aurum ut ignis agit potius quam ut aurum, quale Apocalypsis Ioannis iubet emendum.

## Quo pacto mens deo coniungitur

18   Ad hoc autem ut mens divinam induat[64] substantiam, quasi formam, non propria virtute ducitur, sed divina trahitur actione, si-

species (a desire directed by universal nature) must not be entirely in vain,[90] all minds must be able to see the divine substance without which they see nothing perfectly. And since they cannot see it in any created species, and yet there must exist a form whereby they can see it—a form, I say, proper to the divine substance which enables them to see it, not in an imaginary, but in a proper way—necessarily they are so joined to the divine substance that they are now able to see that substance through itself. Something similar appears in the sight: it sees colors through images of them under the light, but it cannot see light in the main in any other way than through light.[91]

Lest someone think it absurd, however, to join God like a form to the intellect, we must recall that the mind's perfection exists with regard to the truth. But being true, being an entity, and being intelligible are the same. Yet in this very genus [of minds] whatever is compounded from essence and being emerges as an entity and something true rather than as being or truth [in the abstract]; and this entity cannot be the form of other things in the same genus, since the form has already been contracted into itself as into its own matter. Therefore any created mind cannot become the form of the remaining minds. Rather God alone is everywhere the form, so to speak, for the genus of minds, since He alone is being itself and truth in its utmost simplicity—form here in the sense, not of being one part of a composite [of form and matter], but of being the principle of activity. With God as this principle, the mind can operate now as God rather than as mind, just as gold glowing in the fire acts as fire does rather than as gold. In the Apocalypse John tells us to buy this kind of gold.[92]

*How the mind is joined to God*

The mind is not led by its own power to don the divine substance like a form; rather it is drawn to do so by divine action, since an

quidem natura inferior proprietatem formamque superioris absque superioris ipsius actione consequi nequit. Quod in elementis est manifestum, in quibus aer non aliter quam agente igne ignis evadit. Praeterea nihil potest ad excellentiorem actionem aliquando perduci, nisi prius in eo virtus corroboretur. Quod si ad consuetam actionis speciem, sed tamen aliquanto[65] vehementiorem est perducendum, satis utique erit, si modo solita virtus augeatur. Utpote si aer, qui naturaliter uno calefacit gradu, duobus aliquando sit gradibus calefacturus, sufficiet naturalis sui caloris aliquantum intendere qualitatem. Verumtamen si aer actionem specie genereque superiorem sit sibi vendicaturus — videlicet si illuminaturus fuerit, quod corporis est aetherei proprium — novam ab ipso aethere formam iam sortiatur oportet.

19    Quorsum haec? Ut intellegamus mentem non posse ad divinam substantiam per ipsammet perspiciendam attolli per solum naturalis virtutis et luminis augmentum, cum eiusmodi operatio ab ipsa naturali mentis operatione plus quam genere differat, sed opus esse nova quadam virtute novoque lumine ab altiori principio descendente. Quod quidem et gratiae et gloriae lumen appellant, quo illuminata mens et multo magis accensa divinam iam substantiam, cuius calore iam fervet, induit[66] velut flammam — flammam, inquam, non qualem in crinita siccus vapor a terra sublatus subit prope ignis sphaeram, quamvis id admodum simile videatur, immo flammam supercaelestem, lucentem salubriter, non urentem.

20    Negabit forte aliquis mentem per quodvis lumen ad perspiciendum deum posse perduci, quia si nulla est visus ipsius ad sonum proportio, nimirum neque mentis neque luminis a mente suscepti,

inferior nature cannot attain the property and form of a higher nature without the action of the higher. This is obvious in the case of the elements where air emerges as fire only by the agency of fire.[93] Furthermore, nothing can be led at any time towards a more excellent action unless the power in it is first enhanced. If it is drawn towards its usual kind of action, however, and yet this kind is just somewhat more vehement, it will surely be enough if its customary power is merely intensified. With air, for instance, which naturally warms [something] by one degree [but] at some point is going to warm it by two, it will suffice if it intensifies somewhat the quality of its own natural heat. Yet if air is going to appropriate an action for itself that is [qualitatively] higher in species and genus — if it is going to illuminate in other words, illuminating being the property of aethereal body — it now has to be allotted a new form from the aether itself.

To what do these considerations lead? That we may understand   19 that the mind cannot be raised through itself to envisioning the divine substance through the increase only of its natural power and light, since such a contemplative activity differs from the natural activity of the mind more than simply by genus: it needs a new power and a new radiance, one descending from a higher principle. They call this the radiance of grace and of glory, the radiance by which the illuminated mind, and even more so the mind on fire, now puts on the divine substance (with whose heat it already burns) like a flame — not the kind of flame in a comet when a dry vapor lofted from earth comes close to the sphere of fire, although it seems completely like it, but rather a supercelestial flame, one that is dazzlingly bright and beneficial, not one that scorches.[94]

Perhaps someone will deny that the mind can be led to seeing   20 God through any light whatsoever on the grounds that, if no proportion pertains between sight and sound, there is certainly no proportion at all between God in His immensity and either the mind or the light received (and thus made finite) by the mind.[95]

ideoque finiti, ulla ad immensum deum proportio est. Nos autem respondebimus deum, quamvis facultatem intellectus excedat, non tamen sic alienum esse ab intellectu, sicut sonus est alienus a visu vel insensibile quiddam a sensu, cum deus sit (ut Christianis placet theologis) intelligibile primum totiusque intellectualis virtutis et actionis principium mediumque et finis. Est igitur quaedam inter intellectum deumque proportio, non quia sit ulla commensuratio, sed habitudo quaedam potius, quasi materiae intellectualis ad intellegibilem formam et effectus ad causam.

21     Praeterea lumen illud infusum, etsi determinatum[67] evadit in mente, ea tamen virtute praeditum a deo infunditur, qua eam divinae substantiae copulet, non naturali quidem, sed intellectuali potius copula. Id vero efficere nequit radius naturalis, quia iam ab initio totus in suscipientis transivit naturam, per se prius informem, unde et ipse caliginosus evasit et debilis. Neque mens, cum longe a divina simplicitate degeneret, totam potest suam per idem sortiri perfectionem. Ideoque aliud in ea radius est naturalis, per quem, quatenus suae convenit speciei, nonnihil intellegit; aliud vero lumen infusum divinitus, quo sublevante ad gradum super se ultra quam cogitari possit eminentissimum mirabiliter elevatur.

22     Denique infinitas ipsa dei haud privationem formae significat, qualis infinitas materiae convenit, cumque sit inefficax et informis, merito cognitioni inepta censetur, sed absolutam significat excellentiam nullo prorsus subiecto contractam. Haec autem ceu sol natura sua id habet ut mirum in modum lucendo atque illuminando maxime omnium movere intellectualem visum possit atque

But we shall respond that God, though He exceeds the faculty of the intellect, is nonetheless not as foreign to the intellect as sound is foreign to the sight or something beyond the senses foreign to the sense, since God, according to Christian theologians, is both the first intelligible and the principle, mean, and end of all intellectual power and action. So a certain proportion does exist between the intellect and God, not because of its commensurability at all [to God], but rather because it has a certain readiness with regard to Him, as of intellectual matter with regard to intelligible form, and of effect to cause.[96]

Moreover, this light that is poured into [the mind], though it 21 turns out to be enclosed in the mind, is endowed nonetheless with the power poured into it by God, a power that unites it to the divine substance, not with a natural but rather with an intellectual bond. Indeed, the [mind's] natural ray cannot do this, because, from the very beginning, the whole of it has crossed over into the nature of the receiver (a nature in itself originally unformed); hence the ray has become obscure and dim. Nor can the mind, since it has fallen away from the divine simplicity, obtain through this natural ray its own entire perfection. So we have the natural ray in the mind, which enables it (insofar as it is proper to its species) to understand something; and we have the light poured in from the divine and elevating it, so that it is miraculously raised above itself to a degree so sublime it is beyond the possibility of thinking.

Finally, the infinity of God does not signify the privation of 22 form, the kind of infinity proper to matter, which, since it is formless and inactive, is rightly deemed unsuited for knowledge: rather it signifies the absolute excellence that is never entirely contracted into a substrate at all. Like the sun, this infinity by its own nature is such that it can in a wonderful way by lighting and illuminating move the intellectual sight most of all and [itself] be seen; and with the same power that it exceeds the mind it can raise the mind

videri, et qua virtute excedit mentem, eadem possit eandem supra
vires proprias elevare. Neque tamen putandum est mentem essentia divina formatam, quamvis quid ipsa sit intellegat, ipsam tamen
penitus comprehendere. Nam et virtus ipsius terminata est, et lumen in ea determinatum, et divinam cum subit essentiam, non per
omnem divinitatis virtutem inde formatur. Quid ergo? Numquid
partem divinae substantiae cernit quidem, partem vero non cernit?
Non ita sane dicendum, siquidem deus dividi nequit. Immo vero
putandum est eam aspicere deum, haud tamen penitus[68] comprehendere, id est sub tot rationibus et tanta certitudine tantaque
perfectione perspicere deum, sub quot et quanta sibimet perspectus est deus.

23     Accedit ad haec quod non cuncta quae deus et videt et potest,
videndo deum potest ipsa videre. Videt autem potestque deus infinita praeter illa quae in natura consistunt. Quod probavimus alias.
Si enim dei substantiam non comprehendit, certe neque intellegentiam eius atque virtutem, neque igitur cuncta quae et intellegit
deus et potest. Alioquin cum virtus per ea quae potest soleat aesti-
mari, sic quaecumque videt potestque, penitus comprehenderet;
comprehenderet pariter videndi faciendique virtutem atque substantiam. Quid plura? Quo altior intellectus, eo et plura vel numero vel ratione intellegere debet. Ex quo consentaneum est divinam mentem se ipsam undique contuentem tum plura tum
pluribus rationibus videre, quam videat quilibet intellectus.

*Omnes mentium species possunt coniungi deo*

24  Nemo vero diffidere debet mentes humanas, propterea quod in
ipso mentium genere infimae sint, ad ipsam divinae substantiae

above its own capabilities.[97] Yet one should not suppose that the mind, formed by the divine essence, though it understands what that essence is, yet understands it totally. For the mind's power is bounded and the light in it is enclosed, and when it approaches the divine essence it is not formed by way of the whole power of that divinity.[98] What then? Does it see one part of the divine substance, but not [another] part? We surely cannot say this, since God cannot be divided. Rather, we must suppose that the mind looks up at God but does not entirely comprehend Him; in other words, it does not see Him under as many rational principles or with such immense certitude and perfection as God has seen Himself.[99]

Furthermore, by looking at God, the mind cannot see all those things that God sees and can do. But God sees and can do infinite things over and beyond those that exist in nature. We have proved this elsewhere.[100] For if the mind does not understand God's substance, it certainly does not understand either His understanding or His power, and therefore all those things which God both understands and is able to do. Otherwise, since power is ordinarily assessed by what it has the capacity to do, the mind would entirely understand everything it sees and is capable of doing: it would understand the power and the substance of seeing and of doing equally. In short, the higher the intellect, the more it has to understand in terms of both number and rational principle. Accordingly it is proper that the divine mind, in everywhere contemplating itself, sees more and sees subject to more rational principles than any [created] intellect may see.[101]

*All species of minds can be united with God*

Nobody should doubt that all human minds, just because they are the very lowest in the genus of minds, are capable of being led to the contemplation of the divine substance, seeing that the angelic

contemplationem posse perduci, quandoquidem neque ipsae angelicae mentes illuc virtute quadam perveniunt naturali, sed divina
potius et, ut ita dicam, supernaturali trahuntur. Opus autem quod
supernaturali virtute peragitur, propter naturarum diversitatem
impediri non potest, quippe cum immensae potentiae dei nihil alicubi reluctetur. Tam facile divina potestas totam movet machinam
quam facile minimam mundi partem. Tam facile curat aegrotantem graviter, quam facile leviter aegrotantem. Quamobrem qua facultate infusa divinitus mentes altissimae, eadem et infimae ad
sublimia rapiuntur.

25     Praeterea suprema mentium creatarum immenso quodam a
deo[69] spatio distat; infima vero ab[70] hac, cum utraque finita sit,
finito discrepat intervallo. Intervalli vero huius ad illud nulla esse
proportio iudicatur. Quod si finitum additum infinito nullam, ut
apparet, affert varietatem, quidnam prohibet ipsam dei virtutem,
quae spatium ad angelum usque subito percurrit immensum, mox
inde[71] pusillum inter angelum animamque complecti, ut simul tam
anima quam angelus rapiatur?

26     Denique si mentium generi, qua ratione mentes sunt, naturalis
est instinctus ad summum intelligibile pervidendum, quod in
omni intelligibili quaerendo quaerunt et appetunt appetendo, sequitur ut tam naturalis sit instinctus eiusmodi mentibus infimis
quam supremis, atque tam hae quandoque quam illae terminum
consequi possint naturaliter exoptatum. Id autem nobis appetitio
ipsa naturalis ostendit, quae cum trahat ad infinitum, non potest
aliunde quam ab ipsomet infinito inseri ac moveri atque denique
terminari. Quod si quae a natura moventur inferiori non frustra
moventur, multo minus quae a suprema ducuntur. Huius quidem

minds themselves do not arrive there by a natural power, but are drawn there rather by the divine, one might say, the supernatural power. The work enacted by the supernatural power cannot be impeded on account of the diversity of natures, since nothing anywhere can strive against the measureless power of God. The divine power moves the whole world machine as easily as it moves the world's smallest part. It cures a person who is grievously ill as easily as it cures someone who is just mildly sick. This is why the lowest minds are rapturously snatched up to sublimities by the same power, infused from on high, as the highest minds.[102]

Moreover, whereas the highest among created minds is separated by a measureless distance from God, the lowest mind is separated from the highest by a finite distance, since both are finite. But no proportion at all is adjudged possible between this finite interval and that infinite one. But if the finite interval added to the infinite clearly introduces no variation at all [to the infinite], then what is there to prevent God's power itself, which traverses the immense distance down to the angel in an instant, from straightway embracing the paltry distance between the angel and the soul, so that the soul and angel alike are enraptured simultaneously?[103]

Finally, if for the genus of minds, and for the very reason they are minds, a natural instinct exists for gazing up towards the highest intelligible, which they seek and desire in seeking and desiring every intelligible, it follows that an instinct of this kind is as natural to the lowest minds as it is to the highest, and that the lowest and highest minds alike are capable some day of achieving the goal they have naturally chosen.[104] But the natural appetite itself demonstrates this to us: since it drags us towards the infinite, it cannot be introduced from anywhere else and moved and eventually terminated other than by the infinite itself. But if things that are moved by some lower nature are not moved in vain, much less are things led by the very highest nature, whose ray, in transmitting itself through all the orders of minds, illuminates individual minds

radius per omnes sese ordines mentium transferens singulas et
illustrat ut videant, et accendit ut ament. Cum vero ignis atque
sol lumen latius propagare soleant quam calorem, consentaneum
est quousque divini solis radius calefaciendo protenditur, eousque
multo magis posse illuminando protendi. Ergo mentes humanae
sicut inde accensae divinum quotidie appetunt bonum, ita et illic
divinum quandoque verum illuminatae conspiciunt atque conspi-
ciendo vero bono feliciter perfruuntur.

### Diversi in patria gradus
### et quod omnes omnia creata vident

27  Possunt autem aliae mentes aliis clarius pleniusque divinam substantiam contueri, quatenus lumen ipsum, quo ad id quasi materiae perspicuae praeparantur, sub diversis perfectionis gradibus
inde suscipiunt, sive pro naturae sive pro dispositionis acquisitae
diversitate aliter atque aliter praeparentur. Maxima vero nostris
mentibus varietas ex diversis amoris gradibus proficiscitur, quibus
quidem gradibus diversi et visionis et multo magis gaudii gradus
non iniuria congruunt. Forte vero, licet singulae cuncta creata videant, ut probabimus, aliae tamen plura quam aliae ex his quae
non creantur attingunt, et quae vident pluribus rationibus asse-
quuntur, omnes tamen vera ratione perspiciunt. Et cum gaudium
velut terminus amori respondeat, quae amaverunt ardentius, hae[72]
coniunctius, ut solet amor, haerentes interius transferuntur in bonum, sic ipso amoris habitu conferente, suaviusque fruuntur.

28  Proinde si mentium finis est ad divinam substantiam pervenire,
necessario illic tamquam in fine omne mentium desiderium pror-

that they may see, and sets them on fire that they may love. But since fire and the sun both customarily propagate their light farther than their heat, it is proper that however far the ray of the divine Sun extends in heating, it can be extended much farther in illuminating. Just as human minds, therefore, having thence been set on fire, daily desire the divine good, so having been illuminated there too, at some point they contemplate the divine truth; and in contemplating, happily they enjoy the true good.

*In our native land there are different degrees*
*and they all see all created things*

Some minds can gaze at the divine substance more clearly and 27 fully than others insofar as they receive the light — by which they are prepared, like transparent materials, for it — under diverse degrees of perfection, whether they are variously prepared according to the diversity either of their nature or of their acquired disposition. But the greatest variety comes to our minds from the diverse degrees of love, and with these degrees — and not unjustly so — diverse degrees of vision and still more so of joy coincide. But perhaps, though individual minds may see all created things,[105] as we are about to prove, nonetheless of the things that are not created [i.e. things divine] some minds attain more than others and grasp what they see in terms of more rational principles; yet all minds perceive with a rational principle that is true. And since as a goal joy corresponds to love, the minds that have loved more ardently — those that cling more closely in the manner of love — are inwardly transferred into the good, and thus, with the habit of love itself contributing, enjoy with greater sweetness.[106]

Consequently, if the end of minds is to arrive at the divine sub- 28 stance, then necessarily these minds' every desire is totally fulfilled there as at its end. But it would not be fulfilled if the minds there did not in every way comprehend the created order of the uni-

sus impletur. Non impleretur autem, nisi ordinem illic universi creatum undique comprehenderent. Siquidem eiusmodi est consuetum studium intellectus, ut particularia in universalia ad communissimum usque resolvat atque ipsum ens sub absoluta ratione describat perque omnes eius gradus distinctissime dividat, quasi ad id praecipue natus sit ut universi forma quandoque formetur. Quidnam prohibet intellectum, dum fontem conspicit universi, universum effluens inde perspicere? Praesertim cum non sicuti sensus ex summo sensibili ad sentienda minora impeditur ad tempus, sic intellectus ex intelligibili summo impediatur ad reliqua, sed potius mirifice roboretur.

29  Praeterea intellegibile genus amplius est genere naturali. Multa enim ultra illa quae natura facit intellegi possunt. Igitur quaecumque ad esse naturale complendum necessario requiruntur, insuper et multo plura ad complendum esse intellegibile exiguntur. At vero esse intellegibile tunc demum absolutum est, cum intellectus summum attingerit finem, quemadmodum ipsa naturalis esse perfectio in ipsa rerum cunctarum constitutione consistit. Quamobrem deus, quaecumque ad perfectionem universi produxit, in intellectu sibi iuncto producit.

30  Rursus quamvis alius perfectius alio deum videat, singuli tamen ita vident ut capacitas naturalis impleatur ad votum. Haec autem in qualibet mente ad omnia universi genera speciesque extenditur. Adde insuper et ad singula passim subdita speciebus. Nec enim insuper exoptamus. Itaque mentes in deo etiam singula distincte discernunt. Profecto cum virtus superior possit quicquid inferior,

verse. For the accustomed study of the intellect is such that it resolves particulars into universals up to the most general universal,
and describes being itself under an absolute rational principle,
and, by making the maximum distinctions, divides it through all
its grades. It is as though it had been born with the particular purpose of being formed at some point by the form of the universe.[107]
But what prevents the intellect when it sees the fountain of the
universe from seeing the universe flowing out of that fountain?
This is especially the case since, whereas the sense is prevented by
the highest sensible for a time from seeing lesser sensibles, the intellect is not prevented by the highest intelligible from understanding the rest of the intelligibles, but wondrously strengthened
rather.[108]

Moreover, the intelligible genus is more encompassing than the     29
natural genus. For many things can be understood over and beyond those that nature makes. All things whatsoever that are necessarily required to perfect natural being, are therefore required,
and very much more so, to perfect intelligible being. But intelligible being is perfected only when the intellect has attained its highest end, just as the perfection of natural being consists in the very
constitution of all things. Hence whatsoever God has produced
for the perfection of the universe, He produces in the intellect
united to Himself.[109]

Again, although one intellect sees God more perfectly than an-     30
other, nonetheless individual intellects see Him such that their
natural capacity is filled as they would wish. But in every mind
this capacity is extended to all the genera and species of the universe; furthermore it is extended to all the individual things sub-
ordinated everywhere to the species. For we wish for nothing
besides. So in God minds distinctly discern even particulars.[110]
Certainly, since a higher power can do whatever a lower power can
do but more outstandingly still, but souls joined to bodies can
know both universal and particular things, it is proper that minds

atque etiam eminentius, animae vero coniunctae corporibus et universalia cognoscant et singula, consentaneum est mentes ipsi veritati coniunctas una virtute unoque intuitu utraque comprehendere, praesertim cum et ipsae rerum species amplissimae sint in illis, et illae virtutem ibi efficacissimam consequantur, per quam genera speciesque ad singula derivent. Sane opposito quodam ordine rerum species ad intellectum coniunctum perveniunt atque separatum. Hic enim resolutione quadam, a singulis materiae conditionibus separando; ibi vero ex coniunctione quadam mentis cum forma divina, omnium effectrice et iudice etiam[73] singulorum. Quae quidem forma non a singulis abstracta est, sed singulorum ubique creatrix, non formae tantum, sed materiae, in qua singularitatis rerum consistit origo. Quamobrem formae in mentem inde fluentes, ultra communia, etiam singula coniunctis mentibus repraesentant. Quod quidem hinc etiam confirmatur, quod si mentes angelicae caelestia corpora per intellectum movent, necesse est eas hoc ipsum, quod movent situsque qui motu mutantur, non ignorare. Nostrae vero mentes ad angelicam, praesertim quantum ad motum spectat, notitiam perduci possunt, praecipue si quod illic gubernationis officium consequantur.

*Status animae apud deum immobilis*

31 Cum mentes illic unica dei forma rerum creatarum videant formas, consentaneum est ut omnes una videant visione, quae quidem si perfectissima est, statu possidetur potius quam successione quaeratur. Probabile enim est mentes quietis potius quam motionis avidas, ubi finem consecutae fuerint, firmiter conquiescere,

joined to Truth itself understand both universals and particulars with one power and in a single act of intuition. And this is especially so since the species of things that are most encompassing are in these very minds, and there they attain their most effective power, the power through which they lead genera and species down to particulars.[111] Clearly, it is in an opposite order that the species of things become known to both a joined and a separated intellect. For here [in the material world] it is from a kind of resolution—from [the intellect's] separating the species from the individual conditions of matter; but there [in the spiritual world] it is from a kind of joining of the intellect with the divine form, the creator of all things and the judge even of particulars. This divine form indeed has not been abstracted from single things, but is everywhere the creator of single things, not only of their form but of the matter wherein consists the origin of things' singularity. Accordingly, the forms flowing into an intellect from this divine form present single as well as universal things to intellects joined [to the form].[112] This is confirmed too by the fact that if the angelic minds move celestial bodies through the intellect, necessarily they are not ignorant either of the fact that they are doing so, or of the celestial positions that are exchanged in the motion.[113] But our own minds can be guided towards [this] angelic knowledge, especially insofar as it regards motion, principally if they can attain there some governing role.

*The changeless state of the soul in the presence of God*

Since minds there [in the presence of God] see the forms of created things by way of God's unique form, it is proper that all of them see with one vision, which, if it is most perfect, is possessed in rest rather than sought for in successive motion. For it may be assumed that minds eager for quietness rather than for motion are steadfastly at rest when they have reached their end; and especially

31

praesertim quia, si omnes universi species ibi cognoscunt, sub quibusdam vero generibus species procedunt innumerae, ceu sub numero figuraque et proportione, consequens esse videtur ut species quodammodo videant infinitas. At vero cum infinita pertransire non liceat, non praetereundo dinumerant, sed manendo conspiciunt.

32     Rursus si perpetua intellegentia ipsius intellegentis vita quaedam est, atque ibi intellegentia ob stabilitatem suam particeps evadit aeternitatis, sequitur ut beata mens in aeternam vitam iure translata dicatur: merito quidem. Nempe mens humana inter aeterna et temporalia media collocatur. Sicut igitur operatio eius, qua coniungitur temporaneis, temporanea evadere consuevit, sic et illa qua aeternis aeterna. Denique quonam pacto visio ipsa illic mobilis[74] sit non video, ubi et videndi virtus tempus tum ab initio tum vel maxime iam supereminet, et obiectum quod videtur, ac forma qua videtur, status ipse est ipsaque aeternitas. Hinc sequitur animas deo semel haerentes inde discessuras esse numquam, si modo motum iam transcenderunt atque naturale desiderium impleverunt. Quod quidem cum et in substantia stabili sit fundatum[75] et ad stabile obiectum naturaliter dirigatur, nimirum non aliam quam stabilem denique possessionem appetit tamquam finem. Quid mirum si sempiterna mens, quod non propter aliud, sed propter se desiderat, desiderat ut semper habendum?

33     Praeterea ubi naturalia sub se nulla ignorat, certe qualis sua illa possessio sit non nescit. Quocirca si defutura est, defuturam[76] praevidet ac vivit infelix, cum possessione tam cara aliquando,

because, if they come to know there all the universe's species, but countless species proceed under particular genera, as under number, shape, and proportion, it seems to follow that the species appear in a way to be infinite. But since one cannot traverse infinites, minds do not reckon up the species by passing them in review, but see them all together by remaining at rest.[114]

Again, if the perpetual understanding of the understander is a 32 sort of life, and if understanding emerges there because of its stability as a participant of eternity, it follows that the mind in its blessedness can be said with justice to be translated into eternal life;[115] and rightly so, for the human mind is placed as a mean between eternal and temporal things. Therefore, just as the working of the human mind whereby it is joined to temporal things is usually temporary, so the working whereby it is united to eternal things is eternal.[116] Finally, I do not see how vision itself may be moveable there where a) the power of seeing far surpasses time both from the onset [of creation] and now most of all; and b) the object that is seen, and the form by which it is seen, is rest itself and eternity itself. Hence it follows that souls, if in any way they have already transcended motion and fulfilled their natural desire, once they adhere to God will never depart from Him. Since this desire has its foundations in an unchanging substance and is directed naturally towards an unchanging object, it certainly enjoys as its final goal none other than an unchanging possession. What wonder if a sempiternal mind desires to possess for eternity what it desires not on account of another but on account of itself?[117]

Furthermore, where no mind is ignorant of natural things be- 33 neath it, it is certainly not ignorant of the kind of possession [i.e. life] that is its own. If this possession is going to cease, therefore, it foresees it is going to cease and it lives in sorrow, since it reckons it is going to lose such a dear possession at some point in time, nay in a brief while.[118] Besides, whatever naturally adheres to some end, is not wrenched away from that end except by some force

immo brevi se existimet carituram. Adde quod quicquid naturaliter cuidam adhaeret fini, non aliter quam vi quadam illata inde divellitur. Cum igitur deo mens tamquam fini coniungatur, naturaliter prae ceteris exoptato, coniunctionisque[77] huiusmodi efficiens causa ipse sit deus, nullaque vis maior ex adverso queat accedere, quae violenter quandoque seiungat quod deus sponte coniunxit, proculdubio mens a nullo umquam inde recedere compelletur. Quo autem pacto vel a certa veritate per fallaciam vel a puro totoque bono per voluntatem sese avertat, cogitari non potest.

34    Profecto neque mentis substantia permutatur neque intellegendi perspicacia sub lumine deficit continue confirmante, neque lumen subtrahitur umquam, quod ab aeternitate infunditur in aeternum. Neque voluntas vel ob alterius stimulum a totius possessione recedit vel ob taedium satietatemve ab eo umquam obiecto se segregat. Quod cum penitus comprehendi non possit, nimirum et semper occurrit ut novum et cum admiratione summa, ideoque cum desiderio continue possidetur. Denique si quanto quid summo dei statui propinquius est, tanto fit immobilius, mentes substantia iam divina formatas necesse est immobiles prorsus evadere.

*Singuli in deo contenti*

35    Hic vero singuli quaecumque appetunt consequuntur. Philosophi veritatis admodum studiosi hic in ipsa veritate veritatum procreatrice vera cuncta perspiciunt. Hic viri civiles gubernationi ac potentiae dediti cum omnipotente gubernatore mundi potentissimi gubernatores evadunt. Hic victoriae gloriaeque cupidi omnia iam

that is brought to bear. Therefore, since the mind is joined to God as its end—God whom it has naturally chosen before all else—and since the efficient cause of its union is God Himself, and since no greater power can come from something opposed (a power which could at some point violently separate what God has freely joined), then it is beyond question that the mind will never be compelled by anything to depart from God. But it is impossible to ponder how it can turn itself away either through deceit from the unerring truth, or through the will from the pure and entire good.

Certainly, the mind's substance does not change, nor does the clarity of its understanding diminish in the light that is continuously strengthening it and that is poured into it from eternity unto eternity and never withdrawn. Nor does the will recede from the possession of the whole on account of the stimulus of something else, or ever separate itself from that [divine] object on account of tedium or satiety. Since that object cannot be entirely understood, the mind forever encounters it certainly as something new and with the utmost wonder; and it is therefore possessed continuously with desire for it. Finally, if the closer something is to the supreme changelessness of God, the more motionless it becomes, then minds already formed by the divine substance must necessarily turn out to be completely motionless.[119] 34

*In God individual men are content*

Here [in God] individual men obtain all that they desire. Here the philosophers who are wholly concerned with the truth see all true things in the Truth itself, the mother of truths. Here men in public life, given over to government and power, become, with the world's omnipotent governor, the most powerful of governors. Here those who long for victory and glory have already conquered all adversities: all these men know, and are known to, all the 35

adversa vicerunt; noverunt omnes, beatis noti sunt omnibus. Hic voluptatum sectatores, si modo pervenerint in ipsa voluptatum causa, tota voluptate fruentur; nempe quemadmodum corpora umbrae sunt divinorum, ita et sensus oblectamenta divini umbrae sunt gaudii. Nam mens efficacior admodum est quam sensus, ac verum totumque bonum falso quodam bono et potentius — supra quam cogitari queat — et suavius est.

36      Praeterea intellectus obiectum suum undique penetrare solet, cum et intrinseca ab extrinsecis et propria secernat ab alienis, quod numquam efficit sensus. Item intelligibile ob mirabilem puritatem atque virtutem intellectus ipsius penetralibus prorsus illabitur; quod quidem sensibile sensui non potest efficere. Quamobrem puri intellectus voluptas circa intelligibile summum non modo continua puraque est, qualis non est in sensibus, verum etiam intima et integra simulque tota comprehenditur, multoque magis sensus superat voluptatem, quam saporum suavitas illecebras inanes odorum.

37      Solemus cum in habitum proprium restituimur, quocumque id modo fiat, voluptate perfundi. Nulla vero cogitari potest restitutio maior quam ubi animus, qui ab idea, immo vero[78] a se ipso degeneraverat, in ideam suam, immo se ipsum undique restituitur. Ibi rursus ipsa gaudii gaudet idea, unoque in bono bonis fruitur universis. Et cum nos ea delectent quae cupimus, cupiamus autem omnia quia bona, ibi summa voluptate perfundimur ubi, cum sit omne bonum, perfecte quicquid appeti potest consequimur. Variae vero mentes omni quidem bono secundum essentiam boni praecipue, boni autem gradibus secundum varias proprie fruuntur ideas, quatenus varios in primis totius boni gradus amantes, variis

blessed. Here the followers of pleasures, if only they arrive here, enjoy all pleasure in the cause itself of pleasures; for just as bodies are shadows of things divine, so the delights of the sense are shadows of joys divine. For the mind is more capable by far than the senses, and the good that is true and entire is more potent — more potent than one can possibly suppose — than a false good, and sweeter too.

Furthermore, the intellect customarily penetrates its object 36 from every side, since it divides internal from external and its own from alien things, something the sense never does. Again, the intelligible, on account of its marvelous purity and power, flows deep down into the intellect's inmost parts, something the sensible cannot do to the sense. Hence the pleasure of the pure intellect with regard to the highest intelligible not only is continuous and pure — such a pleasure does not exist in the senses — but also is internal and whole: it is simultaneously comprehended in its entirety, and it surpasses the pleasure of the sense far more than the sweetness of tastes surpasses the insubstantial allures of scents.

When we are restored to our proper habit, in whatever way 37 that happens, customarily we are flooded with pleasure. But one cannot think of any kind of restoration that is greater than when the rational soul, having degenerated from the Idea [of the Good?], nay from itself, is everywhere restored to the Idea, nay to itself. Then it rejoices again in the Idea itself of joy, and in the one Good it enjoys all goods. And since the things we desire delight us, but we desire all things because they are good, we are flooded with exquisite pleasure at the moment when, since it is wholly good, we achieve perfectly whatever can be desired. But various minds properly enjoy the whole good chiefly in accordance with the good's essence, but they enjoy degrees of the good in accordance with various Ideas insofar as, in loving first of all the various degrees of the whole good, they too set out on various paths towards the Good itself. Finally, to sum up, the One is entirely what

quoque callibus ad bonum ipsum proficiscuntur. Denique, ut summatim dicam, unum est omnino quo beati fruuntur omnes, etsi aliis alii praecipue modis rationibusque fruuntur, prout varie vel ex affectu vel ex obiecto aliter aliterque alliciente. 'Trahit sua quemque voluptas.' Sic ergo, ut Plato inquit, livor omnis abest a choro divino. Communis enim in eo choro caritas efficit, ut singuli singulorum felicitati tamquam suae congratulentur.

38    Praeterea ubi quisque et quod amavit, et ea qua potissimum eligit ratione et quousque desiderat, ad votum iam consequitur, ibi quilibet absque invidia et procul a stimulo, contentus omnino plenusque vivit. Illic enim tam naturalis quam acquisita capacitas prorsus impletur neque capacitas ab ullo maior[79] desideratur, sua enim cuique naturaliter carissima sunt. Accedit quod nihil gratius est beatis, divino prorsus amore flagrantibus, quam id ipsum: velle quod deum velle cognoscunt, atque ea tum mensura qua capiunt, tum ratione qua cupiunt, tum modo quo deus ipse se exhibet potiundum, deo amato potiri. Quod vero bonum ibi suum omnino comprehendi non posse cognoscunt, et hoc ipso mirifice delectantur, suum videlicet thesaurum eligentes infinitum esse potius quam finitum.

: IX :

*De corporibus beatorum.[80]*

1    Animae purae duplex felicitas convenit: altera ex se ipsa, de qua tractavimus, ex corpore altera, quae apud Platonicos est eiusmodi—praestat enim exemplo quodam hanc cogitare.

all the blessed enjoy, although sundry among them especially enjoy in various ways and for various reasons depending diversely on their desire or on the object attracting them in some way or another: "Each person is drawn to his own pleasure."[120] It is thus, as Plato says, that all envy is absent from the choir divine.[121] For in this choir the shared love ensures that individuals rejoice in the felicity of other individuals as they do in their own.

Moreover, when each person, to his heart's desire, is already attaining what he has loved, and for the reason he chooses it most, and to the degree he desires it, at that point every person lives without envy, far from the goad of desire, and utterly content and fulfilled. For there [in heaven], the natural and acquired capacity alike is completely filled and none desires a greater capacity; for to each person his own things are naturally most dear. Additionally, nothing is more gracious to the blessed, who are utterly on fire with divine love, than this: to will what they know God wills and to possess God whom they love in the measure they receive Him and for the reason they desire Him and in the way which God Himself has shown He should be possessed. But they know that the divine good which then is theirs cannot be comprehended entirely, and they are marvelously delighted in this, choosing, in other words, that their treasure be infinite rather than finite.

38

: IX :

*On the bodies of the blessed.*

A double felicity belongs to the pure soul, one happiness comes from itself (we described it above), the other from the body, and this for the Platonists is of the following kind—for it is better to think about it by way of an example.

1

2    Oculus quidem tuus rotundus est, perspicuus, splendidus, motu celerrimus, mirabilis perspicacia. Oculum meum videt seque ipsum[81] cernit in meo. Affectus animi tui singulos in se ipso figurat ac traducit in meum meosque affectus per meum mutuo recipit. Tales sunt illi animorum currus et in se ipsis et invicem; quisque enim illorum totus est oculus atque in omnibus ferme ita se habent ut oculos ipsos se habere videmus. Igitur quasi oculi quidam rotundi sunt, perspicui, splendidi, motu celerrimi, cuncta undique facillime circumspiciunt. Animorum suorum affectus cogitationesque prae se ferunt ceterisque animis quodam quasi nutu facillime indicant. Accipiunt quoque ab aliis[82] similiter alienorum affectuum cogitationumque indicia. Neque solum undique procul et acutissime vident, sed etiam audiunt. Similiter quoque stellae omnes et daemones voces[que] faciles facile formant, et sicut absque passione ulla sunt ibi sensus, sic et voces, alterius certe speciei generisque quam nostrae. Haec Plotinus et Hermias.

3    Platonicam eiusmodi sententiam confirmat in *Metaphysicis* Avicenna, probans animam a contagione corporis separatam in caelo caelesti quodam instrumento uti quasi suo a corpore caeli accepto perque ipsum imaginationis officium exercere. Vult enim intellectualem animam ex Platonis sententia universae moli corporum naturali dignitate imperioque praeesse. Denique currus illi exuberante suarum mentium splendore repleti mirifice fulgent, eisque tamquam radiis quibusdam totum caelum est pervium. Atque ut multis Platonicorum placet, potissimum in orbe lacteo non aliter quam stellae coruscant. Hinc antiqui poetae dicebant, quando feli-

Your eye is round, clear, brilliant, superlatively quick in its mo- 2
tion, marvelous in its perspicacity. It sees my eye and sees itself in
my eye. In itself it gives shape to the individual desires of your rational soul and transmits them to my soul, and by way of my eye
it reciprocally receives my desires. Such are those chariots of the
souls, both in themselves and in relation to each other; for each of
them is an entire eye and in all things they function almost as we
see eyes functioning. Like eyes they are therefore round, clear, brilliant, superlatively quick in their motion; and everywhere they
look around at all things with the utmost ease. They declare the
desires and thoughts of their own rational souls, and it is easy for
them to indicate these to the rest of the souls by a sort of a wink.
They also receive similarly from other souls the indications of the
desires and thoughts of others. Not only do they everywhere see
them from afar and with great acuity, they also hear them. Similarly all the stars and demons easily form voices too, voices easy [to
hear]; and just as the senses are without any passion there, so too
are the voices, being certainly of another species and genus than
our own. Plotinus[122] and Hermias[123] affirm this.

In his *Metaphysics* Avicenna confirms this Platonic view by 3
proving that in heaven the soul separated from the body's contagion uses a certain celestial instrument as if it were its own, having
received it from the heaven's body; and through it the soul admin-
isters the office of the imagination.[124] For Avicenna wants the intellectual soul, according to Plato's view, to be superior to the universal mass of bodies by virtue of its natural dignity and authority.
Finally, these [celestial] chariots, brimming as they are with the
overflowing splendor of their minds, are marvelously ablaze, and
the whole of heaven is accessible to them as to certain rays of light.
As many of the Platonists agree, the chariots shine brightly for the
most part in the Milky Way exactly as the stars do.[125] Hence the
ancient poets declared that when souls in happiness flew back to

ces animae ad superos revolabant, stellas in caelo novas lucere. Sed haec illi viderint.

4      Accedit ad haec[83] quod Zoroastris et Pythagorae Platonisque sectatores, Plotinus Proclusque praecipue disputant, iisdem quandoque omnino redeuntibus causis eosdem numero prorsus homines redituros. Et Plato in libro *De regno* scribit post praesentem fatalemque mundi cursum hominum animas, imperante deo atque suscitante, corpora sua quae in hoc cursu amiserunt ideo recepturas, ut quemadmodum sub fato quondam corpora humana in terram deciderant, ita sub providentiae divinae imperio ex terra resurgant atque reviviscant. Haec priscorum mysteria philosophorum haud multum discrepant ab Hebraeorum Christianorumque mysteriis, quae etiam a Mahumethensibus confirmantur. Communis enim tribus his legibus sententia est: motum ipsum ideo finem revera esse non posse, quoniam semper ab alio fluit in aliud; hoc ipsum vero, scilicet in aliud tendere, ab ipsa ratione finis praesertim ultimi alienissimum est. Itaque summum ultimumque universi finem, quem mundus quandoque consequi debet — cum et singula mundo minora quandoque finem proprium consequantur — motum non fore, sed statum. Statum enim motu perfectiorem esse quietisque gratia moveri singula. Praeterea mundi corpus in eo statu, utpote consummatissimo, fore pulcherrimum. Expleto tandem caeli cursu quo gignuntur omnia, nihil ulterius generari, sed singula hominum corpora, quorum gratia prius generabantur omnia, e terra iubente deo resurrectura.

5      Quam quidem resurrectionem primum auctoritate divina confirmant. Sic enim deum saepe per prophetas et apostolos prae-

the gods, they shone as new stars in the sky. But this is their concern.

Furthermore, the followers of Zoroaster, Pythagoras, and Plato, 4 especially Plotinus and Proclus,[126] argue that, with the same causes returning in their entirety at some point, exactly the same men will return at the same time.[127] And in the *Statesman* Plato writes that after the present, fatal course of the world, the souls of men, with God commanding and reviving them, will receive the bodies they have lost in this fatal course, with the result that, just as human bodies once upon a time had succumbed to fate on earth, so under the rule of divine providence they will rise from the earth and live again.[128] These mysteries of the ancient philosophers do not differ very much from the mysteries of the Hebrews and Christians, mysteries even confirmed by the Mohammedans. For the view that is common to these three [religious] laws is [as follows]. Motion itself cannot truly be the end, because it forever flows from one thing to another; and this very tendency to move towards something else is utterly alien to the rational principle of the end, especially of the ultimate end. Therefore the highest and ultimate end of the universe, the end that the world has to reach at some point—since individual things that are less than the world do attain their own end at some point—will not be motion but rest. For rest is more perfect than motion and individual things are moved for the sake of rest. Moreover, in this rest—rest being the most perfect condition—the world's body will be incomparably beautiful. At length when the sky's course (wherein all things are begotten) is completed, nothing is to be generated further; but men's individual bodies, for whose sake all things were first generated, will rise again from the earth at God's command.

The three [religious] laws confirm this resurrection in the first 5 place by invoking divine authority. For they say that God had often foretold through the prophets and apostles that He would

dixisse multos[84] variis saeculis mortuos suscitasse. Praeterea sanc-
tos homines etiam vita functos fecisse miracula atque quotidie
facere. Mitto reliqua: innumerabilia enim sunt. Certe nostra aetate
anno MCCCCLXXVII Decembre atque Ianuario reliquiae quaedam Petri Apostoli in urbe Volaterrana repertae miracula duodecim ostenderunt, et ingentia illa quidem et omni populo manifesta. Haec et similia potissima sunt resurrectionis indicia, adeo ut
Avicenna in *Metaphysicis* asserat auctoritati divinae resurrectionem
asseveranti esse credendum. Etsi Avicenna nullam tantae rei rationem afferre tentat, Christiani tamen theologi rationibus eiusmodi
persuadent.

6      Prima ratio. Quoniam ex anima et corpore humano fit unum
quiddam naturale compositum naturalique instinctu anima ad corpus afficitur, ideo patet animam non ex ipso solum universi ordine,
verum etiam secundum suae naturae ordinem corpori copulari.
Quo efficitur ut contra ordinem tam universae quam propriae naturae sit animam seorsum a corpore permanere. Permanent autem
post corporis interitum sempiternae, cumque id quod est contra
naturam sempiternum esse non possit, consequens est animas
quandoque sua corpora recepturas.

7      Ratio secunda. Singulae animae ad corpora singula vivificanda
regendaque naturaliter inclinantur. Sic enim fert et natura et providentia vitae inter aeternitatem tempusque locatae inclinatio-
nemque partim ad aeterna habentis, partim ad temporanea naturalem. Inclinatio vero naturalis manet, semper manente natura.
Quapropter animae a corporibus separatae ad illa naturaliter semper inclinabuntur. Naturalis autem inclinatio proclivitasque inanis
semper esse non debet; id enim ab ordine universi alienissimum

raise many men in various ages from the dead; and that holy men, moreover, even those deprived of life, had performed miracles, and continue to do so every day. I leave aside other instances, for they are numberless. Certainly in our own age, in the year 1477 in December and January, certain relics of the apostle Peter discovered in the town of Volterra made twelve miracles known, and they were prodigious miracles and manifested to the people at large.[129] These and similar facts are the best witnesses of the resurrection, so much so that in his *Metaphysics* Avicenna asserts that one must believe divine authority when it proclaims the resurrection.[130] Although Avicenna makes no attempt to provide any proof for such an important claim, the Christian theologians use the following reasons to persuade us.[131]

First proof. Since one natural composite is made from the soul  6 and the human body, and the soul is affected by a natural instinct for the body, obviously the soul is bound to the body not only because of the universal order but also because of the order of its very own nature. Hence it comes about that it is contrary to the order of the universe and of its own nature alike that the soul remain apart from the body. But after the body's death souls do remain everlastingly; and since that which is contrary to nature cannot be everlasting, the result is that at some point souls are going to receive their bodies back.

Second proof. Individual souls are naturally inclined to give life  7 to and to govern individual bodies. For the nature and providence of a life located between eternity and time, and having a natural inclination in part for things eternal and in part for things temporal, leads them to such. But the natural inclination remains, given that nature always remains. So souls separated from bodies will always be inclined naturally towards bodies. But a natural inclination and proclivity must not remain forever unfulfilled; for this would be entirely foreign to the order of the universe. At some

est. Igitur animae sua ipsa corpora, ad quae secundum naturam semper afficiuntur, quandoque recipient.

8    Ratio tertia. Anima speciei humanae pars altera est, altera vero corpus. Ergo seiuncta a corpore ita, prout est anima, est imperfecta, quemadmodum pars ipsa solet extra totum ad quod constituendum est instituta. Idcirco numquam eius appetitio naturalis quieta erit. Numquam anima ulla beata, nisi ad totum suum resumpto corpore reducatur speretve reduci.

9    Ratio quarta. Virtutibus praemia, vitiis supplicia digna debentur. Haec cum in hac vita non tribuantur, tribuuntur in altera. Corpus autem et virtutum et vitiorum est una cum anima particeps. Ut igitur praemiorum quoque suppliciorumve simul sit particeps, tandem animae redditur.

10    Neque absurdum videri debet animas, postquam a naturali habitu suo discesserint, in eundem iterum redituras, siquidem planetae domicilia sua naturalia et relinquunt et repetunt. Elementorum quoque particulae saepe extra situm proprium expulsae diuque seiunctae, interim continue ad ipsum vergunt ac denique revertuntur. Neque difficile est infinitae dei virtuti ubique praesenti, quae totum creavit ex nihilo, quandoque corpora dissoluta in elementa ex elementis vicissim restantibus revincire. Idem vero corpus ideo retexetur, quoniam eadem erit forma quae quondam, id est anima; eadem quoque prima illa materia sempiterna quae una cunctis subest; eadem denique indeterminata dimensio, materiae comes. Quinetiam in hac vita idem corpus a pueritia ad senectutem habere quilibet dicitur, quamvis effluat iugiter atque refluat.

point, therefore, souls will receive back their own bodies, the ones to which they are always naturally inclined.

Third proof. Of the human species the soul is one part, but the 8 body another. So the soul separated from the body, insofar as it is soul, is imperfect, just as the part is customarily imperfect when outside the whole for the constituting of which it has been appointed. Therefore its natural appetite will never be at rest. No soul will ever be blessed unless, having recovered its body, it is led back (or hopes to be led back) to the whole.

Fourth proof. There ought to be appropriate rewards for virtues 9 and punishments for vices. Since these are not handed out in this life, they are handed out in another. But the body participates in virtues and vices along with the soul. Therefore, in order to participate with it simultaneously in the rewards or in the punishments too, the body is restored eventually to the soul.

It should not seem absurd that souls, after they have deviated 10 from their natural and habitual condition, will be restored to this same condition again, given that the planets leave behind the houses natural to them and then seek them out again. Particular bits of the elements too, expelled from the region proper to them and separated from it in the meantime for a long time, turn towards it continually and are eventually restored to it. Nor is it difficult for the infinite power of God, which is everywhere present and which has created the whole [universe] from nothing, to take the bodies that have been dissolved into the elements, and at some point to reassemble them again from the elements that remain. But the same body will be rewoven because the same form will exist as before, that is, the soul; and the same prime everlasting matter that is one and subject to all things will exist, as too finally will the same undetermined dimension that accompanies this matter. In this present life, moreover, each person is said to have the same body from youth to age, although it passes away and renews itself perpetually.[132]

11    Resurget autem corpus penitus immortale. Nam deus ab initio
sic rerum ordinem temperavit, ut rationali animae, quae est sempiterna vita naturalisque forma corporis, materia sua, id est corpus,
in hoc ipso congrueret, ut per ipsam semper viventem semperque
vivificare naturaliter appetentem, ipsum similiter semper vivere
posset. Potentia eiusmodi bonum quiddam est ordini universi
maxime consentaneum. Igitur quando deus, qui creavit ab initio ac
tale creavit ut posset semper vivere—quando, inquam, recreabit,
proculdubio id quod convenientissimum est implebit, ne potentia
tam bona tamque universo congrua sit semper inanis.

12    Praeterea recreatio illa per deum facta, cessante mundi motu
qui quietis alicuius perfectioris gratia tandem est institutus, ad aliquid dumtaxat stabile dirigetur. Itaque corpus semper coniunctum
animae permanebit. Rursus, intentio naturae in generando ad per-
petuitatem saltem speciei dirigitur, idque ab ipso deo sortita est, in
quo prima perpetuitatis viget radix. Quapropter intentio dei in
regenerando ad perpetuum quiddam multo magis quam natura dirigitur. Hominem ergo incorruptibilem recreabit, non specie tantum—id enim per consuetam generationem expleri satis poterat—verum etiam numero sempiternum, non secundum animam
solum—nam hoc et prius habebat—sed etiam secundum corpus.

13    Accedit ad haec quod in generatione quotidiana corpori iam
facto accedit anima; in regeneratione illa contra animae corpus accedit. Quare sicut vita hominis compositi praesens caduci corporis
conditionem sequitur, ita futura illa vita compositi vicissim condi-

However, the body will rise again entirely immortal. For God has so tempered the order of things from the beginning that corresponding to the rational soul (which is everlasting life and the body's natural form) is its own matter, that is, the body: and the body so corresponds to the soul that through the soul, since it lives forever and desires by nature to give life forever, the body similarly is able to live forever. Such a power is something good, something in absolute harmony with the order of the universe. Therefore when God, who has created from the beginning and who has created something such that it is able to live forever — when, I say, He creates again in the future, He will doubtless fulfill what is absolutely for the best, lest a power which is so good and so in tune with the universe be forever in vain.

Moreover, that second creation (which God will perform after the world's motion ceases, a motion instituted for the sake of some more perfect rest at the end) will be directed towards something that is only at rest. So the body will remain forever conjoined to the soul. Again, in generating, nature's intention is directed to the perpetuity of the species at least, and this it has been allotted by God Himself, in whom flourishes the prime root of perpetuity. Accordingly, in generating a second time, God's intention is directed, much more than nature is, towards something perpetual. So He will recreate man as not only incorruptible in species — for ordinary generation was able to perform that task satisfactorily — but also as everlasting numerically [i.e. individually], not only with regard to the soul alone — for the soul had this [immortality] before — but with regard to the body too.

Add to this the fact that in day-to-day generation a soul approaches a body that has already been made; but in that second generation, to the contrary, a body approaches a soul. Accordingly, just as the present life of the composite human being follows the condition of the fallen body, so that future life of the composite will in turn follow the condition of the immortal soul, with the re-

tionem immortalis animae consequetur, ut privatio tandem secundum perfectissimam saltem naturalium speciem cesset in habitu atque mors tamquam debilissima, ut prophetae aiunt, absorbeatur a vita. Item corpora idcirco resurgunt, ut praemia et supplicia etiam corporibus ita merentibus sempiterna in perpetuum persolvantur; ergo sempiterna resurgent. Adde quod etiam ideo suscitantur, ne animae semper maneant imperfectae. Cum igitur hac in re animae ipsius perfectioni potissimum consulatur,[85] tale reddetur corpus quale convenit animae. Sempiternae vero animae corpus convenit sempiternum, quale etiam ab ipso rerum initio tributum fuisse Litterae Sacrae testantur. Quod quidem munus, inordinato[86] quodam motu ad tempus intermissum, deo tandem ita universum ut melius est ordinante, restituetur.

14    Quod autem naturalis hominis habitus ab initio talis fuerit, hinc ostenditur, quod quanto perfectior homo est quam bruta, tanto facilius, perfectius,[87] saepius finem suum posse consequi debet quam illa suum. In praesenti vero habitu contra contingit. Ex quo patet homines, ob id proprie quod a prima sua temperatione discesserint, ad felicitatem suam maxima cum difficultate contendere facillimeque eam tunc demum assecuturos, cum in habitum priorem restituti iam fuerint. Quae quidem sententia Zoroastris, Mercurii, Platonis mysteriis atque poetis aurea canentibus saecula maxime omnium consentanea esse videtur.

15    Sed ad resurrectionem iam revertamur. Denique dei virtus immensa efficiens resurrectionis causa est. Ergo qua vitae infinitate suscitat mortua, eadem in aeternum a morte libera convenientissime servat. Tantum enim reviviscendi miraculum vita solum sem-

sult eventually that privation, at least in the case of this most perfect species of natural things, will cease to be the composite's habitual condition, and that death, as the feeblest of all, as the
prophets declare, may be swallowed up by life.[133] Again, bodies
rise up a second time so that everlasting rewards and punishments
may be meted out in perpetuity to deserving bodies too so they
will rise again as everlasting bodies. Furthermore, bodies are also
raised lest souls remain forever imperfect. Therefore, since one
pays special attention in this to the perfection of the soul itself, the
kind of body that is restored is one in harmony with the soul.[134]
But in harmony with an everlasting soul is an everlasting body,
such a body, the sacred Scriptures testify, as was given us even
from the very beginning of things. This gift, which was intermit-
ted for a while by a sort of unordered motion, will be restored
eventually by God who orders the universe for the better.

That such has been man's natural habit from the beginning is    14
demonstrated by the fact that to the extent man is more perfect
than the beasts, so the more easily, perfectly, and frequently he
ought to be capable of attaining his end than they are of attaining
their end. But in [man's] present habit the contrary happens.
From this it is obvious that men, precisely because of the fact that
they have departed from their first tempered state, strive with
greatest difficulty for their felicity and that they will attain it most
easily only when they have been restored already to their earlier
habit. This opinion seems to be in harmony most of all with the
mysteries of Zoroaster, Mercury, and Plato,[135] and with the poets
when they sing of the golden ages.[136]

But let us now return to the resurrection. In the end it is God's    15
measureless power that is the efficient cause of the resurrection.
So it is most appropriate that the infinity of life that raises the
dead be the same infinity that preserves the dead free from death
for eternity. For the only proper counterpart to such a great miracle as restoring to life obviously is everlasting life in the future. For

piterna in posterum decere videtur. Qua in re deus omnipotens
reddit corpora usque adeo animarum suarum imperio subdita, ut
vita animae sempiterna sempiterne quoque exundet in corpus.
Quod quidem et praestantissimae formae adversus materiam sibi
subiectam naturaliter convenit et ordini naturae maxime consentaneum est. Ordini vero, ut tradunt theologi, meritorum, id quoque
magnopere congruit, ut corpora non tantum secundum vitam omnibus hominum animabus, quae vitae quaedam sunt, sed puris
etiam secundum qualitates actionesque penitus coniungantur,
quemadmodum animae illae sunt coniunctae deo. Itaque intellectus divino lumine plenus ac voluntas laetitia efficaciaque incompa-
rabili inde repleta splendorem efficaciamque ad motum in corpus
mirabilem omnino transfundunt, ut quemadmodum animae illae
ad caelestium mentium, ita corpora ad corporum caelestium claritatem virtutemque attollantur. Neque mirum videri debet corpus
humanum, natura caelo propter temperantiam non parum simile,
quando rursus dono quodam caelestem formam quandam induitur, subito ad caelestem regionem penitus elevari, trahente videlicet anima infinita dei virtute suffulta. Quae et in terra nunc a deo
disiuncta corpus contra elementorum suorum naturam connectit,
sustinet, elevat, et tunc supercaelesti coniuncta deo potest etiam ad
sublimem attollere secum aetheris regionem. Neque penetratione
tunc vel offendit aetherem vel offenditur purissimum corpus illud,
iam iam virtute factum qualitateque aethereum.

this miracle, God in His omnipotence makes bodies submit to the sway of their souls to such a degree that the everlasting life of the soul flows over everlastingly also into the body. This situation both naturally calls for the most outstanding form (as against the matter subjected to it), and is thoroughly in keeping with the order of nature.[137] But, as the theologians tell us, it also greatly accords with the order of merits that bodies be totally joined not only with respect to life to all the souls of men (souls being particular lives), but also, in accordance with their qualities and actions, to pure souls, just as these souls are joined to God. So the intellect full to overflowing with divine light and the will thence replete with gladness and with incomparable power together transfuse their wonderful splendor and capacity for motion entirely into the body, with the result that, just as souls are elevated to the clarity and power of celestial minds, so are bodies elevated to the clarity and power of celestial bodies. Nor should it seem surprising that the human body, which by nature and on account of its temperance is not dissimilar to the heavens, when it is clothed in a kind of celestial form again as a gift, is suddenly raised on high to the celestial region, having as its leader the soul borne up by the infinite power of God. At present on earth and disjoined from God, the soul unites, sustains, and lifts the body contrary to the nature of its elements; but later, conjoined with supercelestial God, the soul is able to raise it with itself even to the sublime region of the aether. In penetrating [the aether], the purest body neither damages the aether nor is itself damaged, having now been rendered aethereal in power and quality.[138]

: X :

*Status animae impurae.*

1 Ut autem intellegamus qualis sit status animae impurae post mortem, animadvertendum est quales sint viventium mores et habitus. Quales enim sunt adolescentiae mores, tales plurimum sunt habitus senectutis; tales quoque affectiones sunt defunctorum. In vita praesenti virtus nascitur ac vitium. Cum virtute oritur praemium, cum vitio vero supplicium. In futura vita virtus consummatur et vitium; illic praemium impletur atque supplicium. Virtus est exoriens praemium; praemium est virtus adulta. Vitium est supplicium nascens; supplicium est vitium consummatum. Idem enim est quod erat semen, et quod fit seges. Idem quoque quod erat seges, et quod fit pabulum. Qualia igitur in hoc autumno serimus, talia in illa aestate metemus. Talibus aut fusca nocte in Stygia palude pascemur, aut die serena in campis vescemur Elysiis.

2 Quemadmodum natura, providentiae divinae ministra, corpora intrinsecus levitate sursum movet, gravitate deorsum, ita et providentia intrinseca lege et quasi naturali cuidam inclinationi persimili omnia ducit. Hac lege supernae mentes et animae ipsis insita universum sub primo gubernatore gubernant. Hac similiter insita lege mentes humanae sese ad loca suae vitae convenientia ducunt. Et sicut humores in animali duo motus habent principia, naturale videlicet atque animale — naturali quidem leves sursum, graves

: X :

*The condition of the impure soul.*[139]

In order that we may understand the nature of the impure soul's   1
condition after death, we must take note of the nature of the cus-
toms and habits of the living. For whatever the customary ways of
youth, such for the most part are the habits of old age, and such
are the dispositions too of those who are dead. Virtue and vice are
born in the present life. With virtue comes reward, but with vice,
punishment. Virtue and vice are consummated in the future life;
and reward and punishment are fulfilled there. Virtue is reward
springing to life; reward is virtue fully grown. Vice is punishment
being born; punishment is vice having reached maturity. For what
was the seed is the same as what becomes the standing corn. And
what was the standing corn is the same too as what becomes the
food we eat. So whatever seeds we sow [here] in this autumn we
reap [there] in that summer. Either we browse on such food in the
darkness of night in the Stygian marsh or we feast on it in the serenity of day in the Elysian fields.

Just as nature, the minister of divine providence, moves bodies   2
from within by lightness upwards and by heaviness downwards, so
providence leads all things both by an inner law and by a sort of
natural inclination much resembling it. By this law implanted in
them supernal minds and souls govern the universe under the
prime governor. Similarly by this law implanted in them minds
lead themselves towards the places proper to their own life. The
humors in an animal have two principles of motion, the natural
and the animal: by the natural motion light things make themselves go upwards for the most part, heavy things, go downwards;
but by the animal motion they betake themselves for the most
part to the members which need them most, according as the life

deorsum saepius sese transferunt, animali vero ad ea potissimum membra, quae his maxime indigent, prout vita exigit animantis — sic animae duo intus motuum principia possident: alterum quidem vel impetum proprium vel iudicium, alterum vero divinae providentiae legem omnino penetralibus insitam. Illo quidem in hos aut illos se transferunt mores; hac autem post mores contractos ipsaemet in loca, supplicia, munera congrua moribus intrinseca quadam et occulta inclinatione perducunt⟨ur⟩.[88]

3     Hanc Plato sententiam a priscis acceptam saepissime probat; hanc et Platonici omnes ubique confirmant. Eam legem semper bonam in se atque divinam quidam tamen ita distinguunt ut et gratiam et bonum daemonem vocent, quando bonis meritis reddit bona; contra vero aliquando et Nemesim, et furiam, et malum daemonem appellent, quando peccatores ad supplicia ducit. Ea lex intrinsecus more naturae adeoque leviter ducit ut nullus, donec ad terminum perveniat, a providentia sentiat violentiam. Atque interea universum, quod ex primo animorum motus principio saepissime dissonaret, per secundum hoc principium motionis in suam undique consonantiam restituitur, dum sua singuli motu proprio gradatim merita sortiuntur. Praeterea non desunt daemones boni nobis, qui genii nominantur, ingenii duces assidui, qui non vi, sed persuadendo ducant. Sunt et mali, non tamquam duces naturaliter ordinati, sed adversarii, ut ita dixerim, peregrini, quos in hac vita per philosophiam sacrificiaque propulsari Platonici putant. Sed improbas animas post vitam et Plato et Mercurius ait mutato genio[89] incidere in mali daemonis potestatem, scilicet postquam suo

of the animate being requires. Similarly souls possess two principles of motion within: one their own impulse or judgment; the
other, the law of divine providence that has been deeply implanted
in their inmost selves. By the former they give themselves over to
various ways of living, but, having acquired these ways of living,
the law conducts them towards the places, the punishments, and
the rewards best suited to them by a sort of inner and hidden inclination.[140]

Plato frequently approves of this notion that he inherited from     3
the ancients; and all the Platonists everywhere corroborate it.[141]
Yet certain of them introduce a distinction in this law, which is always good and divine in itself, so that when it takes men who have
merited good things and rewards them with good things, they call
it Grace and the good daemon, but they sometimes call it Nemesis
and Fury and the bad daemon when it hauls sinners off to their
punishments. This divine law leads us naturally from within so
gently that until it reaches its goal no one feels constrained by [its]
providence. The universe meanwhile, which would become discordant repeatedly from the first principle of the motion of rational
souls [their own impulse or judgment], is everywhere restored to
its own harmony by way of the second principle of their motion
[the divine law], while individuals are gradually allotted their own
merits by their own motion. Furthermore, we are not without the
good daemons: they are called genii [because] they are tireless
leaders of our own ingeniousness; and they lead us not by force
but by persuasion. There are bad daemons too who are naturally
assigned us not as leaders but as adversaries or, one might say, as
strangers; the Platonists think they are warded off in this life by
philosophy and by sacrifices.[142] But Plato and Mercurius say that
after life wicked souls — their genius having changed — fall into the
power of the bad daemon;[143] after, that is, they have been led by
their own genius to the judge who cannot be deceived. And this
is especially because in souls separated [from bodies] all things

genio ductae fuerint ad iudicem, qui falli non possit. Praesertim cum omnia appareant in animis separatis, et quae ex natura, et quae ex affectibus inerant. Hinc Socrates in *Gorgia:* 'Ceteris, inquit, omissis id considero, quemadmodum iudici sanissimum ostendere animum possim. Summum enim malorum est animo peccatis referto ad inferos descendere.' Addit tum ibi, tum in *Theaeteto* et *Republica,* haec non esse tamquam fabulas deridenda, siquidem quicumque talia negant, ridicula ipsi in medium semper inducunt. Igitur praecipit hoc maxime contendendum, ut mores optimi comparentur. Mores enim esse inquit vias vel ad inferos vel ad superos.

4    Operaepretium fore arbitror repetere latius, quae de his in *Republica* et in libro *De scientia* scribit. Profecto eos inquit esse penitus deridendos, qui vel iustitiam sectandam vel iniustitiam fugiendam humanorum vel praemiorum vel suppliciorum gratia putant; illam vero sententiam esse veram quae asserit illa non esse vera vel praemia vel supplicia, quae aliquando atque sorte,[90] sed illa quae semper necessarioque ordine virtutes vitiaque sequuntur. Addit in libro *De scientia* deum ipsam iustitiam esse nihilque illi iusto similius; nihil contra iniusto dissimilius esse. Veram praeterea sapientiam potentiamque existimandam, quae id cognoscat et consequatur ad votum, contrarium vero habitum extremam inscitiam imbecillitatemque esse censendam. Proinde duo in universo extrema inter se exemplaria ponit, in summo quidem beatissimam divinitatem, in infimo vero oppositum divinitatis expers atque miserrimum. Affirmatque iniustos ob extremam inscitiam numquam animadvertere se propter iniustitiam beatissimo quidem in dies

are made manifest, those that have come from nature, and those that have come from desires. Hence Socrates says in the *Gorgias*, "Leaving all the rest to one side, I consider just this: how can I present my soul at its healthiest to the judge."[144] For the worst of evils is to descend to the depths with a soul laden with sins. He adds there and in the *Theaetetus* and *Republic* that these matters should not be derided as fables, seeing that the people who reject them always introduce ridiculous alternatives themselves.[145] He therefore exhorts us to strive above all to acquire the best moral habits for ourselves. For our morals, he says, are the paths that lead us to those who dwell either in the depths below or in the heights above.

I believe it will help if we take a further look at what Plato writes about these matters in the *Republic* and in the book *On Knowledge* [the *Theaetetus*]. He says, in fact, that we should utterly scorn those who believe that we ought to follow justice or flee from injustice only for the sake of human rewards or human punishments. Rather, the true view is that which asserts that human rewards and punishments, which happen sporadically and by chance, are not the authentic ones, but rather those that always and in a necessary order follow on virtues and vices.[146] In the book *On Knowledge* he adds that God is justice itself and that nothing is more like justice than God; nothing, to the contrary, more unlike injustice.[147] He says that we must consider true knowledge and power to be that which recognizes and freely pursues this, but judge the contrary habit to be utter ignorance and weakness. He then introduces two models in the universe which are completely opposite to each other: up on the summit, divinity at its most blessed; down in the abyss, the contrary, that which is without divinity and most wretched. He affirms that the unjust out of their extreme ignorance never notice that they are becoming daily, because of their injustice, more unlike the most blessed but more like the most miserable; and he affirms too that this unlikeness to one

4

dissimiliores, miserrimo vero similiores evadere. Eiusmodi vero dissimilitudinem similitudinemve esse propriam iniustitiae poenam, sed iustitiae praemium proprie ipsam beatissimi[91] similitudinem miserrimive dissimilitudinem iudicari. His addit iniustos neque in hac neque in altera vita ab ipsa beatitudinis patria, utpote qui sint dissimiles, recipi, immo perverso quodam habitu ad infimum miseriae situm, cuius facti sunt similes, congrue retrahi, semperque in regione maligna sibi persimili inter malos sibi similes pererrare. Subdit denique haec a quibusdam ambitiosis irrideri solere, verum si cogantur in his rationes reddere atque accipere diligenter, eos tandem, ut supra significavimus, revera convictos[92] tamquam pueros deridendos abire.

5    Sed iam redeamus ad mores, quibus ordine distributis, qua ratione praemia suppliciave distribuantur, intellegemus. Ante vero quam distinguamus, meminisse oportet mores bonos ita demum ad felicitatem conducere, si praecipuo erga deum felicitatis auctorem amore quaeruntur; malos autem eas potissimum animas in miseriam praecipitare solere, in quibus amor dei omnis extinguitur. Hinc platonicum illud: 'Sapienti viro lex deus est, insipienti vero libido.' Item illud: 'Beatus ille futurus est, qui humiliter divinae legi se subiicit, miser vero, qui eam superbe contemnit.'

6    Sunt autem mores viventium quatuor. Est homo temperans, continens, incontinens, intemperans. Temperans est, cuius ratio vere iudicat, sensualis affectus libenter obtemperat rationi. Continens, cuius ratio iudicat quoque vere, affectus obtemperat aegre. Incontinens, in quo etsi non male iudicat ratio, praevalet tamen corporea perturbatio. Intemperans, in quo ratio vel consopita est

and likeness to the other is adjudged to be the proper punishment of injustice, while the reward of justice is properly adjudged to be likeness to the most blessed and unlikeness to the most wretched. He adds that neither in this life nor in another does the homeland of blessedness ever admit the unjust, since they have no likeness to it but are properly confined rather, by a perverse habit, to the abyss of wretchedness that they have come to resemble; and they forever wander in a region malign like themselves among those who are wicked like themselves. Finally he notes that these accounts are customarily derided by ambitious sort of men, but that if these men are forced to give their reasons or to give careful ear to others, eventually, as we signified above, they retreat, defeated in fact like boys who deserve our scorn.[148]

But let us return now to ways of behaving and having sorted  5
them in order let us understand the reason behind the distribution of rewards and punishments. Before we can sort out the ways, however, we must recall that the good ones lead to felicity only when they are sought after with a special love towards God, the author of felicity; and that the bad ways usually and chiefly cast those souls into misery in whom the entire love of God is extinguished. Hence the Platonic saying: For the wise man the law is God, for the unwise man, desire.[149] And again: The person who humbly submits himself to the divine law will be blessed, the proud person who treats it with scorn will be miserable.[150]

There are four ways, however, of living life. Man is temperate  6
or continent or incontinent or intemperate. The temperate man is the one whose reason judges truly, and his sensual desire willingly submits to that reason. The continent man is the one whose reason also judges truly, but whose desire submits to it only with difficulty. The incontinent man is the one in whom tumultuous corporeal passion prevails even if the reason does not judge erroneously. The intemperate man is the one in whom the reason has been lulled to sleep or depraved by the dominance of excessive pas-

vel depravata affectu nimium dominante, ubi ad imperium phantasiae omnia fiunt, neque affectui ratio adversatur. Cum hic temperantiam continentiamve dicimus, intellegimus ritu platonico componere vel disponere animum adversus omnes perturbationum species, adeo ut omnium virtutum moralium in his officia comprehendantur.

7 Praeterea cum in anima separata phantasiam ponimus, intellegimus vel ritu platonico sensum intimum, quem in vehiculo et aethereo et aereo collocant, sed cum passione proprie in aereo, vel more peripateticorum, maxime Avicennae, affectum habitumque partis etiam rationalis, quem obsequendo sensibus in se ipsa concepit, ad passiones corporeas declinantem ad materiamque trahentem. Quo Avicenna dicit animam, quasi natura quadam etiam sine electione meditationeque, et hic et in altera vita ab intellegibili mundo ad sensibilem detorqueri atque torqueri.

8 Ut igitur ad institutum iam revertamur, in animo temperato sola vis nutriendi curat corpus, phantasia non amat ipsum, ratio odit. Quapropter impleto curandi huius corporis ministerio, vis illa vivifica, quasi contenta est vehiculo; reliquae vires animae, quaecumque supersunt, sicut in hoc ipso homine temperato solitae fuerant, veritati rerum omnium considerandae sese dedunt, et tanto ferventius quam antea, quanto sunt factae liberiores. Omnes igitur repente communi nixu curruque aethereo recurrunt in aetherem.

9 Animus continentis fertur quidem in caelum ut ille, paulo post, non subito. In hoc enim appetitio phantasiae solita erat vix rationi

sion, and where all things are given over to the sway of the phantasy, and where the reason does not oppose desire. When we refer here to temperance and to continence, we understand in the Platonic manner that they so compose or dispose the rational soul to confront all the species of tumultuous passion that the offices of all the mortal virtues are included in these [two virtues].[151]

Furthermore, when we locate the phantasy in the separated 7 soul, by phantasy either we mean in the Platonic manner the inner sense which the Platonists locate in the aethereal and airy vehicle (but in the airy vehicle it is accompanied by passion, properly so);[152] or we mean in the manner of the Aristotelians, and chiefly of Avicenna, the desire and habit of even a rational part [of the soul].[153] By yielding to the senses, the phantasy has conceived in itself this desire, which deflects it towards corporeal passions and drags it towards matter; and by it, Avicenna says—as by some nature without choice even and without meditation—the soul, both here and in the other life, is wrenched away from the intelligible world and twisted towards the sensible.

So, to return now to our proposed topic, in the temperate soul 8 the power of nourishing alone cares for the body; for the phantasy does not love the body and the reason hates it. Therefore, when the ministry of caring for this body has been completed, this life-bestowing power is confined as it were in the vehicle. The soul's remaining powers, those that live on,[154] give themselves over to considering the truth of all things, just as they were accustomed to doing in the tempered man himself; and to the degree they have been rendered more free, they do so more fervently than they did before. All these powers therefore suddenly wheel back towards the aether in a common effort and in their aethereal chariot.

The rational soul of the continent man is borne to heaven like 9 the soul of the temperate man, but after a little while, not suddenly. For in this soul the desire of the phantasy has been accustomed to obeying the reason, but only with difficulty on account

parere propter corporis blandimenta vel territamenta. Ideo corporea in morte aegre relinquit, qua aegritudine occupat parumper
aciem rationis. Verum ratio quae illam vincere consueverat, silere
iubet. Unde sedata phantasiae querimonia atque expulsa caligine,
caelestis scintilla subrutilat omnibusque animae viribus consen-
tientibus patria superna revisitur.

10   Incontinens autem sero ex his carceribus liberatur, intemperans
vero numquam, siquidem horum animae passionibus infectae corporeis in tantam hac in vita insaniam prolapsae sunt, ut ipsis bonis
bonorum umbras temere praeposuerint; umbras amaverint[93] um-
brasve timuerint. Atque post hanc vitam insanire similiter compel-
luntur, illa quidem diu, haec semper. Quippe incontinentis insania
aliquam reperit medicinam, quia licet dominari solita fuerit perturbatio phantasiae, ratio tamen adversari quandoque consuevit in
vita. Similiter et post mortem reclamat adversus phantasiae cuiusdam furentis insaniam doletque se rerum sublimium possessione
privari. Haec reclamatio paenitentiaque paulatim vim actumque illius phantasiae debilitat, praesertim cum non adsint incitamenta
corporea, quae eiusmodi nutriant phantasiam, et quisque libenter
auscultet medico curaturo taedio diuturni languoris affectus fitque
perinde ac in illo qui, cum horrendis vexatur insomniis, interim
quia somno non premitur profundissimo, secum ipse inquit forte
tunc dormire se et curis inanibus cruciari. Unde pavor laborque
minuitur. Idem forsitan apud inferos contingit incontinenti, et
quantum delirantis phantasiae minuitur strepitus, tantum augetur

of the blandishments and fears of the body. So it relinquishes corporeal things at death with regret, and with this regret it dulls the edge of the reason for a little while. But the reason, which had become accustomed to conquering that desire, commands it to be silent. Hence directly the complaints of the phantasy have been calmed and its gloom dispelled, a heavenly spark is ignited; and with all the soul's powers [now] in accord, the native land in heaven is revisited once more.

The incontinent man, however, is freed from these prisons only 10 at a late hour while the intemperate man is never freed, since in this life the souls of these two fell into such madness, tainted as they were with corporeal passions, that they rashly preferred the shadows of good things to goods themselves: they loved shadows or shadows they feared. Similarly, after this life they are forced to rave on, the incontinent soul for a long time, the intemperate forever. The madness of the incontinent man does indeed find some relief, because, though the perturbation of the phantasy customarily prevailed, nonetheless during life his reason was accustomed at times to opposing the phantasy. After death it likewise protests against the insanity of the raging phantasy, and grieves that it has been deprived of the possession of things sublime. This protesting and repenting little by little weakens the power and action of that phantasy, especially since the corporeal stimuli which nourished such a phantasy are no longer present, and since whoever has been afflicted by the tedium of a lingering torpor willingly gives ear to the doctor who is about to cure him. In this he becomes exactly like the person who, when he is shaken by horrendous dreams, and because in the meanwhile he is not weighed down by the profoundest slumber, says to himself that he is then perhaps sleeping and being tormented by just empty cares. Thence his fear and trouble are mitigated. The same happens perhaps among the dead to the incontinent man, and to the extent the tumult of his raging

absolutae rationis imperium. Sic tandem animus expeditus beatitudinem adipiscitur.

11    In animo autem intemperato, et dum hominis vitam agebat, dormiebat ratio penitus vel affectui prorsus obsequebatur, unde indelebilem habitum ad corporea declinantem secum transfert quasi naturam. Talis est animi huius habitus, qualem cecinit Orpheus:

> Ἄρρηκτοί τ' Ἀιδάο πύλαί καὶ δῆμος ὀνείρων.

Id est: 'Reserari nequeunt portae Plutonis, intus est populus somniorum.' Hunc animum in septimo De republica Plato inquit in hac vita profunde dormire et antequam expergiscatur decedere ac post mortem somno profundiore gravari insomniisque acrioribus perturbari, quod proprie Tartari nomine designatur. Fertur, ut Plato vult, nimio corporis elementalis amore. Terreno igitur corpore dissoluto, alterum sibi quamprimum ex elementorum retexit vaporibus. Solo quasi quodam nutu retexit ex materia facili. Solo haustu reficit quotidie, quasi respirando corpus illud iugiter evanescens. Addit eiusmodi animum circa corpus elementalemque regionem, erga quae affectus fuerat, affectu perseverante revolvi. Neque mirum videri volunt quod anima vaporeum corpus quasi suum formet perque ipsum[94] sentiat, cum id facilius sit animaeque propinquius, atque in hoc corpore per talem spiritum vitam corpori praestet et sensum.

12    Si quaeratur qualis sit corporis illius figura, respondebimus secundum Magos varia simulacra diversorum animalium ex huiusmodi vaporibus fieri. Qualis enim quaelibet animalis vitam moribus imitata est, talem in primis sese facit, talisque omnino eius affectio et dispositio appareret, si sensu aliquo cerneretur. Talem

phantasy abates, the more the rule of the liberated reason is enhanced. Thus freed at last the rational soul attains blessedness.

In the soul of an intemperate man, however, and during the    11
time he lived a man's life, his reason slept entirely or completely succumbed to desire, whence it transformed itself into an ineradicable habit inclining naturally as it were towards things corporeal. The habit of this soul is the one Orpheus sang about: "The gates of Pluto cannot be unbarred: within is the people of dreams."¹⁵⁵ In the seventh book of the *Republic* Plato says that this soul slumbers deeply in this life; that it dies before it awakens; that after death it is weighed down by an even deeper slumber and troubled by even more frightening dreams; and that this condition is properly designated Tartarus.¹⁵⁶ Plato means that the soul is borne away by too intense a love of the elemental body. When this earthly body has been dissolved, therefore, the soul again weaves another body for itself as soon as possible from the vapors of the elements. It weaves it by a single nod of command as it were, and from malleable matter. Just by drinking in [vapors], every day, as though inhaling, it makes that perpetually vanishing body again. Plato adds that such a rational soul is wheeled back by persistent desire towards the [elemental] body and the elemental region, and towards the things it had desired [down there]. They [the Platonists] do not want it to appear extraordinary that the soul forms a vaporous body as though it were its own and senses through it (since it is more malleable and closer to the soul); and that in this body and through such a spirit the soul bestows life and sense on the [elemental] body.

If one asks what is the shape of that [vaporous] body, our reply    12
will be that, according to the Magi, various images of various animals are shaped from such vapors. For the [intemperate] soul imitates the life of any one animal in its manner of living, and whatever that animal's shape is, such primarily is the shape it fashions for itself. And howsoever its affection and disposition might appear as a whole (were it perceived by any sense), such a shape too

quoque figuram quodammodo in umbroso ipsius corpore fingit, si modo ex affectu et habitu animae vehementi colorari possit leve corpus et figurari. Et sicut carnis in vita senserat passiones, ita corporis illius passiones sentit, et tanto acutius quanto corpus est purius. Sed in alio genere sensus illius sunt, in alio carnis. Atque ita forte intellegenda est apud veteres hominum in bestias transformatio.

13    Quidam vero dicunt animam non proprie tale corpus formare perque ipsum sentire, immo sicut arte magica per certam statuarum dispositionem daemonibus certis accommodatam daemones statuis quasi devinciuntur,[95] quod Mercurius confitetur atque Plotinus, sic lege divina animas,[96] quae se corporibus dediderunt, aquae mancipari vel igni, atque id quidem adeo serviliter ut ob hoc vehementer indignentur et doleant. Sed utcumque sit, haec passio Tisiphone furia ab Orpheo nominatur, quae affligat eam ex corpore. Adhibet alias duas animae furias, quae eam crucient ab affectu: Megaera quidem propter odium imaginariique mali timorem, Alecto autem propter imaginarii boni cupiditatem. Quas quidem furias incitari a daemonibus ultoribus Plato inquit Plotinusque probat, et Orpheus ipse magnum daemonem ultorem proprio hymno describit. Tales sunt enim primae[97] animae huius perturbationes, quales sunt eorum qui delirant phrenesi propter febrem, aut eorum qui melancolico terrentur humore. Quod quidem fieri et Avicenna fatetur, et Proclus, cum dicat esse daemones quosdam irrationales, significat nihil mirum esse si animae miserorum irrationales evadant.

14    Quando enim quinque sensuum actiones cessant, actiones interiores maxime augentur. Ac[98] si ratione uti plurimum consueveris,

the soul paints onto its shadowy body (provided this tenuous body can be colored and shaped through the desire and vehement habit of the soul). And just as it had perceived the passions of the flesh in life, so [now] it perceives the passions of the shadowy body, and the purer this body, the more acutely it perceives them. But the senses of that shadowy body are in one genus, those of the flesh in another. And thus perchance we must understand the transformation among the ancients of men into beasts.[157]

Certain people say that the [intemperate] soul properly speak-  13
ing does not form a vaporous body and does not sense through it; but rather, just as the daemons are bound as it were to statues by the magic art and through the predetermined disposition of the statues (a disposition accommodated to certain daemons)—and this Mercurius maintains as does Plotinus[158]—so souls who have devoted themselves to bodies are delivered up by divine law to water and to fire, and this indeed in such a slavish manner that they vehemently rage and grieve because of it. But howsoever this happens, Orpheus calls this passion the fury Tisiphone, being the fury that uses the body to afflict the soul. He introduces two other furies for the soul that torture it with passion: Megaera who uses the soul's hatred and fear of an imaginary evil to torture it and Alecto who uses its desire for an imaginary good.[159] Plato says that these furies are incited by avenging daemons, and Plotinus agrees;[160] and Orpheus himself describes the great avenging daemon in its own hymn.[161] The first such perturbations of this soul resemble the perturbations of those who deliriously rage in a fever or are made subject to fear by a melancholic humor. Avicenna acknowledges this happens;[162] and Proclus—since he declares that certain daemons are irrational[163]—means it is not surprising if the souls of the wretched end up being irrational souls.

For when the actions of the five senses cease, the actions within  14
are most intensified. If you are accustomed chiefly to using your reason, you will speculate then with utmost diligence; if to using

tunc diligentissime specularis; si phantasia, tunc imaginaris vehementissime. Id usque adeo fit in somno ut quae rerum imagines
sunt res veras esse putemus atque horribilibus visis perterriti trepi-
demus, sudemus, vociferemur atque surgamus. Multo magis impiis in morte atque post mortem fallacia terribilium contingit
imaginum. Tunc enim cessant varia nutriendi officia, sensuum
externorum multiplices actiones, humanarum actionum occupa-
tiones rerumque solacia.[99] Solius[100] restat, ut Platonici putant,
phantasiae furentis vel phantasticae rationis imperium in homine
impio. Quae odio (quo dixi) et timore commota versat secum
longo ordine tristes imagines. Nunc caelum ruere in caput suspi-
cit, nunc se terrae profundis hiatibus[101] absorberi, tum impetu as-
sumi flammarum, tum vasto aquarum gurgite mergi, aut umbris
daemonum comprehendi. Itaque corpus suum per infima[102] passim
exagitat quacumque furentis phantasiae depulerit impetus ma-
lusque daemon, ut Mercurius ait et Plato. Quos quidem duos esse
vult hac in re, etiam si non advertant, legis divinae ministros.
Atque id ex odio metuque patitur impius per Megaeram. Ceterum
per Alecto ex amoris habitu, quem ad corporea contraxerat indelebilem, tales quaedam rursus cogitationes surrepunt et affectus,
videlicet quemadmodum senes, qui vixerant in iuventute lascivi,
duplici poena uruntur in senio, scilicet quod ardent voluptatum
cupiditate quodve omni spe potiundi privantur, nisi forte delirent.
Sic miseri apud inferos ob pristinum habitum cupiditatibus humanarum rerum alii aliis sollicitantur, atque ut plurimum non spe-

your phantasy, however, you will imagine with utmost vehemence. This happens in sleep to such an extent that we suppose the mere images of things are truly the things themselves, and we quiver with dread at such horrifying sights and sweat and cry out and start up. To an even greater degree the deceptiveness of terrible images afflicts the impious in death and after death. For then the various offices of nourishing cease, as do the many actions of the external senses, and the busy round of human activities, and the comfort of [earthly] things. In the impious man there remains, so the Platonists believe, the overlordship either of the raging phantasy alone, or of the phantastical reason. Moved by hate, as I have said, and by fear, this phantasy or phantastical reason busies itself with a long succession of gloomy images. The impious man now sees the heavens crashing on his head, or himself being swallowed up in the deep fissures of the earth, next being taken up by the force of flames, and then submerged in a vast whirlpool[164] of waters or encircled by the shades of daemons. Thus he drives his body on everywhere through the depths wherever the impulse of the raging phantasy and the bad daemon will have swept it away, as Mercurius says (and Plato too).[165] He holds that in this matter the two of them are ministers of the divine law even if they do not call attention to it. And the impious man suffers this from hate and fear via Megaera. Via Alecto, moreover, from the habit of love he had [formerly] contracted for corporeal things and which was irremovable, particular thoughts and feelings steal upon him again, ones such as old men experience, who have lived lasciviously in their youth and in their old age are burned with a double punishment, because they are on fire, in other words, with the lust for pleasures and because they are deprived of any hope of enjoying them, unless perchance they do so in delirium. Thus the wretched in hell, on account of their former habit, are variously troubled by various desires for human things. But for the most part they do not hope to be able to attain them, although sometimes, like mad

rant se consequi posse, quamvis nonnumquam velut insani sibi ipsi
videantur propemodum suas delicias adipisci, sed ad poenas acer-
biores se statim ab illis arceri. Sardanapallus arcetur longius ab
amplexu, Midas ab auro, a convivio Tantalus, a potentiae fastigio
Sisyphus. Tanta vis phantasiae est, tantus est impetus, quando vel
ipsa imperat sola vel solus phantasticus quidam habitus et affectus,
ex diuturno ipsius commercio in ratione contractus.

15     Ordinem a nobis in superioribus positum confirmat Olympiodorus in commentariis in *Phaedonem*, tria ex Platonis sententia vi-
tia ponens. Prima quidem quae facile sanabilia sint, quae scilicet
habitu careant. Secunda vero difficile curari posse inquit, utpote
quae habitu committantur, sed repugnantiam quandam paeniten-
tiamque comitem habeant. Tertia denique sanari non posse, quae
videlicet et habitu perpetrentur et repugnantia paenitentiaque penitus careant. Prima igitur Acheronti, secunda Pyriphlegethonti
atque Cocyto, tertia Tartaro apud Platonicos deputantur, unde dicit Plato nullum umquam egredi posse. Totidem gradus bonis in
*Phaedone* distribuuntur, ubi asseritur animas innocentes et pias,
sed expertes[103] philosophiae, in aere una cum aereis corporibus facile vivere, animas autem philosophia civili insuper praeditas in
caelo cum caelestibus lucidisque vehiculis, denique purgatissimas
super caelum absque corporibus beatissime vivere.

16     Orpheus autem novem praecipuas animabus distribuit regiones. Probis quidem vel octavam spheram vel planetas vel aetherem
sub planetis, quae quidem sphaerae novem sunt, si diligentius
partiaris, novem contemplationis gradibus, quos alias diximus,
congruae.[104] Mediis autem aerem aquamve et terram. Reprobis de-

men, they seem about to acquire their pleasures but are straightway snatched away from them and handed over to harsher punishments. Sardanapallus is kept ever further from an embrace, Midas from gold, Tantalus from a feast, Sisyphus from the summit of power. So fierce is the power of the phantasy, so fierce its assault when either it rules alone or a kind of phantastical habit and desire rules alone (one contracted in the reason from its long dealings with the phantasy).

In his commentaries on the *Phaedo*, Olympiodorus confirms the    15
order we established above, positing three vices (following Plato's view).[166] First are those vices that are easily curable because they are not habitual. The second, he says, can only be cured with difficulty given that they are indulged in from habit, yet they are attended by a sort of repugnance and penitence. The third finally cannot be cured, namely those vices which are enacted out of habit and which are totally unattended by repugnance and penitence. Among the Platonists the first kind is allotted to Acheron, the second to Pyriphlegethon and Cocytus, and the third to Tartarus, whence, Plato says, none can ever escape.[167] The same [three] ranks are allotted to good men in the *Phaedo*, where it is maintained that innocent and pious souls, though ones unschooled in philosophy, easily live in the air with airy bodies; that souls provided with civil [i.e. moral and political] philosophy besides live in the heavens with luminous celestial vehicles; and finally that souls who have been utterly purged live in blessedness above the heavens and without bodies.[168]

Orpheus, however, apportions nine principal regions to    16
souls.[169] To upright souls he assigns the eighth sphere or the planets or the aether below the planets; and these nine spheres, if you divide them up carefully, are in accord with the nine degrees of contemplation that we have talked about elsewhere.[170] To intermediate souls Orpheus gives [either] the air or the water and the earth. Finally to reprobate souls he assigns Acheron, Cocytus, and

nique Acherontem, Cocytum, Pyriphlegethontem, ubi 'novies' insuper 'Styx interfusa cohercet.' Novenarius autem numerus inde sumitur, quod vel affectione quadam vel habitu mobili vel habitu immobili peccaverunt, atque quocumque horum modo deliquerint, vel cogitatione vel etiam sermone vel insuper actione peccarunt. Unde novem gradus culparum novemque poenarum merito computantur.

17     Oraculum vero illud Maronis in sexto nullo pacto contemnendum est quasi poeticum, in quo partim Mercurium partim Platonem secutus affectus describit quatuor, qui quatuor sequantur humores, siquidem ex ignea bile appetitum, ex aereo sanguine voluptatem, ex atra bile terrea timorem, ex aquea pituita dolorem mollitiemque nasci consentaneum esse videtur. Deinde subdit ex quatuor his[105] affectibus quatuor tales habitus in animo concipi ad corporea declinantes, quos miseri post obitum secum ferant[106] circa quatuor elementa purgandos. In qua quidem purgatione quatuor praecipuas inferis plagas disponit more platonico, ubi licet Acherontis, Cocyti, Phlegethontis, Tartari strepitum mugitumque audire. His admodum consentaneum esse videtur quatuor vicissim in campis Elysiis disponere regiones, quatuor videlicet in zodiaco signorum triplicitates, quae quatuor congruant virtutum generibus, quibus quatuor expugnantur affectus, unde serena mente lumen caeleste recipitur. Meminisse vero oportet eos non esse inter Platonicos admittendos, qui animas in planetarum sphaeris igneque et aere puro viventes esse inter inferos opinantur. Quo enim pacto inferis deputantur, si et apud beatos sunt et in corporibus adeo levibus obedientibusque imperio animorum, ut inde a divinorum contemplatione non divertantur? Quamobrem solam

Pyriphlegethon, where "the Styx in between encircles them nine times."[171] The number nine [here] is taken from the fact that souls have sinned either because of some desire, or because of a changing habit, or because of an unchanging habit; and in whichever of these ways they have offended, they have sinned either in thought or in word too or in actual deed.[172] Justly enumerated then are nine degrees of guilt and nine degrees of punishment.

In no way should we dismiss as [merely] poetical the oracle that 17 Virgil gives us in the sixth book,[173] where, following Mercurius in part and Plato in part,[174] he describes four passions, which four are a consequence of the humors, since it seems appropriate that appetite is born from the fiery bile [i.e. from choler], pleasure from the airy blood, fear from the earthy black bile, and grief and weakness from the watery phlegm. He adds that from these four passions four like habits are conceived in the rational soul—habits declining towards corporeal things that the wretched bear with them after death and that must be purged with respect to the four elements. In this purgation he allots the four principal regions in the underworld in the Platonic manner, where one may hear the din and roar of Acheron, Cocytus, Phlegethon, and Tartarus. To parallel these it seems wholly appropriate to envisage four regions in turn in the Elysian fields, namely the four triads of signs in the zodiac; and to have these four triads accord with the kinds of virtues by which the four passions are conquered, whence the heavenly light is received in the tranquil mind. But we have to remember that those who think that the souls living in the spheres of the planets, and in the fire and pure air, are living [in fact] in the underworld must not be included among the Platonists. For how can such souls be relegated to the underworld if they are among the blessed; and if they dwell in bodies that are so light and so obedient to the command of their rational souls that they are not distracted by them from the contemplation of things divine? Accordingly, we should in the Platonic manner reserve the term "un-

eam mundi plagam, ubi tumultuaria elementorum confusio disso-
nat, inferorum nomine platonice nuncupare debemus.

18      Denique ut priscorum theologorum sententiam de statu animae
post mortem paucis comprehendam, sola divina, ut alias diximus,
arbitrantur res veras existere, reliqua esse rerum verarum imagines
atque umbras. Ideo prudentes homines, qui divinis incumbunt,
prae ceteris vigilare, imprudentes autem, qui sectantur alia, insomniis omnino quasi dormientes illud. Ac si in hoc somno priusquam expergefacti fuerint moriantur, similibus post discessum et
acrioribus visionibus angi. Et sicut eum qui in vita veris incubuit,
post mortem summa veritate potiri, sic eum qui falsa sectatus est,
fallacia extrema torqueri, ut ille rebus veris oblectetur, hic falsis
vexetur simulacris. Propterea Christus, vitae magister, saepe ita
praecipit: 'Vigilate, inquam, vigilate, ne dormientes vos Dominus
deprehendat.' Rursus: 'Surgite iam atque hinc abeamus.' Quidnam aliud est expergisci quam agnoscere se in sensibus somniare?
Quid vero surgere aliud et abire quam ad deum se ipsa mente
conferre?

19      Neque silentio praetereundam censeo causam quandam suppli-
cii, occultam quidem dolentibus sed potissimam, quam Plato significavit in *Timaeo, Gorgia, Republica* et interpretatus est Origenes.
Deus animam certa quadam spiritalium partium, virium, motuum
harmonia ab eius initio temperavit. Temperatio huiusmodi in hominibus intemperatis iniustisque solvitur paulatim ac dissolvitur
plurimum in damnatis. Necessarium est autem ex solutione et
dissolutione hac non mediocrem oriri molestiam doloremque in
animo, etiam si nesciat unde et cuius gratia doleat, quemadmodum, soluta naturali corporalium spirituum, humorum, membro-

derworld" only for that region of the world where the tumultuous confusion of the elements assaults the ear.

Finally let me summarize the ancient theologians' opinion concerning the status of the soul after death. They think that only things divine, as we said elsewhere, exist as true realities, and that the remainder are images and shadows of things true.[175] So they think that wise men who devote themselves to things divine are awake compared to the rest of us, and that unwise men who chase after other things are entirely deluded by dreams as though they were asleep. However, if they die in this sleep before they have been roused, they are tormented after death by similar but even fiercer visions. And they say that just as he who has devoted himself in life to things true acquires the highest truth after death, so he who has chased after things false is tortured by falsehood in the extreme; and the result is that the former enjoys things true while the latter is tormented by false images. Accordingly, Christ, the master of life, often exhorts us thus: "Keep watch, I say, keep watch, lest the Lord take you as you sleep";[176] and again "Now rise up and let us hence depart."[177] For what else is waking than recognizing that one is dreaming in the senses? What else is rising up and departing than transporting oneself in the mind itself to God?

I believe we should not pass over in silence a particular cause of punishment, hidden even from those suffering it, but the chief cause nonetheless: Plato indicates it in the *Timaeus*, *Gorgias*, and *Republic*, and Origen has interpreted it.[178] God has tempered the soul from its beginning with a fixed harmony of spiritual parts, of powers, and of motions. Such a tempering is gradually weakened in men who are intemperate and unjust, and it is destroyed completely in the damned. But from this weakening and destruction a not inconsiderable vexation and pain necessarily arises in the rational soul, even if it does not know whence and for the sake of what it is in pain. Similarly with a sick person, once the natural tempering of the corporeal spirits, humors, and members has been weak-

rum temperie, dolor necessario sequitur, etiam si aegrotans doloris
sui nesciat rationem.

20    Non negabunt haec omnino Christianorum theologi, sed ad-
dent, ut arbitror, poenam aliquam ex vero quodam animae dam-
natae iudicio, quoniam cogitabit esse se in aeternum divina visione
privatam. Quae ideo maxima poena est, quoniam deus finis est
cuius gratia nati sumus, cuius gratia omnia omnes appetimus
atque agimus. Ideoque multo acrior est naturalis sitis quae ad ipsum quam quae ad potum concitat sitibundum. Sed quemadmodum, si quis opio soporifero fuerit stupefactus, quamvis siti pereat,
tamen sitis stimulum detrimentumque non sentiet, opio vero reso-
luto persentiet vehementiusque vexabitur, sic animus qui Lethaeum, materiae[107] flumen, ingurgitavit, a deo[108] omnium diver-
sissimum, stupore circa divinorum sensum penitus occupatus,
naturalis erga deum sitis tormenta non sentit, sed stupore tandem
expulso et acutissime sentit et vehementissime cruciatur. Ac si
quodammodo in vita cogitare possimus esse nos procul a deo, oc-
cupati tamen vitae solatiis rarius hoc animadvertimus, et quando
animadvertimus, speramus brevi nos redituros ad patrem. Ibi
neque solatium miseros neque spes ulla delectat, quod et Acheron
dici potest. Auget poenam quod sua se culpa tanto bono privatos
existimant; propterea sibi ipsis perpetuo indignantur, quod Stygis
nomine significari potest. Accedit Tartarea locorum aut vilium aut

ened, pain necessarily ensues, even if he does not know the reason for his pain.

The theologians of the Christians are not going to deny this entirely, but they will add, I think, that a particular punishment comes from a particular authentic judgment made by the damned soul [itself], because it is going to ponder the fact that it has been cut off from the divine vision for eternity.[179] This is the greatest punishment, because God is the end for whose sake we were born and for whose sake all of us desire and do all things. Accordingly, the natural thirst we have for Him is more ardent than the one that incites a thirsty man to drink. Take someone who has been stupefied by the narcotic effects of opium: though he may be dying of thirst, he nonetheless does not perceive the pangs of that thirst and the harm to himself; but when the opium has disappeared, he perceives it clearly and is tormented with even greater vehemence. Similarly the rational soul, which has become addicted to Lethe (the river of matter and the farthest of all things from God), and which has become utterly seized by a stupor with regard to the perception of things divine, does not feel the torments of its natural thirst for God. But when this stupor has been sloughed off, it experiences its thirst most acutely and is racked most vehemently by it. If we are able to think of ourselves in this life, however, as being in a way distant from God, we nonetheless very rarely notice it, preoccupied as we are with life's comforts; and when we do notice it, we hope that we are going to return soon to our Father. But no solace exists there for the wretched and no hope seduces them at all; and this state can be referred to as Acheron. Augmenting the punishment is that the wretched mull over the fact that they have been deprived of so great a good by their own fault, and on this account they are perpetually angry with themselves; and the Styx can be the name that signifies this state. The Tartarean dwelling place of the vile or most hideous things is next; and fi-

teterrimorum habitatio, ac tandem humani huius corporis crucia-
tus, qui in sensu Phlegethon, in animo Cocytus esse videtur.

: XI :

*De medio animorum statu,*
*praecipue secundum philosophos.*[109]

1 Solet de animabus illorum saepe quaeri, qui ante electionis aeta-
tem e corporibus decesserunt. Plato scribit Herum Pamphilium,
qui a morte surrexit, de aliorum statu animorum multa et stu-
penda narrasse; de his autem alia[110] quaedam non multum memoria digna. Avicenna vero in *Metaphysicis* eos animos, qui nondum
vel bonum vel malum habitum contraxerunt, ex divinae clementiae
largitate boni aliquid reportare. Nos igitur, si philosophicis hac in
re coniecturis liceret incedere,[111] forsitan diceremus ordine rerum
ita currente eiusmodi sortem illis quodammodo praeter apparen-
tem ordinem contigisse, sed a divina sapientia, quae nihil usquam
esse permittit ordinis totius expers, in ordinem quendam, nobis
quidem occultum, superis autem manifestissimum redigi.

2 Quid si deus, quemadmodum inter omnia extrema quae inter
se longissime distant, plura semper media interponit, ita inter ipsas beatissimorum miserrimorumve sortes, tamquam maxime om-

nally there is this human body's torture: this seems to be Phlegethon in the sense, and Cocytus in the rational soul.[180]


: XI :

*The middle state of rational souls, especially*
*according to the philosophers*

People often inquire about the souls of those who depart from  1
their bodies before the age of choice. Plato writes that Er the
Pamphylian, who rose from the dead, had narrated many extraordinary things about the condition of other rational souls, but that
the sundry other things he said about the newly born are not worthy of being much remembered.[181] In his *Metaphysics* Avicenna
[says] that those souls who have not yet acquired a good or a bad
habit win from the abundance of the divine clemency something
of good.[182] But we ourselves, if it is permissible for us to engage in
philosophical conjectures on this matter, would say perhaps, given
the changing order of things, that a portion has been allotted
them which is in a way over and beyond the visible order, but that
they are brought by the divine wisdom (which permits nothing
ever to be without a share in the whole order) back to some particular order, one hidden indeed to us but fully manifest to those
above.

Why? If God always interposes many means between all the  2
extremes which are furthest apart, so has He interjected as many
grades as possible between the lots of the most blessed and the lots
of the most miserable, these being at the greatest possible distance
of all things from each other. And if He has done this, it is so that
there would be no fewer grades in the invisible orders of rational
souls than in the visible orders of bodies; and so that there would

nium inter se distantes, gradus quam plurimos interiecit, ut non
pauciores in occultis animorum ordinibus quam in manifestis corporum gradus existerent, essentque hinc beatissimi multi, multi
inde miserrimi, rursus hinc alii minus beati, inde alii miseri minus,
omnium vero medii pariter, qui neque miseri sint proprie neque
beati? Siquidem beatus est qui divinis in deo saporibus fruitur,
miser vero qui numquam[112] divinum aliquem sentit odorem semperque esurit;[113] minus autem inde beatus qui in illo paucioribus
fruitur. Vicissim minus hinc miser qui esurit[114] doletque minus;
medius tandem, qui in creatura quosdam creatoris sentit odores
vivitque odore contentus. Quamobrem dicent forte philosophi infantum animas non debere de divina iustitia conqueri, quia si forte
facultate summi boni privatae sunt, etiam extremi mali discrimine
liberatae.

3      Rursus probabile est non conqueri, si modo in perspicuitatem
animae nullis corporalium affectionum nubibus obfuscatam lumen
divini solis naturalia creans naturalium formarum influat plenum
eique, ut inquit Timaeus,[115] ordinem universi demonstret atque simul ordinatorem in ordine, quantum ordo ipse capit ordinatoris,
et hoc bono iubeat faciatque esse contentam. Itaque sicut in homine inter crassum corpus et animam spiritus est, atque in affectu
dolorem inter et voluptatem est indolentia, item in ratione inter
scientiam et ignorantiam opinio recta, rursus in universo perspicua
inter lucidum et opacum, sic in spiritibus segregatis esse videntur
qui in caelis tam luce quam lumine dei beate formentur atque con-

hence be multitudes of the most blessed and multitudes correspondingly of the most miserable, and some who were less blessed
on the one hand and others who were less miserable on the other,
and as the means equally of all, those who were neither miserable,
properly speaking, nor blessed. For the blessed person is he who
relishes in God the savors divine; but the miserable is he who
never detects a divine aroma and is always hungry. The less blessed
is he who enjoys fewer things in God; and the less miserable in
turn is he who is less hungry and who grieves less. And the person in the middle, finally, is he who detects certain of the Creator's aromas in the creature and lives content with that fragrance.
Wherefore the philosophers will say perhaps that the souls of infants ought not to complain about the justice divine, because, even
if they have been perchance deprived of the ability to reach the
highest good, they have also been freed from the hazard of the
greatest evil.

Again, it is probable that [a freed infant soul] will not complain 3
provided: a) that the splendor of the divine Sun, in creating natural things, flows replete with the natural forms into its clarity, a
clarity obscured no longer by the clouds of corporeal affections;
b) that, as Timaeus says, this splendor shows it the order of the
universe and simultaneously the arranger of that order (to the extent the order itself receives the arranger); and c) that it tells it
to be content with this good and makes it so.[183] As in man, therefore, the spirit exists between the gross body and the soul, and in
feeling the experience of being without pain is midway between
pain and pleasure, and in reason right opinion is midway between
knowledge and ignorance, and in the universe finally the transparent is midway between the clear and the opaque; so among
the segregated spirits there seem to be those who are blessedly
formed in the heavens by both the light (*lux*) and the splendor
(*lumen*) of God.[184] But each of these is miserably lacking, by way
of contrast, to the spirits on earth. Between the [two extremes],

tra, quibus circa terram miserabiliter utrumque desit, inter hos autem in puriore aere medii, quibus etsi non lux ipsa proprie, tamen lumen aspiret.

4 Meminisse vero oportet, quod significamus alias, quemadmodum aliud est lux in sole permanens, aliud lumen inde manans perque cuncta diffusum, aliud radius quidam oculis inde naturaliter insitus, sic aliud esse infinitam in deo lucem, per quam solam et deus se ipso fruitur et beatae mentes divina bonitate fruuntur; aliud commune lumen inde per omnes perspicuas mentes se abunde diffundens, per quod quasi creatum externumque mentes singulae, modo inde non divertantur, creata cuncta conspiciunt. Creatorem vero ipsum proprie in se ipso nequaquam, nisi per lumen accensae transferantur in lucem; aliud radium quendam iam singulis proprium factumque ab initio mentibus naturalem, in eisque restantem quodammodo etiam inde diversis atque discedentibus. In gradu quidem primo beati sunt; in secundo vero neque beati proprie neque miseri, modo hoc ipso contenti vivant; in tertio denique animae sunt humanae sive corporibus sive corporeis affectibus alligatae atque ex hoc ipso paene iam miserae, sola vero spe quasi felices. Miserrimi vero sub hoc ipso gradu sunt, quibus solus restat radius, atque ille quidem iam et caliginosus et urens lucisque purae fiducia destitutus.

5 Forte vero Platonicus aliquis ita coniiciet. Si deus mentes primae lucis gratia procreavit atque ipsae ad eam consequendam tum divinae bonitatis agnitione tum vel maxime amore parantur, quippe cum agnitio lumine inde formet et amor hinc illuc luce re-

however, are the middle spirits in the purer air, and upon them breathes, if not [God's] light itself properly speaking, yet its splendor.

We must recall what we indicate elsewhere. Just as the light re-  4
maining in the sun is one thing, but the splendor emanating from it and diffused through all things is another, and still another is a ray from it naturally implanted in eyes, so the infinite light in God is one thing — the light through which alone God enjoys Himself, and blessed minds enjoy God's goodness — but another is the common splendor thence diffusing itself in abundance through all transparent minds. This is the splendor through which, as through something created and external, individual minds, provided they are not diverted from it, see all created things. But they do not see the Creator in Himself at all properly speaking, unless, set ablaze through the splendor, they are transformed into the light. Still another thing is the particular ray proper indeed to individuals which was made natural to minds from the very beginning and which in a way remains in them even when they have been diverted from or are departing from it. In the first degree are the blessed; in the second, are those who are neither properly blessed nor properly wretched, provided they live content with this; and in the third finally are human souls tied either to bodies or to bodily desires, and because of this they are wretched in the present or virtually so but happy as it were in hope alone. The utterly wretched are those beneath this third degree: only a ray is left to them and that is already murky and scorching and robbed of the pledge of the pure light.

Perhaps some Platonist will come up with the following conjec-  5
ture. If God has created minds for the sake of the first light, and if they are made ready to acquire that light both by knowledge of the divine goodness but most of all by love of it — given that knowledge forms them thence with splendor (*lumen*) and love re-forms them hence and thither with light (*lux*) — it is probable that justice

formet, verisimile fore divinam iustitiam velle nulli omnino mentium agnoscendi amandique dei semper facultatem omnem occasionemque deesse. Quoniam vero multis ante rationis usum morientibus rursusque quibusdam ab initio stolidis utrumque maligna fati necessitate subtrahitur, ideo consentaneum fore facultatem eiusmodi per divinam providentiam vel in hac quandoque miro quodam pacto vel in altera saltem vita rependi, ne quis absque propria culpa fine speciei praecipuo careat. Quamobrem horum animas, etsi hic numquam, tamen a corporibus segregatas in illo quod[116] diximus lumine, dum creatorem in creaturis agnoscunt, tanto gradatim accendi creatoris amore, ut ad consequendam lucem certo quodam tempore disponantur. Tempore, inquam, quoniam solae angelicae mentes, tamquam in aeternitate totae, momento sive proficiant sive deficiant; animae vero quasi iam naturaliter quodammodo ad temporalia declinantes suam tempore operam peragant, sed longiori quidem in corpore, extra vero corpus admodum breviori, momento vero dumtaxat, cum primum fuerint in angelicam ferme translatae naturam. At si animae in purgatoriis constitutae suppliciis, quamvis in deteriori habitu locoque sint, tamen ad beatitudinem usque resurgunt, nihil mirum videri debere illorum animas in regione indolentiae media beatitudinique propinquiore positas ad beatitudinem usque posse proficere. Haec de infantibus maxime philosophi opinarentur.

6 Verum de his, qui ab ipsa natura omnino stolidi sunt, difficilior admodum quam de infantibus quaestio esse videtur. Hi enim si diu vixerint, aliquem circa materiam, quae est infimum universi,

divine wishes absolutely none of the minds to be lacking in any faculty and occasion for knowing and loving God forever. But because both knowing and loving have been withheld by the malign necessity of fate from many who die before the use of reason and again from those who are stupid from the onset, it is appropriate that divine providence compensate them for such a faculty, either in this life on some occasion and in some marvelous way, or at least in another life, lest someone be deprived of the principal end of [our] species without any fault of his own. Accordingly, with the souls of these [infants and idiots], though it never happens here [on earth], yet when they are released from bodies and dwell in that splendor we have described and recognize the Creator in His creatures, they are set ablaze step by step with such an ardent love of the Creator that they are made ready to receive the light itself at an appointed time. At an appointed time, I say, because only the angelic minds, all of them being in eternity, either advance or fail to do so in a moment, but souls which already and in a way naturally turn aside towards temporal things enact their own work in time — for a longer time in the body, but for a much shorter time outside the body. They do so in a moment only when they have been wellnigh transformed into the angelic nature. But if souls confined to the punishments of purgatory, though they are in a much worse condition and location, nonetheless rise again even to blessedness, then it should not appear surprising that souls placed in the middle region of painlessness, closer as it is to blessedness, can advance all the way to blessedness. Philosophers have formed these opinions in the main about infants.

As to those who are naturally wholly stupid, the question 6 seems much more difficult than it is for infants. For if they live for a long time, they contract a habit centered on matter, which is at the nadir of the universe, a habit that customarily turns them away from God in that He is the summit of the universe. This habit, when accompanying even the separated soul, still turns perchance

habitum contrahunt, qui a deo, quod est universi summum, diver-
tere solet. Hic habitus animam comitans etiam separatam adhuc
forte ad materiam vertit atque interim avertit a deo. Beatitudo autem nullis nisi in deum conversis convenire censetur. At vero si hi
miseri sunt, cum converti nullo modo ad summum fato prohibente potuerint, nulla sua culpa sunt miseri ac deus frustra converti iussisset eos qui non possent.

7      Respondebit hic forte peripateticus aliquis in stultis ob nimiam
phantasiae ipsius intensionem[117] rationem adeo vacavisse, ut non
agendo habitum non creaverit; habitum vero proprium phantasiae,
qui non tam in anima est quam in corpore animato, cessare statim
composito dissoluto. Quo efficiatur ut mens statim, nullo prohibente naturali radio, convertatur in deum et divinum lumen, quod
ubique adest, accipiens accendatur. Deinde amet accensa et
amando vehementius se convertat brevique tempore nonnihil pro-
merendo beatitudinem consequatur. Platonici vero, qui habitum et
in phantasia quodammodo remanente restare putant et in rationem illi consentientem, si modo quisquam,[118] et tunc quidem
coacta, consenserit, inde transfundi, respondebunt oportere prius
habitum ad opposita divertentem omnino deleri[119] quam superius
erigatur. Sed in hoc delendo tum genii tum dei virtutem mirabiliter operari. Non enim sub divina providentia minus consultum
provisumque esse mentibus quam corporibus. Igitur sicut corporibus aegrotantibus, ubi natura morbum non potest expellere pro-
priaque in sanitatem virtute redire, arte medicorum confirmata
expellere consuevit, similiter et in mentibus, quibus naturalis fa-

towards matter and in the meantime away from God. But blessedness is thought to befit none except those who have been brought back to God. But if souls are wretched simply because, with fate forbidding them, they could not be brought back in any way to the Highest, then they are wretched through no fault of their own, and in vain would God have ordered the conversion of those who could not be converted.

Here perforce some Aristotelian will reply that the reason in stupid men has been so emptied out because of the extreme intensity of their phantasy that in not doing [anything] it will not have created a habit; and that a habit proper to the phantasy — a habit which is not in the soul so much as in the ensouled body — immediately ceases when the composite [of soul and body] is dissolved. Consequently, if there is no natural ray preventing it, the mind is straightway converted to God, and in receiving the divine splendor which is present everywhere, it is set aflame; then, having been set aflame, it loves, and in loving more ardently, it converts itself; and in a brief time, since it deserves something, it acquires blessedness. But the Platonists who suppose that the habit does remain in the phantasy (that itself remains in a way), and is thence transfused into the reason in harmony with it (provided the reason, being then under compulsion, gives its consent) — these Platonists will reply that a habit diverting [the reason] towards its opposites must be utterly destroyed before it may be lifted higher; but that in this destroying, the power both of the [daemon] genius and of God are marvelously at work. For under divine providence, they say, there is no less careful consideration of and provision for minds than of and for bodies. Therefore, just as in ailing bodies, where nature cannot expel the disease and return to health under its own power, nature usually does expel the disease when strengthened by the art of doctors, similarly in minds too, where the natural faculty for purging the corporeal habit and for returning to God is lacking, the all-powerful Doctor, either solely through His own power

7

cultas corporei habitus expurgandi revisendique dei deest, omnipotentem medicum vel propria dumtaxat virtute, vel ministrorum felicium ministerio feliciter utrumque peragere. Neque id quidem ordine carere putabunt, ut divina clementia, quae maxime probatur in principe, hic apertissime luceat, dum et nullus absque culpa propria condemnatur, et qui extra culpam ad tempus meriti facultate privatur, in facultatem quandoque divinitus restituitur — facultatem, inquam, tutam, quae et aberrare non possit et brevi multum deo adiuvante promereatur. Haec illi.

8 Verum ne de pueris stultisque pueriliter stulteque sentiamus, ita iam concludendum esse videtur. Huc nos ferme coniecturalis philosophorum ducit via, sed quoniam humana coniectio circa divina saepe multumque fallitur, multo satius tutiusque censemus, nos sanctioribus apud Christianos ducibus obedienti humilitate committere.

: XII :

*Conclusio.*[120]

1 Postquam terminus vitae non idem nobis atque ceteris animantibus est a deo tributus, quemadmodum primo communibus rationibus, secundo argumentationibus propriis, tertio tum signis tum solutionibus quaestionum ostendimus, summa diligentia cavendum, arbitror, ne incertum hoc fugacis vitae momentum saeculis infinitis anteponamus. Meminerimus autem, si sapimus, non

or with the aid of His blessed ministers, blessedly accomplishes both. Nor will the Platonists deem it extraordinary that divine clemency (which is most approved of in a prince) should be most luminously manifest here where no one is condemned without its being his own fault; and where he who is deprived for a time, without its being his fault, of the deserving man's faculty is at some point divinely restored to that faculty — that vigilant faculty which cannot err and which can in an instant, with God's help, deserve [so] much. These are the Platonists' views.

In order not to judge in a childish and unintelligent way, how- 8 ever, about children and people who lack intelligence, it seems we must now conclude. Up till now, the way of conjecture, the way of the philosophers, in general has conducted us, but because, with regard to matters divine, human conjecture is often grossly deceived, we judge it much more satisfactory and much safer to commit ourselves in humble obedience to those who are more venerable guides among Christians.

: XII :

*Conclusion.*

Inasmuch as God has not given us the same goal in life as He has 1 given the rest of living beings — as we have shown first by general reasons, second by arguments proper to particulars, and third by signs and by solutions to questions — we must exercise the utmost diligence, I think, lest we prefer this uncertain moment of fleeting life to the infinity of the ages. We should remember, however, if we are wise, that we cannot live for eternity, or live well or perfectly, or understand blessedly, unless: a) we are formed by the essence of Him through whose creative activity we receive the possi-

posse nos in aeternum aut bene esse aut perfecte vivere aut feliciter intellegere, nisi eius formemur essentia, quo creante, ut essemus, accepimus; eius vita vivamus, quo afflante spiramus atque movemur; eius intellegentia intellegamus ipsum perque ipsum omnia, quo illustrante quotidie et creata consideramus et quaerimus creatorem. Perveniemus autem deo duce ad hunc gradum naturae supremum, si modo ab ipsa materia, quae naturae gradus est infimus, affectum animi pro viribus segregabimus, ut quantum ab ea discedimus, tantum accedamus ad deum, et cui nunc posthabito fallacis huius vitae momento[121] quoad possumus vivimus, tandem eius vita vivamus in aevum.

FINIS

THEOLOGIA PLATONICA
MARSILII FICINI FLORENTINI
DE ANIMORUM IMMORTALITATE[122]

IN OMNIBUS QUAE AUT HIC AUT ALIBI A ME
TRACTANTUR, TANTUM ASSERTUM ESSE VOLO QUANTUM
AB ECCLESIA COMPROBATUR.[123]

bility of existence; b) we live by the life of Him through whose inspiration we breathe and are moved;[185] and c) we understand both God Himself and all things through God by the understanding of Him through whose daily illumination we consider all that is created and seek for the Creator. But we will arrive, led by God, at this the highest degree of nature only if we summon up the strength to separate [our] rational soul's desire from matter itself (which is the lowest degree of nature), so that, to the extent we depart from matter, we may thereby approach God, and, having set aside the moment of this deceptive life and living now for Him as best we can, we may at last live His life for eternity.

### THE END

## THE PLATONIC THEOLOGY
## OF MARSILIO FICINO, THE FLORENTINE,
## ON THE IMMORTALITY OF SOULS

IN ALL I DISCUSS, EITHER HERE OR ELSEWHERE, I WISH TO MAINTAIN ONLY WHAT MEETS WITH THE APPROVAL OF THE CHURCH.[186]

# APPENDIX

*Argumentum Marsilii Ficini Florentini*
*in Platonicam Theologiam*
*Ad Laurentium[1] Medicem Patriae Servatorem[2]*

1 Marsilius Ficinus Laurentio Medici viro magnanimo s. d.[3]

Decrevi, Magnanime Laurenti, antequam grande illud *Platonicae Theologiae* volumen ederem tuo nomini dedicatum, in quo adhuc superest nonnihil quod examinatione indigeat, edere, si tibi placuerit, argumentum. Non ut huiusmodi argumento quasi quodam *Theologiae* praeludio exercitatus accedas promptior ad ludendum, cum mihi videaris ipsam ludi[4] palmam iam consecutus, sed ut hoc interim pignore admonitus memineris et meminisse me tibi debere quod iamdiu iure promiseram et solvere quandoque velle quod debere cognosco. Praesertim cum non tam[5] hoc ipsum debeam quia promisi, quam id promiserim quia cuncta debebam.

2 Postquam vero hoc in *Theologiam Platonicam* argumentum legeris, deinceps quantum per negotia licebit leges quae sequuntur quinque Platonicae sapientiae claves.[6]

*Tres contemplationis Platonicae gradus.*

3 Tres vero sunt praecipui contemplationis platonicae gradus. Primus quidem a corpore per animam ascendit ad Deum. Secundus autem consistit in deo. Tertius denique ad animam corpusque descendit. Tres quoque gradus nostrum continet argumentum.

# APPENDIX

*The Introduction of Marsilio Ficino, the Florentine,
to [His] Platonic Theology.
Dedicated to Lorenzo de' Medici, the Savior of the State.*[1]

Marsilio Ficino to the great-souled Lorenzo de' Medici, greeting.  1

Great-souled Lorenzo, before I publish that massive volume of the *Platonic Theology* which is dedicated in your name and in which there is something still remaining that needs my scrutiny, I have decided, if it seems agreeable to you, to publish an introduction. And I have decided to do so, not that you might use such an introduction as a kind of run-up to the *Theology* and in order to enter the race with greater alacrity—since it seems to me you have already won the palm of victory—but that, alerted in the meanwhile by this pledge, you will keep in mind both that I have kept in mind the debt I owe you, a debt I had duly promised some time ago; and that I wish to pay at some point this debt I acknowledge. This is especially since I owe this, not so much because I promised it, as because I promised it since I was indebted to you for everything.

But after you have read this introduction to the *Platonic Theol-*  2
*ogy*, then, insofar as your affairs will allow, peruse the five keys to Platonic wisdom that follow.[2]

### The Three Steps of Platonic Contemplation

There are three principal steps to Platonic contemplation. The  3
first ascends from the body through the soul to God. The second comes to a halt in God. The third finally descends to the soul and the body. Three steps also comprise our introduction.[3]

*Contemplationis primus gradus est ascensus
ad animam, angelum, deum
ac de divina intellegentia et amore.*[7]

*Caelum est forma sine materia, ut nonnullis placet.*

4  Considerabam nuper diligenter Aristotelis illud paradoxon, caelum materia caret. Rationem quoque Averrois meditabar qua paradoxon aristotelicum comprobat. Quod videlicet materia cum natura sua informis sit, ideoque ad quamlibet formam aeque se
habeat omnesque vicissim capere valeat, a formis iugiter fluit in
formas,[8] unde fit ut quod ex materia constat, formam suam quandoque possit amittere. Caelum vero formam propriam amittere
nequit, tum quia nulla usquam est illi contraria qualitas, sicut
neque motus circulari motui suo contrarius reperitur, tum quia
motum habet sine ulla digressione semper aequalem indefes-
sumque qui et in idem redit, principiumque rursus incohat ubi
finiri videtur. Ex his concludit Averrois caelum esse formam quandam per se sine materia existentem, quae quamvis subiecta materia
non indigeat, ipsa tamen subiecta est quantitati motuique secundum locum. Eiusmodi formam inter physicas formas et metaphy-
sicas esse vult mediam. Naturales enim formae cum quantitate
quadam et in materia sunt; formae vero omnino super naturam
tam quantitate quam materia carent. Mediam quandam formam
esse vult ne ab extremo ad extremum absque medio transeatur,
quae quamvis habeat quantitatem, materiam tamen non habet,
qualem esse substantiam caelestem existimat. Proclus quoque
platonicus caeleste vehiculum animae corpus esse putat, nullam
tamen habere materiam.

*The first step of contemplation is the ascent*
*to the soul, to the angel, and to God.*
*On the divine understanding and on love*

*For many the sky is form without matter.*

A short while ago I was considering that paradox of Aristotle's,   4
namely that the heavens lack matter.[4] I was also reflecting on
Averroes' additional reasoning for the Aristotelian paradox,
namely that, since matter is by its nature unformed and therefore
equally open to any form and has the power to receive all forms in
turn, it flows unfailingly out of forms into forms. Hence what is
made from matter is able at some time to lose its own form. But
the heavens are unable to lose their own form both because no
quality is ever contrary to them (just as we find no motion contrary to their own circular motion), and because they have motion
which is always uniform and never digresses and never tires, a motion which returns to the same point and makes a new beginning
when it seems to be finishing. Averroes concludes from this that
the heavens are a certain form existing through itself without matter, a form (though a substrate) that does not need matter, yet is
itself subject to quantity and to motion in space.[5] Averroes wants
such a form to be the mean between physical and metaphysical
forms. For natural forms exist with a certain quantity and in matter, but forms that are entirely above nature lack both quantity
and matter. He wants there to be a mean form, so that we do not
pass from one extreme to another without a mean, a form which,
though it has quantity, nevertheless does not have matter; and he
believes the heavens' substance is such a form. The Platonist
Proclus also believes that the soul's celestial vehicle is [extended]
body though it does not have any matter at all.[6]

*Forma sine quantitate magis quam sine materia potest existere.*

5 His ego Aristotelis Averroisque et Procli gradibus ad caelum usque directis conatus sum pro viribus ascendere super caelum. Profecto cum formarum genus[9] queat alicubi se a materia liberare, sicut in caelo modo nobis apparuit, potest etiam alicubi absolvere seipsum a quantitate, ac etiam multo magis, quippe si ab alterutro dependeret, penderet potius a materia a qua substantialis forma saepe sustinetur quam a quantitate, quam substantialis forma forte non minus sustinet quam sustineatur ab illa. Quod maxime in caelo conspicitur, ut placet Averroi, ubi forma talis sustinet quantitatis dimensiones. Adde quod multo magis cum materia quam cum quantitate congruit in ordine quodam generis atque naturae. Quare si absque materia potest esse, longe facilius[10] absque quantitate consistere potest, praesertim forma illa quae substantia est.[11] Substantia enim, cum accidens antecedat, absque quantitate, quae accidens est, alicubi potest existere.

*Forma sine qualitate[12] magis quam sine*
*mole esse potest.*

6 Ita formarum ordo, quemadmodum ab elementis in caelum proficit in melius, dum ab umbra materiae liberatur, ita super caeli verticem in aliquid longe melius proficit, dum in animis angelisque etiam a mole quantitatis absolvitur. Depositaque divisionis debilitate ob indivisibilis naturae unitatem fortitudinem adipiscitur. Consummatur tandem super illos in optimo, cum in deo etiam liberatur a qualitate accidentisque defectu. Potest autem a qualitate secerni facilius quam a mole. Substantialis enim forma ubique in natura ipsa sustinet qualitates, nusquam[13] vero sustine-

*Form can exist without quantity more than it can without matter.*

Climbing up these steps of Aristotle, Averroes, and Proclus, which 5
reach as far as the heavens, I have tried as best I can to rise above
the heavens. Certainly, since the genus of forms can somewhere
liberate itself from matter, as we have just seen in [the case of] the
heavens, it can also somewhere free itself from quantity; and much
more so even, for if this genus depended on either one, it would
depend on matter, by which substantial form is often sustained,
rather than on quantity, which substantial form perchance sustains
no less than it is sustained by it. This is principally seen in the
heavens, in Averroes' view, where such a [substantial but matter-
less] form sustains the dimensions of quantity. Moreover, form is
considerably more in accord with matter in a particular order of
genus and of nature than it is with quantity. So, if form is able to
exist without matter, then it can exist without quantity much
more easily, and especially the form which is [an independent]
substance. For substance, since it precedes accident, can somewhere exist without quantity that is accident.

*Form can exist without quality⁷ more than it can
without mass [i.e. quantity].*

Thus the order of the forms, just as it gets better as it proceeds 6
from the elements to the heavens (being liberated from the
shadow of matter), so above the heavens' pole it proceeds to something far better still when in souls and angels it is also freed from
quantity's mass. It acquires strength, having cast off the weakness
of division by virtue of the unity of [its] indivisible nature. Finally,
above souls and angels it is perfected in what is best, when in God
it is liberated even from quality and the defect of accident. But it
can be separated from quality more easily than from mass. For everywhere in nature substantial form itself sustains qualities but is

tur ab illis; alicubi tamen in quantitate iacere videtur. Quod in formis[14] naturae infimis plane conspicitur.

*Caelum aut est vita quaedam visibilis aut natura vitae proxima.*

7  Caelum quidem, cum sine materia sit, spiritale quiddam quodammodo esse videtur Platonicis magis quam corporale. Quid ergo
caelum est? Lux circularis circulusque lucidus sine materia, quemadmodum oppositum eius, quod est terrae imum, est materia sine
luce. Caelum igitur, ut Platonicis placet, aut vita quaedam est non
occulta, ut anima, sed ob dimensionem, si vis, oculis manifesta,
aut saltem, cum sit natura quaedam vitae propinquior quam cetera
corpora, vita quadam vivit sibi magis admodum familiari quam
cetera.

*Differentia lucis in caelo atque elementis*
*apud Platonicos ac Peripateticos.*

8  Sed iuvat gradatim a luce ascendere rursus ad lucem. Videmus in
elementis ubi minus crassae materiae[15] inest, facilius lucem adesse;
accensamque materiam quo magis extenuatur rarescitque eo purius perlucere. Quamobrem caelum, quoniam fulget summopere,
materia carere probatur, et ob hoc ipsum, quia caret materia,
maxime fulget. Quod si quis dixerit partes caeli densiores magis
lucere quam alias, respondebunt Platonici rariores partes lucere
quidem magis, sed ob nimiam tenuitatem lucem[que] videri non
posse. Respondebunt rursus Peripatetici aliud esse ex se, aliud ex
alio coruscare. Ideo elementa, quia fulgorem capiunt alicunde,
quae[16] rariora sunt facilius capere; caelestia vero quae ex se splen-

nowhere sustained by qualities; yet in some places we do see it embedded in quantity. This is obvious in the lowest forms of nature.

*The heavens are either a sort of visible life or a nature proximate to life.*

The heavens, since they are without matter, seem to the Platonists 7
to be something in a way more spiritual than corporeal. What are
the heavens then? They are circular light and a light-filled circle
without matter, just as its opposite, which is earth's lowest part, is
matter without light. So the heavens for the Platonists are either a
sort of life — a life not hidden like the soul but manifest to the eyes
on account, if you will, of dimension — or at least, since they are a
sort of nature closer to life than other bodies are, they live by a life
which is much more intimately their own than the others do.[8]

*The difference among the Platonists and the Aristotelians
between the light in the sky and in the elements.*

But it behooves us to ascend once more from light to light. We see 8
that light dwells more easily in those elements where less heavy
matter is present; and that in the case of ignited matter, the more
it is thinned out and rarified, the more purely it is transparent.
Therefore the heavens, since they are radiant in the extreme, are
proved to lack matter; and because of this fact — that they lack
matter — they are radiant in the extreme. But if someone asserts
that the denser parts of the heavens are more radiant than the others, the Platonists will respond that the rarer parts do in fact shine
more, but because of their extreme thinness the light cannot be
seen. The Aristotelians will again counter that to exist from oneself is one thing, to shine from another is something else. Thus,
[with] the elements, because they receive light from elsewhere,
the ones which are rarer receive more easily; but [with] celestial
things, which are resplendent of themselves, the denser they
are, the more abundantly they are ablaze. But let us leave such

dent, quo densiora sunt[17] eo uberius refulgere. Verum mittamus his[18] quaestiones huiusmodi. Mittamus caelum parumper, ne splendore corporeo prorsus allucinemur.

*Quando purgamus lucem caelestem,*
*primo reperimus animam, deinde angelum.*

9  Age caelesti naturae; relicto, si vis, lumine atque motu; subtrahe quantitatis dimensiones. Licet enim cogitatione subtrahere, nam aliud est lumen caeli motusque, aliud est[19] dimensio. Forma quae superest spiritus quidam est tanto lucidior velociorque caelo, quanto caelum est lucidius et velocius elementis. Substantia haec incorporea animus rationalis esse videtur. Deme rursus huic motum; relinque lucem et qualitatem. Potes enim demere, nam aliud lux et qualitas est, aliud motus. Forma quae deinde restat est angelus, clarior admodum et velocior animo,[20] quia neque disgregat lucem suam motu neque actionem propriam sicut anima distrahit tempore.

*Praestat ascendere ad substantiam,*
*in qua virtus non sit aliud quam substantia.*

10  Ceterum nondum satis naturam rerum purgasse videmur. Restat nobis adhuc, nisi me ratio fallit, accidens a substantia secernendum. Angelus enim substantiam habet et qualitatem. Verum quaerendum est primo numquid fieri hoc praestet, deinde utrum

questions to the Aristotelians. Let us abandon the heavens for a little while, so that we are not dazzled utterly by [their] corporeal splendor.

> *When we purge away the heavens' light,*
> *we come upon first the soul and then the angel.*

Well then on to the heavens' nature. Having subtracted, if you will, their light and motion, subtract the dimensions of quantity; for in thought it is permissible to subtract them, since the heavens' light and motion are one thing, their dimension another. The form that remains is a certain spirit; and to the degree that the heavens are brighter and quicker than the elements, so this spirit is correspondingly brighter and quicker than the heavens. This incorporeal [i.e. dimensionless] substance seems to be the rational soul. Again, subtract motion from this soul and leave light and quality; for you do have the capacity to subtract it, since light and quality are one thing, motion another. The form that then remains is the angel, a form much clearer and quicker than the rational soul, because it neither separates its light in motion nor divides its own action up in time like the soul.

> *It is better to ascend to the substance*
> *in which power is nothing else but substance.*

But for all that, it seems we have not yet purified the nature of things sufficiently. We still have the task, unless reason deceives me, of separating accident from substance. For the angel has substance and quality. But we must inquire first whether it is better for this separation to happen; then whether it can occur. It is certainly better; for where substance is one thing, quality another, such a substance, since its nature is unformed and imperfect, is formed and perfected by another; and in receiving and sustaining a quality, it is in a way acted on. And that quality, since it is a form

possit? Praestat nimirum, nam ubi substantia aliud est, aliud qualitas, substantia huiusmodi, cum sua natura informis imperfectaque sit, aliunde formatur atque perficitur, et in capienda sustinendaque qualitate quodammodo patitur. Atque qualitas illa, quia est forma quaedam in alio,[21] scilicet in subiecto, se sustinere non potest, multoque minus ex se potest existere; eget ergo tam causa quam subiecto. Nec est integra plenaque omnino, cum pro capacitate subiecti suscipiatur. Unde necessario fit ab altiore forma, quae quidem, ne sine fine vagemur, in seipsa sit, per se sufficiens ipsa sibi atque plenissima, sitque virtus undique infinita, cum neque excedatur ab altiore neque a suscipiente aliquo finiatur. Adde quod totum illud quod ex substantia qualitateque componitur, quia dividitur in partes, in virtute debilitatur; et quia componitur, pendet tum ex partibus tum ex eo artifice qui partes illas in unum conciliavit, quae, cum diversae sint, ex seipsis invicem non coissent. Quamobrem cum huiusmodi compositum, neque quantum ad partes neque quantum ad totum spectat, sit optimum, meliusque aliquid futura sit[22] et substantia quae non distinguatur a qualitate sua, et qualitas quae non sit aliud quam substantia propria, ut tandem actus quidam omnino purus immensusque reperiatur, quis dubitet melius esse ut super id quod ex substantia accidenteque componitur ad id quod est melius ascendamus?

*Rationes multae quod necessarium sit esse actum purum et infinitum.*

II  Praestet igitur huc ascendere, sed numquid possibile est? Quid si est possibile fore rogas, quandoquidem iam esse ita, est necessarium ut probavimus?

*Prima ⟨ratio⟩.*[23] Quod si aliam exigis rationem, conducit ad idem huiusmodi ratio: quod substantia, quia accidentis est fundamentum, prior est accidente; et quia quod prius est a posteriore non

in another, that is, in a substrate, cannot sustain itself, much less can it exist of itself; therefore it needs both a cause and a substrate alike. Nor is this form entire and utterly complete, since it is received according to the capacity of the substrate. Hence it necessarily comes from a higher form, which indeed (lest we are to wander on endlessly) must be in itself, and sufficient through and for itself, and wholly complete, and be everywhere an infinite power, since it is neither exceeded by something higher nor confined by any sustaining substrate. Moreover, all that is compounded from substance and quality, because it is divided into parts, is weakened in power; and because it is compounded, it depends both on its parts and on that artificer who has harmonized those parts into one—parts that, since they are different, cannot in turn be assembled out of themselves. Therefore, since such a compound, neither inasmuch as it looks to the parts nor inasmuch as it looks to the whole, can be what is best; and since substance which is not distinguished from quality and quality which is nothing other than its own substance is going to be something better—so that finally we come upon a certain act that is utterly pure and measureless—since this is so, who will doubt that it is better for us to rise above what is compounded from substance and accident to that which is better?

*There are many reasons for the necessity of a pure and infinite act.*

Let it be better then to ascend hither, but is it possible? Why do you ask if this is going to be possible, seeing that it is already necessary it should [actually] be so as we proved?   11

(i) But if you demand another proof, the following proof will lead to the same [conclusion], namely that substance, because it is the foundation of accident, is prior to accident; and since what is prior does not depend on what succeeds, somewhere substance can exist without accident.[9] And this is [intrinsically] better as we

dependet, potest substantia alicubi absque accidente consistere. Atque hoc melius est, sicut ostendimus. Quare ne ab aeterno in aeternum huiusmodi potentia, in rerum principio tam bona, sit frustra, operaepretium esse videtur ut iam sit actu.

*Secunda.* Praesertim cum ubi summus actus[24] est et summa perfectio, ibi potentia actusque posse et esse sint idem.

*Tertia.* Ac si in rebus inferioribus minusque bonis, scilicet elementis, mixtis, plantis et animalibus, quantum ad partes eorum spectat et reliqua, quod praestat ut sit, iam est a natura provisum, quanto magis in rebus admodum melioribus et in summo naturae, quicquid melius esse probatur, iamiam est et verius.

*Quarta.* Praeterea, quod melius esse monstratur in universo, non ob aliam causam melius esse censetur nisi quia verae rationi consentaneum est, conducit maxime ad rerum ordinem, decet praecipue rerum ordinatorem. Tale vero nefas dictu est impossibile esse vel falsum.

*Quinta.* Rursus potentia et veritas tamquam bona naturaliter appetuntur, atque hoc ipsum quod sunt, aut sunt ipsa bonitas aut a[25] bonitate. Ergo quod in[26] universi natura possibilius veriusque est, hoc est et melius, atque e converso, quod universo melius, iudicatur, idem possibilius est et verius.

*Sexta.* Item quod est melius magis est boni particeps, non est igitur impossibile. Nam impossibile nullius boni particeps iudicatur.

*Septima.* Accedit quod si actus purus infinitusque, quem disputando excogitavimus, infinite melior est quam angelus et quam universum cuius pars est angelus, quod totum est terminatum, necessario est infinite potentior ad existendum, cum potentia bonum sit bonumque potestas. Immo etiam, cum vere actuque esse bo-

have shown. Therefore, lest a power like this, which was so good in the beginning of things, exist from eternity to eternity to no purpose, it seems important to have it exist already in act.

(ii) And especially since, where the highest act and highest perfection exists, there power and act can be and are the same.

(iii) In inferior things, however, and in things less good, that is, in the elements, in things mixed [from the elements], and in plants and animals, and insofar as it regards their parts and so forth, what is important for their existence has already been provided by nature. If this is so, then whatever is proved to be better in things wholly superior and at the summit of nature already exists there and more truly so already.

(iv) Moreover, what is shown to be better in the universe is deemed to be better for no other reason than because it is in harmony with true reason [and] most conduces to the order of things [and] principally befits the bestower of that order on things. But to say that such is impossible or false is impious.

(v) Again, power and truth are naturally desired as goods, and the very thing they are is either goodness itself or it comes from goodness. Therefore that which is more possible or more true in the nature of the universe is also better. Conversely, what is adjudged better for the universe, the same is more possible and more true.

(vi) Again, what is better participates in the good, so it is not impossible; for the impossible is judged not to participate in any good.

(vii a) Moreover, if the pure and infinite act, which we have been searching for in this argument, is infinitely better than the angel and better than the universe that is whole and determined (the angel being part of it), necessarily it has infinitely more power to exist, since power is the good and the good is power. Or rather, since to be truly and to be in act is the good, and nothing of the good is wanting in measureless good, measureless act is already

num sit et nihil boni immenso desit bono, immensus actus infinite verius iam actu est quam cuncta. Si infinita potestas duratione infinita nondum venit in actum, nulla umquam alia potentia venit.

Immo si infinitus actus qui idem est ac illa potestas, non sit semper in actu, alius certe nullus erit. Si est semper in actu potentia quaedam sua natura omni carens actu quae est infinite passiva, id est materia, proculdubio est semper in actu potestas illa quae actus est totus atque est efficax infinite, a qua passiva potentia sit possitque pati et patiatur.[27]

*Octava.* Sed quid curiose inepteque quaerimus, utrum possibile verumve sit in universo esse immensum bonum necne, cum nihil sit possibilius veriusque eo quo nihil potest potentius cogitari? Non esset autem immensum bonum, nisi esset in eo quicquid melius iudicatur ut sit.

*Nona.* Atque excederet mens nostra cogitatione affectuque, quibus per boni gradus absque fine progreditur, principii summi naturam, si quid boni cogitari posset quod in eo non esset, ac nisi illud esset immensum.

*Decima.* Quid plura? Si in summo principio omnium atque fine, ubi summopere invenitur quicquid est appetendum, summa bonitas est, et summa ipsa bonitas idem est prorsus ac summa potentia veritasque, sequitur quicquid circa ipsum melius iudicatur, possibilius fore, immo iam verius esse.

12 Omnino autem meminisse oportet potentiam alicuius boni capacem esse revera aliquid atque in re aliqua vera fundari; praeterea dependere ab alio quodam quod iam actu id habeat bonum; rursum quod actu bonum possidet, ab alio proficisci quod actu sit ipsum bonum actusque cuiuslibet actus.

infinitely and more truly in act than all else. If infinite power still does not come into act from infinite duration, no other power at all ever comes [into act].

(vii b) Or rather, if infinite act, which is the same as that [infinite] power, is not always in act, certainly nothing else will be in act. If a particular potency by its nature lacking all act (its nature being infinitely passive) is always in act, namely matter, then doubtless that power which is total act and infinitely powerful is always in act. From it comes the passive potency that is able to suffer and does in fact suffer.[10]

(viii) But why out of curiosity and silliness do we seek whether it is possible or true that measureless good exists or does not exist in the universe, since nothing is more possible or true in that nothing can be deemed of greater power? But it would not be the measureless good unless whatever is deemed better that it exist were in fact in it.

(ix) And our mind would exceed the nature of the highest principle in thinking and feeling (by which it proceeds endlessly up the steps of the good), if it were able to think about some aspect of the good that was not in fact in that [highest] principle, and if that principle were not measureless.

(x) In short, if in the highest beginning and end of all (where we most find whatever is desirable) the highest goodness exists, and if this highest goodness is exactly the same as the highest power and truth, it follows that whatever is judged better with regard to it will be more possible, or rather is already more true.

But we must remember in general that the power capable of any 12 good is in fact something and is based in something true; and furthermore, that it depends on something else which has that good already in act; and again that what possesses the good in act proceeds from another which is the good itself in act and is the act of any act whatsoever.

*De luce dei ac de umbra materiae.*

13   Ceterum alicui fortasse videbitur natura illa in qua qualitas non discernitur a substantia sine forma luceque esse. Sed meminerit ille probavisse nos ad formam in se existentem ascendendum esse. Est ergo illa substantia forma. Profecto sicut in rerum infimo, id est materia prima, idem est esse et informe tenebrosumque esse, sic in summo idem est esse et formosum lucidumque esse, immo formam lucemque esse. Materia enim apud Moysem tenebrarum abyssus est formarumque informe subiectum; deus, lux, abyssus luminum formaque fons formarum. Materia infinita est patiendi potentia; deus infinita virtus agendi, immo infinitus est actus. Illa ergo potentia est potentiarum omnium quae in patiendo versantur; hic actus est actuum. Et sicut innumere de materia vere dicitur: materia neque forma haec est neque illa, ita de deo innumerabiliter dicitur et vere dicitur: deus haec forma est et illa. Una materia est umbra rerum umbratilium infima; unus deus lux summa luminum. Materia ob nimias tenebras ignota est; deus ob nimiam lucem est incognitus. Nam si lux, quae est purior, est et lucidior, nimirum deus cum solus sit purus actus, solus lux est revera dicendus. Si lux in forma quadam consistit potius quam subiecto et formositas consistit in luce, ibi solum vera lux, ubi mera sine subiecti inquinamento forma, ibi solum vera formositas, ubi solum lux vera veraque forma.[28] Quapropter omnis forma et lux, quae vel videtur oculis vel cogitatur, quia finita est, umbra quaedam est ad dei formam atque lucem. Merito deus infinitus est actus, quoniam vel subiecti vel causae limite, sicut diximus, non contrahitur. Hinc fit plane ut sit lumen immensum.

*On God's light and on the shadow of matter.*

Furthermore, someone will assume perhaps that the nature in   13
which quality is not distinct from substance is without form and
light. But he will recall that we have proved that we must ascend
to the form existing in itself. So this [self-subsistent] substance is
form. Just as in the lowest of things, that is, in prime matter, being
is identical with unformed and shadowy being,[11] so in the highest
of things being is identical with beautifully formed[12] and light-
filled being, or rather it is form and light. For according to Moses
matter is the abyss of shadows[13] and the unformed substrate of
forms, [whereas] God is light,[14] the abyss of lights and the form
and fountain of forms. Infinite matter is the potency of being
acted upon; God is the infinite power of acting, or rather He is
the infinite act. So the former is the potency of all the potencies
that are involved in being acted upon; the latter is the act of acts.
Just as it is truly said of matter and on innumerable occasions that
it is neither this form nor that form, so it is said of God on countless occasions and truly so that God is this form and is that form.
The one matter is the lowest shadow of shadowy things; the one
God is the supreme light of lights.[15] Matter is unknown on account of its dense shadows; God is unknown because of His intense light. For if light which is purer is also brighter, certainly
God, since He alone is pure act, alone must truly be called light. If
light consists of a certain form rather than a substrate, and if formal beauty[16] consists of light, then true light only exists where
pure form exists without the impurity of a substrate, [and] true
formal beauty only exists where true light and form only exist. So
all form and light that is seen with the eyes or contemplated, being
finite, is a shadow compared to God's form and light. God is with
justice infinite act because He is not constrained[17] by the limit of a
substrate or a cause, as we said. Hence clearly He is measureless
splendor.

*Quantum lux dei supereminet superficiem intellectus,*
*tantum dei calor centrum penetrat voluntatis.*

14  Cum vero a lumine calor trahat originem, est etiam ardor immensus, ardor in bono infinito infinite beneficus. Hunc nos ardorem
voluntatis ardore potius quam scintilla mentis attingimus. Nam
deus quantum intellectus sui luce nos supereminet, tantum ferme
bonitatis ardore se nobis inurit, ut nihil deo excelsius sit, nihil
quoque profundius. Quo amplior eius lux, eo intellectui naturaliter est ignotior; quo vehementior ardor, eo, ut ita dicam, certior
voluntati. Deus ergo in summa intellectus cognitione quodammodo nox quaedam est intellectui; in summo voluntatis amore
certe dies est voluntati. Unde Orpheus deum appellat noctem
atque diem et David inquit, 'ut tenebrae eius, ita et lumen eius.'[29]
Verumtamen divinus splendor in animo beatorum, quando nox
appellatur, omni temporali die longe clarior advenit. Atque ob divinum munus tanto paene clarior quanto et deus est, ut ita dicam,
[et][30] lucidior sole et animus purior ac serenior aere.

*Lux in elementis, caelo, anima, angelo, deo.*

15  Lux in elementis facile perspicitur oculis, quorum complexio constat ex elementis. Lux in caelo, quamvis amplior, difficilius tamen
aspicitur; remotior enim oculorum qualitas est a caelo. Lux in
anima nullo modo videtur, sicuti neque lux solis a noctua, quia ni-
mia est neque ad eam corporalis sensus ullam habet proportionem, sed rationalis animae discursu aliquo cogitatur. Lux in an-

*To the extent God's light towers above the plane[18] of the intellect,*
*to that degree God's heat penetrates to the center of the will.*

Since heat takes its origin from light, it is an infinite heat, an    14
infinitely beneficial heat in the infinite good. We attain this heat in
the heat of the will rather than in the spark of the mind. For to
the extent God towers over us with the light of His intellect, so
He burns Himself into us with the heat of His goodness, so that
nothing is loftier than God, nothing too more profound. The
more radiant His light, the more unknown it is naturally to the intellect; the more vehement His heat, the more certain so to speak
it is to the will. So God in the highest knowing of the intellect is
in a way a kind of night to the intellect; [but] in the highest love
of the will, certainly He is day to the will. Hence Orpheus calls
God both night and day[19]; and David says, "as are the shadows of
Him, so is the light of Him."[20] Nonetheless the divine splendor in
the rational soul of the blessed, when it is called night, dawns far
more clearly than any temporal day. And to the extent that God is,
so to speak, brighter than the sun and the rational soul purer and
more serene than the air, so is the soul, on account of this divine
gift, clearer or almost so [than sun or air].

*Light in the elements, in the heavens, in the soul, in the angel, in God.*

Light in the elements is easily seen with the eyes whose complex-    15
ion derives from the elements. Light in the heavens, although it is
ampler, is seen nonetheless with greater difficulty; for the quality
of eyes is more distant from the heavens. Light in the soul is not
seen in any way, just as the sun's light is not seen by an owl,[21] because it is too intense and has no proportion at all to the light of
the corporeal sense; it is thought about, however, by the rational
soul in a discursive way. Light in the angel is neither seen nor even
thought about discursively; for it is above the proportion of the

gelo neque videtur neque etiam cogitatur; est enim super sensus proportionem et super temporalis discursionis capacitatem, verumtamen intellegitur. Congruit enim anima cum angelo in sua quadam intellegentia stabili potius quam mobili cogitationis discursione. Lux in deo, quia etiam limites intellectus excedit omnino, naturali hominis intellegentia non intellegitur, sed creditur potius et amatur, atque amata gratis infusa videtur. Nempe huius amore accensus animus quo flagrat ardentius, eo refulget[31] clarius; discernit quoque verius fruiturque suavius. Hinc Plato asserit divinam lucem non rationis digito demonstrari, sed perspicua piae vitae serenitate capi.

*Quid caelum, anima, angelus,*
*deus atque de differentia visibilis lucis et invisibilis.*

16    Ut autem nostrae disputationis ambages aliquando paucis colligamus, caelum esse dicimus lucem quandam absque materia quodammodo corporalem; animam lucem quandam sine quantitate magnam; angelum lucem sine motu celerrimam; deum lucem absque qualitate optimam atque potentissimam. Cuius calorem voluntate prius certiusque et vehementius experimur, quam intellegentia lumen. In hoc potissimum differt lux invisibilis a visibili, quod visibilis quidem, tam in igne quam in caelo, extrinsecus veniens illuminat priusquam calefaciat; invisibilis autem contra intrinsecus agens quodammodo calefacit[32] antea quam illuminet. Ideo in[33] illa a visu ad tactum; in hac quasi a tactu quodam in visum progredimur. Humana pulchritudo videtur priusquam ametur; divina vero amatur ut videatur. Sed in illa qui videt saepe miserabiliter possidetur; in hac videre nihil est aliud quam feliciter

sense and above the capacity of temporal discourse, and yet it is understood. For the soul is in harmony with the angel in its so to speak stable understanding rather than in its mobile discursive thinking. Light in God, because it utterly exceeds even the limits of the intellect, is beyond the natural understanding of man, but is rather believed and loved; and being loved, it seems infused with every grace. For when the soul is on fire with love of this light, the more ardently it burns, the more brightly it shines; and it discerns more truly too and enjoys with greater sweetness. Hence Plato asserts that the divine light is not demonstrated by the skill of the reason but understood in the clear serenity of a devout life.[22]

*What are the heavens, the soul, the angel, and God;*
*and on the difference between visible and invisible light.*

But to sum up finally the intricacies of this debate in a few words, 16 we declare that the heavens are a sort of light that is in a way corporeal without matter; that the soul is a sort of light that has magnitude [extension] without quantity; that the angel is light at its swiftest without motion; that God is light at its best and most intense without quality, light whose heat we experience earlier and more certainly and vehemently in the will than whose splendor we experience in the understanding. The main difference between invisible and visible light consists in the fact that visible light in the fire as in the sky, coming as it does from without, illuminates us before it warms us; but that invisible light, to the contrary, operating as it does from within, warms us so to speak before it illuminates us. So in the former we proceed from sight to touch; in the latter, from a touch to sight. Human beauty is seen before it may be loved; but divine beauty is loved so it may be seen. But the person who gazes on human beauty is often miserably possessed [by love]; whereas to gaze on divine beauty is nothing other than to possess in happiness. Whosoever believes he is going to possess

possidere. Igitur frustra nimium contraque ordinem naturae laborat, quicumque deum absque singulari eius amore cultuque credit se possessurum vel reperturum[34] sperat antequam amaturum.

*Secundus contemplationis Platonicae gradus consistit in deo.*[35]

*Artificium uniforme et omniforme*
*pendet ab arte uniformi et omniformi.*

17  Communis omnium opinio credit et diligens sapientum ratio probat artificium hoc mundi quod circa naturam suam ac motum artificiose rationabiliterque disponitur atque agitur, esse regique ab arte quadam rationali artificiosaque ratione. Profecto quantum ex huiusmodi artificio coniicere licet, quod et unum et universum est atque circa totum partesque undique tam mirabili ratione constat et agitur ut vix ulla possit ratio assequi, nulla queat omnino ratio imitari, absque dubio una cum Timaeo argumentamur artem illam mundi effectricem esse rationem quandam et unam et universam, uniformem, ut ita loquar, et omniformem — rationem, inquam, mundi totius rationes omnes in seipsa omnium mundi partium complectentem.

*Deus nominatur ars, ratio, substantia, natura,*
*vita, sensus, intellegentia, certitudo.*

18  Si ratio haec absolutissima est et fons omnium rationum a qua substantia omnis, natura, vita, sensus, intellegentia producitur penitus atque ducitur, nemo usque adeo irrationalis esse debet ut ne-

God without a singular love and worship of Him, or hopes to discover Him before he loves Him, is thus laboring utterly in vain and against the order of nature.

## *The second step of Platonic contemplation consists in God.*

*Artistry that is uniform and omniform*
*depends on a uniform and omniform art.*

The common opinion of all men supposes, and the diligent reasoning of the wise proves, that this workmanship of the world, which arranges and acts in an artful and rational way with regard to its own nature and motion, exists and is ruled by a certain rational art and artful reason. Indeed, insofar as we are permitted to conjecture from such a workmanship that it is both one and universal and that everywhere, with regard to the whole and the parts, it stays constant and is moved by such a marvelous reason that another reason can scarcely attain it and no other reason can entirely imitate it — insofar as this so, we conclude along with Timaeus[23] that the art creating the world is without doubt a sort of reason that is both one and universal, uniform one might say and omniform: it is the whole world's rational principle embracing in itself all the rational principles of all the world's parts. 17

*God is called art, rational principle, substance, nature, life, sensation,*
*understanding, and certainty.*

If this entirely absolute rational principle is also the fountain of all rational principles from which all substance, nature, life, sensation, and understanding is wholly produced and led forth, nobody should be so irrational as to deny that this principle is utterly unchanging substance, nature at its most fertile, eternal life, sensation 18

get huiusmodi rationem esse substantiam stabilissimam, naturam fecundissimam, vitam aeternam, sensum perspicacissimum, intellegentiam lucidissimam—lucidissimam inquam, id est certissimam. Quod enim in corpore mundi lux et luminum et videntium est, id in ratione mundi effectrice est certitudo, luce hac tanto lucidior quanto certior et praestantior, certitudo scilicet cuiuslibet certitudinis quae ex se certa sit sui, in se certa cunctorum, per se serenis mentibus clara certaque faciat omnia.

*Deus est veritas, verorum omnium fons,*
*causa veritatis rerum atque mentis.*

19  Unde etiam summa cuiusque veritatis veritas nominatur a qua vera omnia fiunt, per quam indagantur vera,[36] in qua vere cernuntur. Quam rerum perscrutatores pro arbitrio ubicumque volunt de veris consulunt, cuius scintilla naturaliter insita vera rimantur, cuius radiis per omnia fusis vera inventa[37] discernunt a falsis, cuius examine vera iam discreta comparant invicem et diiudicant. Et cum species a singulis abstractas, in quibus rei cuiusque veritas consistit, intellegunt non nisi veritatem ipsam, id est Deum, intellegunt qui complexio et fons est omnium abstractorum, id est idearum, sicuti solis lumen fons est colorum.

*Descriptiones dei communes secundum Platonicos.*

20  Quid ergo Deus est? Ratio rationum, fons rerumque artifex omnium; forma uniformis et omniformis; substantia immobilis omnia movens; in motu status; in tempore aeternitas; in loco continens; in summis profunditas; summitas in profundis; in multitudine unitas; in debilitate potestas; natura fecundissima natura-

at its most acute, understanding at its most lucid—most lucid, meaning most certain. For what in the world's body is the light both of lights and of those seeing them is certitude in the rational principle making the world; and it is more lucid than that earthly light to the degree that it is more certain and more excellent. It is the certitude, that is, of every certitude that is certain of itself from itself, that in itself is certain of all things, and that through itself makes all things clear and certain to serene minds.

> God is truth, the fountain of all true things,
> the cause of things' truth and the mind's truth.

Hence God is also called the highest truth of every truth from 19 which all truths are made;[24] through it they are tracked down; and in it they are clearly seen. Those who elect to search into things, wherever they wish to, use it to consider truths. By its spark which is naturally innate they look for truths; by its rays which are infused through all things they distinguish truths they have discovered from falsities; and by examining it, they mutually compare and adjudge truths which have now been distinguished. And when they understand species abstracted from individual things (species in which the truth of each thing consists), they do not understand them without the truth itself, that is, God, who is the totality and fountain of all abstract [things], that is, ideas, just as the sun's light is the fount of colors.

*Common descriptions of God according to the Platonists.*

What is God therefore? He is the rational principle of rational 20 principles and the fount of things, the artificer of all, the uniform and omniform form, the immobile substance moving all, the rest in motion, the eternity in time, the continuous in space, in the heights the depth, in the depths the height, the unity in multiplicity, in weakness the power, the most fertile nature of natures, the

rum; fecunditas fecunditatum naturalissima; aeterna viventium vitarumque vita; sensus sensibiliumque[38] lumen et sensuum perspicacia;[39] sensus medullas sensibilium in corticibus sentiens, cortices in medullis; intellegentia quoque talis ut ipsa et[40] rerum intellegendarum bonitas sit, et intellectus cuiuslibet veritas et gaudium voluntatis.

*Rationes multae quod gaudium contemplantis*
*superat sensuum voluptates.*

21   *Prima ⟨ratio⟩.*[41] Gaudium, inquam, ex verissima bonitate et optima veritate optimum et verissimum.[42] Hinc Plato divinus inquit, ab his quae sensibus offeruntur, quia veniunt ab extrinseco nec vere existunt, sed impura breviaque sunt, externam quandam titillationem circa corporis et animae cutem falsamque et dolori permixtam et brevem fieri voluptatem. Ab his autem quae menti ab intrinseco penitus se insinuant, quia intima veraque et pura et stabilia summaque sunt, intimam, veram, meram, stabilem summam voluptatem animae medullis infundi.

*Secunda.* Proinde sensus atque sensibile ita se invicem habent, ut propter eorum crassitudinem debilitatemque sese prorsus penetrare non possint. Intellegibile vero[43] sua tenuitate vique mirabili illabitur in[44] intellectus interiora atque intellectus subtilitate virtuteque sua undique intellegibile penetrat. Alioquin non posset mens rei intellegendae naturam ab alienis secernere, in partes suas distinguere, intima eius cum extimis comparare. Quo fit ut voluptas mentis, si quando rite contemplando revera percipitur, interior vehementiorque sit quam sensus oblectamenta.

most natural fertility of fertilities, the eternal life of living things and of lives, the light of sense and sensibles, and the perspicacity of the senses, the sense sensing in the outer rinds the very pith of sensibles and in the pith the outer rinds, and such an understanding that it is itself the goodness of the things to be understood and the truth of every intellect and the joy of the will.

*Many reasons why the joy of someone contemplating exceeds the pleasures of the senses.*

(i) The joy that derives from the truest goodness and the best truth is itself the best and truest joy. Hence the divine Plato says that from the things which are offered to the senses, because they come from without and do not truly exist but are impure and brief, is derived just an external titillation centered on the skin of the body and soul, a false and transient pleasure mingled with pain.[25] But he says that from the things that insinuate themselves into the mind entirely from within, because they are innermost, true, pure, unchanging, and supreme, then an innermost, true, pure, unchanging, and supreme pleasure is infused into the very pith of the soul.

(ii) Accordingly, the sense and the sensible are reciprocally such that they cannot on account of their thickness and weakness entirely penetrate each other. The intellegible, however, by its thinness and its extraordinary power slips into the inmost parts of the intellect; and the intellect by its subtlety and power everywhere penetrates the intellegible. Otherwise the mind could neither separate from externals the nature of the thing to be understood, nor distinguish it into its parts, nor compare its innermost aspects with those without. The result is that the pleasure of the mind, if ever in contemplating rightly it is actually perceived, is an interior one and more vehement than the delights of the sense.

*Tertia.* Si tunc vehementer delectari solemus cum circa calorem vel frigus siccumve et humidum aut evacuationem repletionemve habitum corporis naturalem, contrariis quasi amissum, contrariis iam recipimus, ceu quando nimium calefacti refrigeramur, in ceterisque similiter, quanta illum voluptate perfundi putamus, qui naturalem mentis habitum tenebris et malignitate deperditum, iamiam luce et bonitate resumit totusque ad suam reformatur ideam?

*Quarta.* Ac si ex rebus magis magisque convenientibus maior gradatim maiorque nascitur delectatio, atque si nihil convenientius homini quam ipsa humanitatis idea, quae verus est homo, quid suavius quam et eam intellegendo in se complecti et in eam amando restitui?

*Quinta.* Praeterea in omnibus pulchris bonisque amandis revera nihil aliud, quamvis forsitan inscii, quam pulchritudinem ipsam bonitatemque amamus, a qua et ex qua pulchra bonaque sunt singula. Perinde ac si quis dixerit gustui dulcedinis avido pomum vinumque placere, non quia pomum vinumve sit, sed quia dulce, atque idcirco nihil aliud in his quam ipsam dulcedinem affectari et in dulcedine bonitatem. Igitur si omnium iucundissimum est re amata potiri, quid potest iucundius cogitari quam illo potiri qui ipsa pulchritudo est et ipsa bonitas? Nusquam[45] enim alibi re amata sed eius umbra potimur.

*Sexta.* Ibi ergo placet idea nostra; est enim sibi quisque[46] carissimus. Ibi solum plenissime delectamur ubi solum verissime nos reperimus. In nostra idea ideae placent omnes. Pulchritudo oblectat in omnibus, omnes in bonitate nos implent.

*Septima.* Atque secundum formam proprie ibi ipsa gaudii idea gaudemus. Quo fit ut tota gaudii illic solum plenitudine gaudeamus.

(iii) We are usually vehemently pleased, when, with regard to heat or cold, dryness or wetness, emptiness or fullness, we recover from these contraries the body's natural habit, one lost as it were in the contraries—when, for instance, having been heated too much, we cool down again and similarly with the rest. If this is so, then we are in a position to judge how intense a pleasure suffuses that man, who, having lost the natural habit of his mind completely in shadows and evil, even now recovers it in light and in goodness and is wholly reformed to accord with his own idea?

(iv) But if a greater and still greater delight is gradually born from more and more suitable things, and if nothing is more suitable to man than the very idea of humanity, the idea which is the true man,[26] what is sweeter than to embrace it in itself by understanding it, and by loving it to be restored to it?

(v) Moreover, in loving all beautiful and good things, we really are loving nothing else, though perhaps we do not know it, than beauty and goodness itself, by which and from which derive individual beautiful and good things. It is as if someone were to say that an apple or wine pleases a taste eager for sweetness, not because they are an apple or wine, but because they are sweet; and therefore nothing else is attractive in these except the sweetness itself, and in the sweetness, the goodness. So, if the most delightful of all delights is to possess the beloved object, what can be supposed more delightful than possessing that object which is beauty itself and goodness itself? For nowhere else do we possess the beloved object, but only its shadow.

(vi) Our own idea delights us there, for each person is dearest to himself.[27] We are totally delighted only there where we most truly find ourselves. In our own idea all ideas please [us]. In all ideas beauty delights us, in goodness all ideas fill us.

(vii) And there, according to form, appropriately we rejoice in the idea itself of joy, with the result that we rejoice only there in the complete fullness of joy.

*Octava.* Si ubi est bonum hoc et illud, ibi gaudet hic et ille, certe ubi est ipsum bonum, ibi est ipsum gaudium.

*Nona.* Si nullus vere vivit aut sapit nisi qui proprie vita ipsa vivit et sapientia ipsa sapit, proculdubio nullus vere pleneque gaudet nisi qui proprie gaudio ipso gaudet.

*Decima.* Denique cum finito pulchro et bono finite laetemur, certe infinita pulchritudine bonitateque innumerabilium formarum bonorumque fonte infinite gaudemus.

*Gustus animi amaro corporis humore infectus,*
*divinorum saporem aut nullo modo aut vix et rarissime gustat.*

22 Sed tanti huius gaudii vix et raro admodum, ha nimium miseri! in terris participes sumus, et tunc[47] quidem exilem quandam eius umbram ac momento praetereuntem nostrae mentes aegrotae percipiunt. Quarum naturalis gustus, proh dolor! amaro corporis huius humore nimium est infectus, unde efficitur ut caelestis ille saluberrimusque sapor vel non sentiatur vel offendat interdum vel leviter breviterve delectet. Acutius inter nos aliquando gustant vehementiusque et diutius oblectantur qui magis sordes labemque corporis morum contemplationisque studio a natura mentis abstergunt. Sed

> pauci, quos aequus amavit
> Iupiter, aut ardens evexit ad aethera virtus.

Quinam isti sunt, o amice? Hi certe sunt quibus a vitae magistro dicitur. 'Iterum videbo vos et gaudebit cor vestrum; gaudium vestrum erit plenum, nec a vobis umquam auferetur.'

(viii) If this or that man rejoices where this or that good is present, then certainly where the good itself is present, joy itself is present.

(ix) If no man truly lives or knows unless it is he who properly lives in life itself and knows in knowledge itself, then certainly no man truly or fully rejoices unless it is he who rejoices properly in joy itself.

(x) Finally, since we delight in a finite way in a good and beautiful object that is finite, we certainly rejoice in an infinite way in the infinite beauty and goodness of numberless forms and in the fountain of good things.

*The rational soul's taste, tainted by the body's bitter humor,*
*savors either not at all or scarcely or very rarely the flavor of things divine.*

But we participate in such an immense joy scarcely or very rarely  22
on earth—ah we who are in too much misery!—and our sick minds now perceive just a poor shadow of it, one that is passing in a moment. The natural taste of our minds—ah the pain of it!—is too much tainted by the bitter humor of this body; and its effect is such that the heavenly flavor, that which endows us most with health, is either not perceived or displeases on occasion or pleases but barely and briefly. But amongst us those who taste more acutely at times and enjoy more intensely and for a longer time are those who take greater pains to cleanse the mind's nature from the body's filth and stain by the study of morality and contemplation. But: "There are a few whom just Jupiter has loved or blazing virtue has carried to the upper air."[28] But who are these, my friend? They are certainly those to whom the Master of life declared, "I shall see you again and your heart shall rejoice and your joy shall be full and it shall never be taken from you."[29]

*Tertius contemplationis Platonicae gradus.*
*Cur anima in corpore difficile divina cognoscat*
*et quod sit immortalis.*[48]

*Primum mentis obstaculum ad lucem intellegibilium*[49] *intuendam:*
*quia est coniuncta corpori.*

23    Igneus est ollis vigor et caelestis origo
Seminibus, quantum non noxia corpora tardant,
Terrenique hebetant artus moribundaque membra.
Hinc metuunt cupiuntque dolent gaudentque, nec auras
Respiciunt, clausae tenebris et carcere caeco.

Quid in his carminibus platonicus Maro noster voluerit, videamus. Anima, tenebroso corporis huius carcere circumsaepta, mirabile veritatis lumen et vera, quae mirifice in illo refulgent, minime percipit, quia minimam ad illud habet proportionem. Defectus autem proportionis huiusmodi tribus ex causis provenit.

24    Prima est, quoniam anima forma quaedam est coniuncta corpori; illud vero lumen est forma penitus a commercio corporum segregata. Huc tendit quod inquit in *Metaphysicis* Aristoteles: 'Intellectus noster se habet ad illa quae in natura clarissima sunt, tamquam noctuae oculus ad solis lumen.' Ad idem spectat quod scribit in *Metaphysicis* Avicenna: quemadmodum paralytici lingua, oppressa quodam humore, certum gustum saporis amittit, quo expurgato recipit gustum; ita intellectus humanus ob corporis mortalis coniunctionem quasi paralyticus, id est naturali eius sensu orbatus[50] est, ad illa quae incorporea penitus sunt et aeterna. Atque

*The third step of Platonic contemplation.*
*Why the soul in the body can know divine matters*
*only with difficulty, and that the soul is immortal.*

*The mind's first obstacle to intuiting the light of intellegibles is*
*because it is joined to the body.*

"Fiery is the vigor and celestial the origin in those seeds, insofar as    23
harmful corporeal things do not retard them nor earthly limbs and
mortal members dull them. For such corporeal things make the
souls fear and desire and grieve and rejoice and never look again to
the wafting breezes, pent up as they are in shadows and a sightless
dungeon."[30] Let us see what our Maro, a Platonist, intends by
these verses. The soul immured in the shadowy prison of this
body least sees the marvelous light of truth and the truths that are
wondrously refulgent in it, because it has the least proportion at
all to that light. But such a defective proportion derives from three
causes.

The first cause is because the soul is a certain form joined to the    24
body, but light is a form entirely separated from any commerce
with bodies. Aristotle refers to this in his *Metaphysics* when he
says: "Our intellect with regard to those things which are clearest
in nature is like the eye of an owl with regard to the sun's light."[31]
Avicenna refers to the same when he writes in his commentary on
the *Metaphysics*: just as the tongue of someone paralyzed, which is
afflicted by some humor, loses the authentic taste of the flavor, and
when the humor has been purged, recovers the taste, so the human intellect, on account of its conjunction with a mortal body,
has been paralyzed as it were (that is, orphaned by its natural
sense) with regard to those things which are entirely incorporeal
and eternal. And just as the tongue's humor takes away the act of
tasting, not the power to do so, because the power appears in the

sicut humor linguae actum gustandi adimit, non virtutem, quod in
eo apparet qui iam purgatus gustandi recipit actum, ita corpus actionem intellectus circa incorporalia interturbat, sed potentiam
non disperdit. Quod ex eo coniicimus, quia quanto longius animus
tam morum cultu quam speculationis frequentatione se a corpore
sevocat, tanto clarius incorporalia cernit. Atque una cum his etiam
semetipsum, qui etiam ipse est[51] incorporeus, quandoquidem actione sua et affectu quodam innato aliquando corporum transcen-
dit ordinem atque virtutem.

*Secundum obstaculum ad intellegibile lumen:*
*quoniam animus ad corpus afficitur.*

25 Altera causa quae proportionem quam ab initio diximus impedit
est eiusmodi; quod anima coniuncta corpori, cum eo pacto quo
hic est naturaliter moveatur et agat, certe naturalem convertit
affectum in primis ad corporalia, qualis affectus eam ab incorpora-
libus longe divertit.

*Tertium obstaculum ad intellegibile lumen:*
*quoniam animus vertit aciem ad corporea.*[52]

26 Tertia quod aciem cognoscendi frequenter vertit ad sensum et
sensibilia eorumque imagines in phantasia reconditas. Hae vero
imagines tamquam nubes quaedam usque adeo aciem mentis
obumbrant, ut lucem intellegibilium mirabilem non discernat,
dum splendorem eorum ut plurimum non in seipso, sed in his nubibus intuetur, ubi iam a seipso degenerantem, et quasi corporalem iam factum aspicit, et ob hoc neque verum ipsum videt neque
clarum, sed imaginum caligine obfuscatum. Similis autem esse videtur haec affectio mentis oculis rubra ophthalmia laborantibus,

person who, once purged, recovers the act of tasting, so the body muddies the action of the intellect with regard to incorporeals but does not destroy its power.[32] We conjecture this from the fact that the longer the rational soul, by its ethical behavior and frequency of speculation alike, cuts itself off from the body, the clearer it discerns incorporeals, and along with these incorporeals it sees itself too, being incorporeal too itself, since by its action and a sort of innate desire [for incorporeals] it transcends at times the order and power of bodies.

*The second obstacle to the rational soul's intuiting the intellegible light is because it is drawn to the body.*

The second cause which impedes the proportion we spoke of at the outset is the following: the soul joined to the body, since it is naturally moved and acts in the manner it does here, certainly turns its natural desire primarily towards corporeals, and this kind of desire diverts it totally from incorporeals.                                    25

*The third obstacle to the rational soul's intuiting the intellegible light is because it turns its acuity towards corporeals.*

The third cause is that the soul often turns the edge of its understanding towards the sense and sensibles and towards their images hidden away in the phantasy. But these images, like certain clouds, dim the mind's edge to such an extent that it cannot discern the wondrous light of intelligibles while it gazes on their splendor for the most part not in itself but in the clouds. There it sees the light already falling away from itself, already rendered as it were corporeal. On this account it sees neither the true nor the clear but what is obscured by the murk of images. But this affection of the mind seems to resemble eyes suffering from red inflammation: in them light is seen not as clear (which it is) but as red, and also the colors in the light are not seen as they truly are but as red. There are some people too whose rational soul is so dimmed at times by   26

quibus lux non clara sicuti est, sed rubra videtur, colores quoque in luce non quales sunt, sed rubri. Sunt etiam nonnulli quorum animus aliquando ita et corporis contagione et corporalium nebulis obfuscatur, ut rerum spiritalium radios omnino nusquam videat, instar oculi qui opprimitur cataracta. Ceterum quando corporales hae sordes quodammodo abluuntur, ab animo incorporalia aliquantum prospiciuntur. Quando vero penitus diluuntur, subito intellegibile lumen, intellegibilium omnium radiis plenum, intellegentiae oculis sese prorsus infundit. Quod quidem ubique est, et natura sua intellectualem oculum, cum primum fuerit purgatus, illustrat, sicut lumen visibile visum. Atque sensibilia omnia multo clarius in luce intellegibili tamquam in primo fonte refulgent, quam in luce visibili, quae revera illius est umbra. Meminisse vero oportet animam, occupatam in mole corporis fabricanda regendaque et in diversas actiones distractam et perturbatam, ad spiritalium radios aut nullo modo aut ut plurimum neglecte et leviter aciem vertere,[53] adde et oblique.

27 Quippe etiam quando paulo attentius pro viribus aspicit, quia ipsa coniuncta est corpori, saepissime ad coniuncta se flectit,[54] id est ad corporalium nubes in phantasia volantes.

28 Phantasia etiam radios spiritalium, cum primum menti subrutilant, corporalium simulacris induit, ideoque mens aut nullo pacto aut vix obscureque videt. Sed quando et seiuncta est a corpore et a corporis labe mundata ad incorporalia solum tota intentione convertitur, quorum uberrima luce refulget ad votum, cuncta in ea clare discernit tamquam et clarissima in seipsis et intellegentiae intima. Hoc autem assequitur quando

> perfecto temporis orbe
> Concretam exemit labem purumque relinquit
> Aethereum sensum atque aurae simplicis ignem.

the body's contagion and by nebulous corporeals that it does not see the rays of things spiritual anywhere at all, like an eye dominated by a cataract. But for all that, when these corporeal stains are in a way cleansed, the incorporeals are glimpsed a little by the rational soul. And when they are washed wholly away, suddenly the intelligible light, replete with the rays of all the intelligibles, pours its entire self into the eyes of understanding. This light is indeed everywhere and by its own nature it enlightens the intellectual eye as soon as it has been purified, just as the visible light brings light to the sight. And all the sensibles shine in the intelligible light as in the primal fountain much more clearly than they do in the sensible light, which is really a shadow of it. But we must remember that the soul occupied in assembling the bulk of the body and in ruling over it, the soul distracted and disturbed by diverse actions, turns its acuity either not at all or for the most part negligently and casually towards the rays of spiritual things, and does so moreover indirectly.

Certainly, even when the soul looks somewhat more attentively 27 as best it can, yet since it is bound to the body, it turns itself most often towards the things it is bound to, that is, to the clouds [the images] of corporeals floating in the phantasy.

The phantasy too takes the rays of things spiritual as soon as 28 they glimmer in the mind and decks them in the images of corporeals; and so the mind sees either not at all or scarcely and obscurely. But when it [the mind], now disjoined from the body and cleansed of the body's filth, is turned back with its whole attention towards incorporeals only, with whose overflowing light it gleams in answer to its prayer, then in that light it sees all things clearly both as they are most clear in themselves and as they are innermost to understanding. But the mind attains this when, "with the completion of time's cycle, it has removed its ingrown blemish and it lays aside [even] the pure aethereal sense and the fire of the unmixed air."[33]

*Ratio immortalitatis animi:*
*quoniam intellegit incorporea sine corporis instrumento,*
*attingit formas separatas separatque coniunctas.*

29  Quod autem animus noster queat secundum substantiam separari a corpore atque deinde in seipso manere, ex hoc in praesentia intellexisse sufficiat quod intellectus agit sine ullo instrumento corporeo, quando scilicet per omnia corporalium genera speciesque discurrens, ascendit inde superius ad ordinem spiritalium, illaque in genera sua speciesque[55] distinguit. Per instrumentum vero corporeum, quod etiam particulare esset, non posset nisi corporea et particularia comprehendere. Si absque corpore potest agere, potest et seorsum ab illo vivere atque intellegere. Adde quod secundum actionem quae et a substantia eius est et in substantia permanet, ipse non modo attingit quae separata aeternaque sunt (quando invitis etiam phantasiae fallaciis probat talia quaedam in rerum ordine esse debere), verum etiam vi sua separat a materia formas, quando in rebus naturalibus secernit a singulis speciei cuiusque naturam.

30  Plotinus et Proclus aiunt, quoniam essentia actionis et principium est et fundamentum, ideo mentem, quae actione se a corpore sevocat, abstrahendo posse multo magis secundum essentiam seorsum a corpore vivere. Themistius arbitratur difficilius esse naturas separare coniunctas quam formas percipere separatas; unde concludit intellectum posse separatas formas attingere, quandoquidem coniunctas naturas pro arbitrio separat.[56]

*Proof of the immortality of the rational soul:*
*because it understands incorporeals without the instrument of the body,*
*arrives at forms that are separate, and separates those that are joined.*

But [to show] that our rational soul can be substantially separated    29
from the body and then remain in itself, it is enough for the present to have understood that the intellect acts without any corporeal instrument; when, that is, in discoursing through all the genera and species of corporeals, it thence ascends higher to the order
of spiritual things and distinguishes them into their genera and
species. However, it would be unable through a corporeal instrument, which would also be particular, to comprehend anything
but corporeals and particulars. [But] if it can act without a body,
it can live and understand while apart from it. Moreover, in accordance with its action, which comes from its substance and remains
in its substance, the rational soul not only attains what are separate and eternal, when, in spite of the deceptions of the phantasy,
it proves that some such entities must exist in the order of nature;
but also it uses its power to separate forms from matter, when in
natural things it separates the nature of each species from individuals.

Plotinus and Proclus say that because the essence of action is    30
both its beginning and its foundation, the mind, which by its action divorces itself in abstraction from the body, is much more
able in terms of its essence to live apart from the body.[34] Themistius thinks that it is more difficult to separate joined natures than
to perceive separated forms; whence he concludes that the intellect, since it can separate joined natures at will, is [certainly] able
to attain separated forms.[35]

*Ratio immortalitatis animi:*
*ex proportione ad formas separabiles*
*atque ex accessu ad separatas.*

31  Naturae huiusmodi naturalia familiariaque obiecta sunt intellectus humani, quamdiu naturale hoc corpus inhabitat. Continue namque et naturali quodam instinctu intellegit eas a singulis separando; unde inter hunc et illas necesse est ut proportio sit non parva. Ex quo concluditur intellectum esse ea conditione corpori iunctum ut sit separabilis, immo etiam iam[57] quodammodo separatus, quandoquidem obiecta eius domestica sunt species coniunctae quidem singulis, sed non ut coniunctae, immo ut separabiles atque separatae. Nempe communis intellegendi modus hic est, ut quando phantasia hominem hunc et illum imaginatur, tunc intellectus, praetermissis mortalibus hominis accidentibus, praetermisso hoc situ temporeque et illo, ad humanitatem ipsam se conferat singulis communem hominibus, ubique semperque vigentem similiterque in aliis speciebus. Maxime vero tunc separatus apparet, quando interdum, ultra conditionem qua hic habitat, species illas[58] rerum naturalium resolvit prorsus[59] in rationes ipsas ideasque super naturam, ab omni materia penitus absolutas. Et sicut ab imagine in phantasia, reperta ante naturali quodam intuitu, processit ad speciem abstrahendo, sic deinde a specie argumentando ad speciei rationem prorsus aeternam, videlicet quia necessarium sit naturam in multis unam a forma una super multitudinem proficisci.

*Proof of the immortality of the rational soul*
*from its being proportional to the separable forms*
*and from its accessing those that are separate.*

Such [potentially separable] natures are the natural and familiar    31
objects of the human intellect as long as it inhabits this natural
body. For continually and by a certain instinct it understands them
by separating them from individuals; and so between this intellect
and such natures there has to be no minor proportion. The conclusion from this is that the intellect is joined to the body but with
the condition that it is separable; or rather it is even now separated in a way, seeing that its day-to-day objects are species joined
indeed to individuals, but they are its objects not insofar as they
are joined but as they are separable and separated. Certainly, the
common way of understanding is such that when the phantasy
imagines this or that man, then the intellect, having dismissed the
man's mortal accidents, and having dismissed this or that particular situation or occasion, betakes itself to humanity itself, to [the
species] common to individual men, the humanity thriving always
and everywhere. And similarly with the other species. But the intellect is separated most when now and then, going beyond the
condition in which it dwells here, it completely resolves the species
of natural things into the rational principles themselves and into
the ideas above nature that are divorced entirely from all matter.
And just as from the image in the phantasy (an image discovered
beforehand by a natural glance) it has proceeded by abstracting to
a species, so it next proceeds by arguing from that species to the
species' wholly eternal rational principle. This is because it is necessary for a single nature in many things to originate from a single
form above that many.

*Ratio immortalitatis animi:*
*quia intellegit nonnihil ad cuius intuitum proprium*
*phantasma aliquando non est necessarium.*

32  Profecto quoniam ab essentia provenit actio, semper qualis essendi
conditio est talis agendi, atque e converso. Quamobrem animus
noster, quia nunc ita iunctus est corpori ut separabilis sit aliquando et ut permaneat separatus, ideo cognoscendo, quamvis
conditione loci incipiat a singulis rerum formis omnino materiae
iunctis, tamen deinde procedit ad species coniunctas quidem
effectu, sed et sua quadam natura et virtute intellegentiae separabiles. Tertio vi sua, discussis a se parumper phantasiae simulacris, ad
rationes iam separatas, quas in rerum ordine omnino absolutas
existere numquam excogitare posset, nisi saltem ad brevissimum
tempus ab acie phantasmatum nubes expelleret. Sed cito ob regio-
nis huius naturam consuetudinemque congregatae iterum nubes
caelestium impediunt claritatem. Ex illa autem subita abstractione
coniiciunt metaphysici posse intellectum aliquando absque phan-
tasmatibus intellegere. Unde etiam sequitur posse seorsum a corpore vivere et clarissime intellegere.

*Proof of the immortality of the rational soul:
that it understands something for whose proper intuition
a phantasmal image is sometimes not needed.*

Certainly, because action proceeds from essence, then whatever the    32
condition of existing is like, such always is the condition of acting,
and the reverse. Hence our rational soul, because at present it has
been so joined to the body that occasionally it may be separable
and remain in a separated state, so in knowing, though it may begin, being subject to the condition of a place, from the individual
natural forms that are entirely joined to matter, it then proceeds
nonetheless to species that are effectively joined yet are separable
both in their own particular nature and by the power of understanding. Thirdly, having for a brief while dispelled from itself the
images of the phantasy, it [proceeds] by its own power to already
separated rational principles. [But] it could never think about
these existing in the universal order entirely as absolutes, unless, at
least for a very brief moment, it were to drive the clouds of phantasmal images away from its attention. Straightway, however, on
account of the nature and customary state of this region [of the
soul], the clouds congregate once more and dim the brightness of
the celestials. From that momentary abstraction, however, the
metaphysicians conjecture that the intellect can understand occasionally without phantasmal images. Whence it also follows that it
is able to live apart from the body and to understand with the
utmost clarity.

*Anima[60] in corpore secundum Platonicos procedit cognoscendo a singulis*
*ad species, a speciebus ad ideas. Extra corpus e[61] converso progeditur,*
*scilicet ab ideis ad species,*
*a speciebus ad singula.*

33 Verum quando separatus animus est, progreditur aliter quam in
corpore, nam in corpore animus a singulis ad species, a speciebus
transit ad rationes. Separatus autem contra nempe a familiaribus
suis naturaliter tunc incipiens, in divinis rationibus naturali intuitu naturales videt species, ac in speciebus, quasi subita quadam
argumentatione et tamen momento, inspicit singula. Hinc circulus
ab eo fit a tempore ad aeternitatem, ab aeternitate rursus ad tempus. Ergo quemadmodum ita coniunctus materiae fuit ut separabilis foret et aliquando separatus existeret, sic deinde ita separatus
existit[62] ut rursum iungibilis sit et aliquando iunctus. A naturis
procedunt vires, naturae a viribus indicantur. Natura ab infinita
potentia, sapientia bonitateque regitur. Non igitur frustra vires
sunt naturales. Hac argumentatione ad animorum circuitum sempiternum uti verisimiliter fortasse possunt Platonici. Eadem verissime ad corporum humanorum resurrectionem Hebraei, Christiani, Mahumetenses uti posse videntur.

*Quam obscure animus in corpore,*
*tam clare extra corpus intellegit incorporea.*

34 Proinde anima, dum in materia et quodammodo sub tempore vitam ducit, naturales formas in materiae infimae videt umbra; supernaturales autem formas, ut plurimum, sub naturalium videt

*According to the Platonists, the soul inside the body proceeds in knowing*
*from individuals to species, and from species to Ideas.*
*Outside the body it proceeds conversely, that is, from Ideas to species,*
*and from species to individuals.*

In truth, when the rational soul is separate it proceeds otherwise    33
than it does in the body; for the soul in the body proceeds from
individuals to species and from species it crosses over to rational
principles. Separate from the body, however, the reverse happens,
for beginning from the things that are naturally familiar to it then,
in the divine rational principles it sees by natural intuition the natural species; and in the species, by a sudden process of argumentation as it were and yet in a moment, it examines individuals.
Hence it makes a circle from time to eternity and from eternity
back again to time. Therefore, just as it was joined to matter such
that it would be separable and occasionally exist as separate, so
thereafter it exists as separate but such that it is joinable again and
occasionally is joined. Powers proceed from natures, natures are
revealed by their powers. Nature is ruled by infinite power, wisdom, and goodness. Therefore natural powers are not in vain. The
Platonists can use this argument perhaps for the sempiternal circuit of souls with some plausibility.[36] But the Hebrews, Christians, and Mohammedans are obviously able to use the same
argument with incontrovertible truth[37] for the resurrection of human bodies.[38]

*As obscurely as the rational soul understands incorporeals in the body,*
*so as clearly does it understand them outside the body.*

Therefore the soul, while it leads a life in matter and in a way in    34
time, sees natural forms in the shadow of the depths of matter;
but it sees the supernatural forms for the most part during the

eclipsi. Quando vero extra materiam et super tempus agit vitam, tunc supernaturales quidem formas in summae formae lumine conspicit; naturales autem sub radiis supernaturalium intuetur. Tunc igitur omnia clare, omnia nunc obscure, siquidem temporalia non aliter percipit quam per eorum imagines sensibus haustas, in eisque quasi purgatas. Non enim aliter inter haec et animam est proportio. Ad aeterna vero, quamdiu in mortali[63] corpore occupata est, difficile parumque convertitur, et conversa occursu imaginum corporalium saepissime allucinatur[64] et fallitur. Hinc illud Platonis nostri mysterium in *Phaedone:* 'Animus in alio vivens', scilicet in corpore, 'perque aliud aspiciens', scilicet per sensuum fenestras atque phantasmata, 'aspiciens, inquam, quae sunt in alio', id est tam species in singulis quam formas singulas in materia, 'nihil usquam dare discernit. Quando autem vivens in se per se aspicit atque in se illa quae sunt in seipsis', id est rationes rerum, quae dum in summa omnium ratione sunt in seipsis existunt, 'tunc omnia clarissime perspicit', quia et intima et clarissima,[65] quae tanto fulgentiora in se et illi[66] sunt quam ista quanto puriora, veriora, potentiora.

*Praestantior sensus est in phantasia quam in nervis,*
*longe praestantior in mente quam in phantasia.*

35  Sed numquid illa sensibus comprehendit? Sensibus certe quibusdam, sensuum videlicet sensu, quoniam praeter sensus illos quos[67]

eclipse of the natural ones. But when it lives a life outside matter and above time, then it catches sight of the supernatural forms in the light of the highest form, but it gazes at the natural forms subject to the rays of the supernatural ones. So it then sees all things clearly, whereas now it sees them obscurely, since it perceives temporal things in no way other than through images of them drawn from the senses and purged as it were in them. For otherwise there is no proportion between them and the soul. But as long as it has been busy in a mortal body,[39] with difficulty and just barely is it converted towards things eternal; and [even when] converted, it most often dreams and is deceived by the throng of corporeal images. Hence that mystery of our Plato in the *Phaedo:* "The rational soul living in another" (that is, in the body) "and gazing through another" (that is, through the windows and phantasmal images of the senses) — "gazing I say at the things which are in another" (that is, at the species in individuals and at the individual forms in matter) — "never discerns anything clearly. But when, living in itself it gazes through itself and in itself at those things which are in themselves" (that is, at the rational principles of natural things, which, as long as they are in the highest universal rational principle, exist in themselves), "then it sees all things with greatest clarity,"[40] because they are the innermost and clearest things — things which are more dazzling, in themselves and for the rational soul, than other things are to the extent that they are purer, truer, and more powerful.

*The more outstanding sense is in the phantasy rather than the sensory nerves,[41] and the more outstanding sense by far is in the mind rather than the phantasy.*

But can it be said that it [the rational soul] understands with senses? It does so certainly with certain senses, that is, with the senses' sense, because beyond those senses which the Platonists

in aethereo animae vehiculo exerceri Platonici opinantur, sunt et sensus nonnulli admodum clariores, quibus uti mens potest etiam absque corpore.[68] Sane quinque sensus qui in nervis et spiritibus exercentur, emanant ab iis[69] qui vigent in phantasia. Sed in hac quinque illi sensus unus sunt, amplior illis et perspicacior, adde et stabilior. Servat enim quae illi non servant. Unus est rursus in mente tanto latior, stabilior, perspicacior quam in phantasia, quanto mens praestantior est quam illa. Si latior est, nimirum ultra illa rerum porrigitur genera, quae sensibus et phantasia comprehenduntur. Si stabilior est, etiam servat diutius quam phantasia. Si perspicacior, certius, clarius, splendidius quam illi cernit et quam illa. Cernit, inquam, interdum per illos et per illam imagines atque singula quando eo sese vertit. Cernit per se, excitatus ab illa, species, et clarius quia propinquius. Inspicit in seipso seipsum, quando ad se reflectitur. Potest autem ad se reflecti, si se amat, quaerit, intellegit. Ubi apparet prorsus indivisibilis et in seipso consistens (nam forma, quae vel divisibilis est vel necessario iacet in alio, numquam reflectitur in seipsam). Clarissime tandem rationes discernit, quando ex se ad summam omnium respicit rationem, in qua mentis visus rationem vimque lucis videt atque colorum; tanto hac luce hisque coloribus fulgentiorem, quanto ibi, scilicet in idea sua, est integrior et praestantior quam in corporibus inde formatis. In qua etiam mentis auditus rationem sonorum

hold are exercised in the soul's ethereal vehicle are several senses that are much more perspicacious and that the mind can use even without the body. The five senses in fact which are exercised in the nerves and spirits emanate from those that flourish in the phantasy. But in the phantasy these five are one sense: it is more comprehensive than they are and more perspicacious and indeed more stable; for it preserves what they do not preserve. Again, there is one sense in the mind which, to the degree that the mind is more outstanding than the phantasy, is that much more comprehensive, more stable, and more perspicacious than the sense in the phantasy. If it is more comprehensive, certainly it reaches beyond those genera of natural things that are understood by the senses and by the phantasy. If it is more stable, it also preserves for a longer time than the phantasy. If it is more perspicacious it sees more unerringly, more clearly, and more brilliantly than the [five] senses or the phantasy. Meanwhile it sees, I repeat, images and individuals through the senses, and through the phantasy when it turns itself towards it. It sees [various] species through itself when it has been roused by the phantasy, and sees more clearly being closer to them. It gazes at itself in itself when it is turned back upon itself. But it can be turned back upon itself if it loves, seeks, and understands itself. Then it appears entirely indivisible and abiding in itself (for form, which is either divisible or lies necessarily in another, is never turned back upon itself). At last, with greatest clarity, it sees the rational principles, when of itself it looks back to the highest rational principle of all, wherein the mind's gaze sees the rational principle and the power of light and of colors. The principle is more dazzling than either this light or these colors to the extent that there (in its own idea, that is) it is more complete and more outstanding than in the bodies formed from it. In this highest principle the mind's hearing too hears the rational principle of sounds more sonorously and more harmoniously than all the sounds that it can hear in the ears or imagine in

audit sonantiorem consonantioremque[70] sonis cunctis quos vel au-
ris audire vel phantasia queat imaginari. Eadem ratio est de ceteris
intelligentiae sensibus. Quibus quisquis suavissime optat frui, det
operam imprimis oportet, ut corporis sensibus utatur quidem, sed
non fruatur.

the phantasy. The same principle pertains for the rest of the understanding's senses. Whoever elects to enjoy with utmost sweetness these [intellectual] senses, should pay attention to the fact that it especially behooves him to use the body's senses but not to enjoy them.[42]

# Note on the Text

❧❧❧

As in previous volumes, the Latin text of the *Platonic Theology* is based on the two independent witnesses, *A* and *L*. Differences between the present edition and the texts in the *Opera* and Marcel's edition are noted where appropriate.

| | |
|---|---|
| *A* | The *editio princeps*, Florence, 1482, with printed corrigenda as noted below. |
| *L* | Florence, Biblioteca Mediceo-Laurenziana, MS Plut. LXXXIII, 10, the dedication copy written for Lorenzo de' Medici. |
| *Marcel* | The reading of Raymond Marcel's edition, *Marsile Ficin: Théologie Platonicienne de l'immortalité des âmes* (3 vols., Paris: Les Belles Lettres, 1964–70). |
| *Opera* | The reading of the text in *Marsilii Ficini . . . Opera* (Basel: Henricpetri, 1576; repr. Turin: Bottega d'Erasmo, 1959, 1983; Paris: Phénix Éditions, 1999). |

Also included in this sixth and last volume is the *Argumentum in Platonicam Theologiam*, the independent text most closely related to the *Theology* itself. First drafted late in 1476, it was subsequently presented (in *Laur.10*) to Lorenzo de' Medici, probably after 1480, as a kind of pledge that the *Theology*, which had been composed between 1469 and 1474 and whose dedication had been promised him, would soon be in his hands.[1] Hence the *Argumentum* was less a working paper than a retrospective overview, a *praegustatio* of the larger work that finally appeared in 1482. Later, in 1491, Ficino assembled the *Argumentum* and seven other short theological texts from Book II of his epistolary (mostly datable to 1476–77) in a collection he called *Opuscula Theologica*.[2]

Thus the text of the *Argumentum* comes down to us in two traditions: that of the manuscripts containing Book II of Ficino's letters; and that presenting the *Argumentum* as a self-contained work. The latter tradition

consists of the two presentation copies (the earlier and the later), both from Lorenzo de' Medici's own library and no doubt intended for his personal use:

| | |
|---|---|
| *Laur.10* | Florence, Biblioteca Medicea Laurenziana, Plut. LXXXIII, 12. The dedication copy, written by Ficino's amanuensis Sebastiano Salvini, probably 1480/82. |
| *L5* | Florence, Biblioteca Medicea Laurenziana, Plut. LXXXIII, 11. A later redaction, copied by Ficino's amanuensis Luca Fabiani in 1491.[3] |

Our present text is based on these two witnesses to the independent tradition and is in principle that of the later redaction (*L5*); but the variants of *Laur.10* have been recorded and mistakes in *L5* corrected on occasion from *Laur.10*. Both manuscripts have been recollated and the *Opera* text (vol. I, pp. 706–716) and Marcel's text (3: 266–289) have been cited where appropriate. Readers interested in the (mostly trivial) variants of the epistolary tradition may consult the edition of Marcel.

This translation of the *Argumentum* is the first into English, though there is both an important sixteenth century Italian translation by Felice Figliucci in his *Divine lettere del gran Marsilio Ficino*, vol. I (Venice, 1546, 1549; photo reprint, Rome: Storia e letteratura, 2001), dedicated to Duke Cosimo, and a modern Italian one by Eugenio Garin in his *Filosofi italiani del Quattrocento* (Florence: Le Monnier, 1942), pp. 328–372, based on a collation of the *Opera* text with three MSS (see Marcel's strictures in his edition, 3:260). There is also a recent German translation by Elisabeth Blum, Paul Richard Blum, and Thomas Leinkauf in their *Marsilio Ficino: Traktate zur Platonischen Philosophie* (Berlin: Akademie Verlag, 1993), pp. 44–105, which reproduces en face Marcel's Latin text, and to which we are indebted for some of our references.

## NOTES

1. For the date of composition, 1476, see Marcel, 3: 247–249. The use of the honorific *patriae servatorem* in the dedication of *Laur.10* indicates a *terminus post quem* for that manuscript of February 1480 or after, when this title began to be applied to Lorenzo.

2. Edited in vol. 3 of Marcel's edition of the *Platonic Theology*.

3. For the description of these MSS, see *Marsilio Ficino, Lettere. I: Epistolarum familiarium liber I*, ed. Sebastiano Gentile (Florence: Leo S. Olschki, 1990), pp. XCIV-XCV. We have adopted Gentile's sigla.

# Notes to the Text

༄༅༅

## CAPITULA

1. Quinta quaestio . . . post discessum: *in the internal titles this part of the rubric is given as the title of Cap. I*

2. *in the internal titles this chapter title is omitted*

3. scilicet mundum fuisse creatum *after* communi *in L and after correction in the internal titles of A*

4. in corpore vivens] dum in corpore vivit *in the internal titles of AL*

5. *in the internal titles the rubric is given as* De statu animae purae, praecipue secundum Platonicos

6. *in the internal titles the rubric is given as* De corporibus beatorum

7. *in the internal titles the rubric is given as* De medio animorum statu, praecipue secundum philosophos *and not preceded by a chapter number*

8. *in the internal titles the rubric is given simply as* Conclusio *and is not preceded by a chapter number*

## BOOK XVII

1. Marsilii Ficini Florentini Theologie De animorum immortalitate liber xxvii incipit *L*: XVII LIBER *A*

2. *chapter rubric given as* Ordo sex priscorum theologorum et sex academiarum *in the* Capitula librorum *printed at the beginning of A*

3. hausit *L*

4. Zenocrate *A*

5. *omitted before correction in A*

6. aliam *before correction in A*

7. in corpora *before correction in A*

8. corpora *A, Opera, Marcel*

9. Missa *before correction in A*

10. *omitted in Opera, Marcel*

11. terminatamque *L*

12. si multitudo] similitudo *before correction in A*

13. referas *before correction in A*

14. individuo statui *Marcel:* in dividuo statu *L, Opera:* in diuiduo statu(i) *A, but the sense demands* individuo statui *(Ficino's correction of* statu *to* statui *in the corrigenda is ambiguous, and could apply to this* statu *or the* statu *in note 16)*

15. in dividuo *A, Opera:* individua *Marcel*

16. statui *L (and A after correction? See note 14)*

17. *thus AL:* ἀπλανὲς *Opera, Marcel*

18. obtinet *before correction in A*

19. prius *L*

20. et fluere] effluere *L*

21. distinctae *L*

22. harmonia *before correction in A*

23. pythagorei mysterii *transposed in L*

24. *corrected following Opera:* quatrinitatem *LA, Marcel (but perhaps F.'s coinage)*

25. Ita *L*

26. *corrected to* permanentis *by Marcel*

27. his *L*

28. *corrected to* deo *by Opera, Marcel:* de *AL*

29. *omitted in L*

30. virtutem *A*

31. his *L*

32. fuerit atque] fuit et *L*

33. modis *L*

34. vita *L*

35. quod *added silently after* oportet *by Opera, Marcel*

36. *omitted in Opera, Marcel*

37. ea *L*

38. incerta *A, Opera*

39. Ac *L, A before correction, Marcel*

40. explicavitque *before correction in A*

41. ut scribitur *omitted in L*

42. his *L*

43. discrepant *before correction in A*

44. Zenocrates *AL*

45. Zenocratis *AL*

46. miserias *L*

47. ut *A*

48. *added interlinearly in L*

49. et Hermeiam *omitted before correction in A*

50. muscarum *before correction in A*

51. inficitur *Marcel*

52. Eleatam *before correction in A*

53. illum *before correction in A*

54. in *added after* et *Opera, Marcel*

55. adeo *Opera, Marcel*

56. Legum sexto *transposed in Opera, Marcel*

57. ignorat *before correction in A*

58. supponitur *L*

59. Idem *Opera, Marcel*

60. solemus *before correction in A*

## BOOK XVIII

1. Marsilii Ficino Florentini Theologiae De animorum immortalitate liber XVIIIus incipit L: XVIII Liber A

2. scilicet . . . creatum *omitted in the capitula librorum printed before the text in A and, before correction, in the internal titles of A*

3. animos *Opera, Marcel*

4. ideo quod *before correction in A*

5. *Marcel corrects silently to* moverique

6. indissolubili L

7. *Opera and Marcel correct to* illud, *but* illum, *given in AL, is more likely an authorial error*

8. *omitted in L*

9. Zeno- AL

10. affluere *before correction in L*

11. *omitted in L*

12. illic L

13. aeternitates A

14. quiquis *before correction in A*

15. *omitted in L*

16. nascentem *before correction in A*

17. iis L

18. *corrected silently to* id *by Marcel*

19. anima L

20. quidam L

21. *omitted by Marcel*

22. materiae *before correction in A*

23. capiunt *Marcel*

24. illa *Opera, Marcel*

25. *omitted in L*

26. quem *L*

27. infinitam] in infinitam *before correction in A*

28. *omitted by Marcel*

29. et *before* momentoque *deleted in A*

30. est proprie *transposed in Opera, Marcel*

31. et *before* animalium *deleted in A*

32. quam *L*

33. atque ab] absque *L*

34. rationali *Marcel*

35. In esse *A, Opera*

36. dent *before correction in A*

37. in *before correction in A*

38. -tantur *L*

39. dum . . . vivit] in corpora vivens *in the Capitula librorum of A*

40. -erit *AL*

41. turbam *before correction in A*

42. qui *L*

43. iis *A*

44. substentaculum *L*

45. *chapter rubric given as* Ubi est anima pura et qualis corpore mortuo *in the Capitula librorum of A*

46. *omitted before correction in A*

47. -que *omitted in L*

48. *omitted by Marcel*

49. *omitted before correction in A*

50. primum *before correction in L*

51. enim *before correction in A*

52. Saturni *Marcel*

53. -ratur *before correction in A*

54. Hinc *Opera, Marcel*

55. *omitted before correction in* A

56. perspectam *Opera, Marcel*

57. -tissimae *L, Opera:* -tissim(a)e *A:* -tissime *Marcel*

58. Hic *L*

59. primum *L*

60. sapientia *L*

61. eandem qu(a)e *L*

62. aut *L, Opera*

63. formam *before correction in* A

64. induatur *AL (perhaps an authorial error; see note 66)*

65. aliquando *Opera, Marcel*

66. *corrected from* induitur *as in AL, Opera, Marcel*

67. terminatum *A, Opera, Marcel (but see 18.8.22)*

68. potest *before correction in* A

69. adeo *AL*

70. vero ab] vera ob *Marcel*

71. tamen *before correction in* A

72. haec *before correction in* A

73. et *L*

74. nobis *before correction in* A

75. fundamentum *before correction in* A

76. defutura *before correction in* A

77. cognitionis *L*

78. *omitted in* A, Opera, Marcel; *Marcel mistakenly reports* L's vero *after the* immo *in the next line*

79. magis *L*

80. *chapter rubric given as* Status animae purae *in the Capitula librorum of* A

81. seque ipsum] seque ipsumque *Opera, Marcel*

82. illis *Opera, Marcel*

83. hoc *Opera, Marcel*

84. multosque *Opera, Marcel*

85. consulitur *before correction in A*

86. in ordinato *A*

87. perfectiusque *L*

88. *corrected by Marcel from* perducunt *in AL, Opera*

89. mutato genio *omitted before correction in A, added in the margin of* L

90. forte *Opera, Marcel*

91. -tissimis *before correction in A*

92. coniunctos *before correction in A:* convictas *Marcel*

93. amarint *L*

94. ipsam *before correction in A*

95. devincuntur *before correction in A*

96. animae *before correction in A*

97. purae *L*

98. At *L*

99. sollertia *L*

100. Solus *before correction in A*

101. habitus *before correction in A*

102. infimam *before correction in A*

103. experte *before correction in A*

104. congruae *L:* congru(a)e *A:* congrue *Opera, Marcel*

105. iis *L*

106. miris, ut inquit, modis *after* ferant *deleted in A*

107. mere *L, A before correction, Opera*

108. a deo] adeo *AL*

109. *chapter heading given as* Status animae mediae, id est infantum atque similium *in the Capitula librorum; the chapter number is also omitted in AL but given in the Capitula*

110. talia *L, A before correction*

111. incidere *Opera, Marcel*

112. nusquam *A*

113. exurit *AL:* esurit *Opera, Marcel*

114. exurit *AL:* esurit *Opera, Marcel*

115. Timaeus inquit *transposed in A*

116. quidem *before correction in A*

117. intentionem *Opera, Marcel*

118. quicquam *L*

119. omnino deleri] modis inolescere miris *before correction in A*

120. *chapter heading given as* Conclusio exhortatoria *in the Capitula librorum; the chapter number is also omitted in AL but given in the Capitula*

121. momentum *L*

122. THEOLOGIA . . . IMMORTALITATE *omitted in L*

123. *L adds* LAUS DEO: *A adds* Impressum Florentie per Antonium Miscominum anno salutis MCCCCLXXXII, VII Idus Novembris.

### INTRODUCTION TO *PLATONIC THEOLOGY*

1. Magnanimum virum *before* Laurentium *Laur.10*

2. *in L5 followed by the rubric* Tres sunt contemplationis platonicae gradus: *deleted as a duplication of the rubric before §3*

3. *address omitted in Laur.10*

4. *omitted by Marcel*

5. *omitted in L5*

6. Postquam vero . . . claves *omitted in Laur.10*

7. *rubric in Laur.10:* In primo contemplationis platonicae gradu ascendimus primo a materia elementorum ad caelum sine materia, secundo ad animam sine quantitate, tertio ad angelum mutationis expertem, quarto ad Deum sine accidente substantiam

8. informas *L5*

9. formarum genus cum *Laur.10*

10. materia . . . facilius *omitted in Laur.10, probably an eyeskip (but a marginal addition has been erased)*

11. praesertim . . . est *omitted in Laur.10*

12. quantitate *L5*

13. nunquam *Laur.10*

14. in formis *added in the margin of L5*

15. crasse naturae *L5*

16. aliunde quale *Laur.10*

17. *interlinear addition in Laur.10*

18. hic *Marcel*

19. *interlinear addition in Laur.10*

20. anima *Marcel*

21. alios *before correction in L5*

22. fit *Opera, Marcel*

23. *this and the rest of the italicized ordinals in this chapter are written in the margin of Laur.10, but are omitted by L5, Opera and Marcel*

24. actus summus *Laur.10*

25. *superscript in L5*

26. *superscript in Laur.10*

27. *this paragraph omitted in Laur.10*

28. *interlinear addition in Laur.10*

29. et David . . . lumen eius *omitted in Laur.10*

30. *omitted in Laur.10, Opera, Marcel*

31. fulget *before correction in L5*

32. Invisibilis . . . calefacit *added in the margin of L5*

33. mihi *L5*

34. possessurum vel reperturum] reperturum vel reperturum *Laur.10*

35. *rubric in Laur.10:* In secundo contemplationis platonicae gradu qui consistit in deo, agitur de providentia nominibusque dei et de gaudio contemplantis [*corrected from:* contemplationis]

36. Cuncta *before* vera *deleted in Laur.10*

37. reperta *Laur.10*

38. -que] *emended from the* quidem *found in Laur.10, L5, Opera, Marcel*

39. perspicacitas *Laur.10*

40. ipsa et *after correction in Laur.10:* et ipsa *L5*

41. *this and the rest of the italicized ordinals in this chapter are written in the margin of L5 and Laur.10, but are omitted by Opera and Marcel*

42. Gaudium . . . verissimum *is the last sentence of the previous paragraph in Laur.10*

43. vera *Marcel*

44. *omitted in Laur.10*

45. Numquam *Laur.10*

46. est enim sibi quisque] quisquis enim sibi *Laur.10*

47. nunc *Opera, Marcel*

48. *rubric in Laur.10:* In tertio contemplationis Platonicae gradu a deo ad animam corpusque descendimus atque consideramus quid animus in corpore possit, quid extra corpus

49. intellegibilem *before correction in Laur.10*

50. privatus *before correction in Laur.10*

51. est ipse *before correction in Laur.10*

52. corpora *Opera, Marcel*

53. Meminisse vero oportet . . . vertere] *Laur.10 preserves an earlier version:* Meminisse oportet quod anima occupata in mole corporis fabricanda

regendaque et in diversas actiones distracta et perturbata . . . et leviter aciem vertit.

54. reflectit *before correction in Laur.10*

55. discurrens . . . speciesque *added in the margin of L5*

56. *this paragraph omitted in Laur.10*

57. *omitted by Opera, Marcel*

58. *interlinear addition in Laur.10*

59. *interlinear addition in Laur.10*

60. Animus *Laur.10*

61. *omitted in L5*

62. existeret *before correction in Laur.10*

63. in mortali] immortali *Laur.10, L5 (see the relevant note to the translation):* in mortali *is the reading of some MSS of Ficino's epistolary.*

64. caligatur *Laur.10*

65. clariora *before correction in Laur.10*

66. in se et illi] in se illa *Opera*

67. quos *Ficini epistulae, Opera, Marcel:* quo *L5 (omitted in Laur.10; see note 68)*

68. Quoniam . . . corpore *omitted in Laur.10*

69. his *Laur.10*

70. constantioremque *before correction in Laur.10*

# Notes to the Translation

ꙮꙮꙮ

## ABBREVIATIONS

Allen, *In Phaedrum*    Michael J. B. Allen, *Marsilio Ficino and the Phaedran Charioteer* (Berkeley and Los Angeles: University of California Press, 1981).

Allen, *In Philebum*    Marsilio Ficino, *The Philebus Commentary*, ed. and tr. Michael J. B. Allen (Berkeley and Los Angeles: University of California Press, 1975; repr. Tempe, Arizona: Arizona Center for Medieval and Renaissance Studies, 2000.

Allen, *In Sophistam*    Michael J. B. Allen, *Icastes: Marsilio Ficino's Interpretation of Plato's Sophist. Five Studies and a Critical Edition with Translation* (Berkeley and Los Angeles: University of California Press, 1989).

Baeumker    Clemens Baeumker, ed., *Avencebrolis Fons vitae ex arabico in latinum translatus ab Iohanne Hispano et Dominico Gundissalino*, 2 vols., continuously paginated (Namur: Aschendorff, 1892-95).

Bidez    Joseph Bidez, *Vie de Porphyre, le philosophe néoplatonicien, avec les fragments des traités Περὶ ἀγαλμάτων et De regressu animae* (Leipzig: Teubner, 1913; repr. Hildesheim: Olms, 1980).

Bidez-Cumont    Joseph Bidez and Franz Cumont, *Les mages héllenisés: Zoroastre, Ostanès et Hytaspe d'après la tradition grecque* (Paris: Les Belles Lettres, 1938).

Blum et al.    Marsilio Ficino, *Traktate zur Platonischen Philosophie*, ed. Elisabeth Blum, Paul Richard Blum and Thomas Leinkauf (Berlin: Akademie Verlag, 1993).

Clarke et al.    Iamblichus, *De mysteriis*, translated with an

|                      | introduction and notes by Emma C. Clarke, John M. Dillon and Jackson P. Hershbell (Leiden: Brill, 2004). |
|----------------------|------|
| Cousin | Proclus, *Commentarium in Platonis Parmenidem*, ed. Victor Cousin (Paris, 1864; repr. Hildesheim: Olms, 1961). |
| Colonna | Aeneas of Gaza, *Teofrasto*, ed. Maria Elisabetta Colonna (Naples: S. Iodice, 1958). |
| Couvreur | Hermias, *In Platonis Phaedrum scholia*, ed. P. Couvreur (Paris: E. Bouillon, 1901). |
| Crouzel-Simonetti | Henri Crouzel and Manlio Simonetti, eds., *Origène: Traité des principes*, 4 vols. (Paris: Éditions du Cerf, 1978-84). |
| Des Places, *Oracles* | Édouard Des Places, ed., *Oracles Chaldaïques, avec un choix de commentaires anciens* (Paris: Les Belles Lettres, 1971). |
| Des Places, *Numenius* | Numenius, *Fragments*, ed. Édouard Des Places (Paris: Les Belles Lettres, 1973). |
| Des Places, *Porphyry* | Porphyry, *Vie de Pythagore-Lettre à Marcella*, ed. and tr. Édouard Des Places (Paris: Les Belles Lettres, 1982). |
| Diehl | Proclus, *In Platonis Timaeum commentaria*, ed. Ernest Diehl, 3 vols. (Leipzig: Teubner, 1903; repr. Amsterdam: Hakkert, 1965). |
| Diels-Kranz | Hermann Diels and Walther Kranz, eds., *Die Fragmente der Vorsokratiker*, 3 vols. (Berlin: Weidmann, 1906-1910). |
| Dillon-Hershbell | Iamblichus, *On the Pythagorean Way of Life*, text, translation and notes by John Dillon and Jackson Hershbell (Atlanta, Georgia: Scholar's Press, 1991). |
| Dodds | *Proclus: The Elements of Theology*, ed. E. R. Dodds, 2nd ed. (Oxford: Clarendon Press, 1963). |
| Ficino, *Opera* | Marsilio Ficino, *Opera omnia* (Basel: Heinrich |

Petri, 1576; repr. Turin: Bottega d'Erasmo, 1959; Paris: Phénix Editions, 1999).

Finamore-Dillon    Iamblichus, *De anima*, text, translation and commentary by John F. Finamore and John M. Dillon (Leiden: Brill, 2002).

Hiller    Theon of Smyrna, *Expositio rerum mathematicarum ad legendum Platonem utilium*, ed. E. Hiller (Leipzig, 1878).

Kristeller    Paul Oskar Kristeller, *Supplementum Ficinianum*, 2 vols. (Florence: Olschki, 1937).

Kern    *Orphicorum fragmenta*, ed. Otto Kern (Berlin: Weidmann, 1922).

Kroll    Proclus, *In Platonis Rem publicam commentarii*, ed. Wilhelm Kroll, 2 vols. (Leipzig: Teuber, 1899-1901; repr. Amsterdam: Hakkert, 1965).

Laurens    Marsilio Ficino, *Commentaire sur le Banquet de Platon, de l'Amour*, ed. and tr. Pierre Laurens (Paris: Les Belles Lettres, 2002).

Marg    Timaeus of Locri, *De natura mundi et animae*, ed. Walter Marg, editio maior (Leiden: Brill, 1972).

PG    *Patrologiae cursus completus. Series Graeca*, ed. Jacques-Paul Migne, 161 vols. (Paris: Migne, 1857-1866.)

PL    *Patrologiae cursus completus. Series Latina*, ed. Jacques-Paul Migne, 221 vols. (Paris: Migne, 1844-1891).

Ricciardelli    *Inni Orfici*, ed. Gabriella Ricciardelli (Rome: Fondazione Lorenzo Valla and Milan: Mondadori, 2000).

Saffrey-Westerink    Proclus, *Théologie platonicienne*, ed. H. D. Saffrey and L. G. Westerink, 6 vols. (Paris: Les Belles Lettres, 1968-97).

Sirinelli et al.    Eusebius of Caesarea, *La préparation évangélique*,

|  | ed. J. Sirinelli et al., 9 vols. (Paris: Éditions du Cerf, 1974-1991). |
|---|---|
| Smith | *Porphyrii philosophi fragmenta*, ed. Andrew Smith (Leipzig: Teubner, 1993). |
| Sodano | Porphyry, *In Platonis Timaeum commentariorum fragmenta*, ed. Angelo Raffaele Sodano (Naples: s. n., 1964). |
| Tambrun-Krasker | Brigitte Tambrun-Krasker, *Oracles chaldaïques, recension de Georges Gémiste Pléthon* (Athens: Academy of Athens, 1995). |
| Thom | Johan C. Thom, *The Pythagorean Golden Verses with Introduction and Commentary* (Leiden: E. J. Brill, 1995). |
| Van Riet, *De anima* | *Avicenna: Liber de anima, seu sextus de naturalibus*, ed. Simone van Riet, 2 vols. (Louvain: Éditions orientalistes and Leiden: E. J. Brill, 1968). |
| Van Riet, *Liber* | Avicenna, *Liber de philosophia prima sive Scientia divina*, ed. Simone van Riet, 2 vols. (Louvain: E. Peeters, 1977-1980). |
| Vian | Francis Vian, ed., *Les argonautiques orphiques* (Paris: Les Belles Lettres, 1987). |
| Waszink | Plato, *Timaeus a Calcidio translatus commentarioque instructus*, ed. J. H. Waszink, 2nd ed. (Leiden-London: Brill and The Warburg Institute, 1975). |
| Westerink | L. G. Westerink, ed., *The Greek Commentaries on Plato's Phaedo*, 2 vols. (Amsterdam and New York: North Holland Publishing Company, 1976-77). |
| Willis | Macrobius, *Saturnalia, ... in Somnium Scipionis commentarios*, ed. James Willis (Leipzig: Teubner, 1963). |

For Ficino's debts to Aquinas we have noted below two kinds of parallel passages from the *Summa contra Gentiles* assembled by Collins in *The Sec-*

*ular Is Sacred*, those indicating either "almost verbatim copying" or "a close similarity in thought" (p. 114). A third category, consisting of similarities "not marked enough to justify any conclusion about the presence of Thomistic influence," has been ignored. We follow Collins throughout in citing the paragraph numbers from the 1961 Marietti edition of the *Summa*; thus, in the citation 1.43.363, "363" refers to the paragraph number of the Marietti edition.

## CAPITULA

1. The other four questions had been raised and resolved in Books 15 and 16; see our note 1 for Book 16 and the Outline of Ficino's *Platonic Theology*.

## BOOK XVII

1. For this account of the history of ancient Platonism, see Allen, *Synoptic Art*, chap. 2. Ficino means Ammonius Saccas, the teacher of Plotinus, not Ammonius the teacher of Plutarch.

2. *curiosius* in the medieval pejorative sense: "with too much curiosity."

3. *Parmenides* 137CD (and in general 137C-142B, the first hypothesis of the second part).

4. *Philebus* 23C; see Ficino's *In Philebum* 2.1 (ed. Allen, pp. 386–389) which also cites the *Parmenides* 137C-142B.

5. Cf. Plotinus, *Enneads* 5.5.10, 6.6.9–10, 6.7.32.

6. It is possible, given the chapter's title, that Ficino means "Platonists" here in the restricted sense of "the last two schools of Platonists;" but the binary concepts from the *Philebus* were central for all the Neoplatonists.

7. *Fons vitae* (ed. Baeumker, p. 327.12–17).

8. This is all summarized from Aquinas' short treatise *De esse et essentia*.

9. *Sophist* 254B-256D — cf. Ficino's *In Sophistam* 34–35 (ed. Allen, pp. 254–261), *Parmenides* 136A-C, *Timaeus* 35AB, 36C-37C, 40AB. See Allen, *Icastes*, chap. 2, especially pp. 59–64, for a study of the whole problem.

10. Cf. Ficino, *In Sophistam* 34–35 (ed. Allen, pp. 254–261; cf. pp. 59–64); idem, *In Philebum* 2.2 (ed. Allen, p. 405).

11. *Parmenides* 156B.

12. *Timaeus* 35AB; see n. 9 above.

13. Cf. Plato, *Timaeus* 40B4 (cf. Aristotle, *Meteorology* 1.6.343b9) and in general 34A, 38BC, 40B; also Macrobius, *In somnium Scipionis* 1.6.18, 9.10, 11.6, 11.10, 14.23 (ed. Willis, pp. 21, 41, 46–47, 60); Origen, *De principiis* 2.3.6–7 (ed. Crouzel-Simonetti, 1: 268, 272).

14. Plato, *Timaeus* 35B-36B, 43D; Timaeus Locrus, *De natura mundi* 209–212 (ed. Marg, pp. 125–130); Macrobius, *In somnium Scipionis* 1.6.41–47, 2.1.13–25 (ed. Willis, pp. 25–26, 97–98); Plutarch, *De animae procreatione in Timaeo = Moralia* 1027A-1030C.

15. Cf. Plato's analysis of the divided line in *Republic* 6.509D-511E.

16. This is the famous sevenfold lambda figure in the *Timaeus* 35B-36B, 43D. See Macrobius, *In somnium Scipionis* 1.6.34–36 (ed. Willis, pp. 24–25); and Allen, *Nuptial Arithmetic*, pp. 29, 46–47, 62–63.

17. Philolaus *apud* Proclus, *In Timaeum* 2 (ed. Diehl, 1: 176.28–177.2), in the context of Proclus' argument there. The quotation from Philolaus declares that the world is constituted from contraries, "from things limiting and things limitless" (ed. Diels-Kranz, frag. 44 B 1.2), and it appears earlier in the commentary at 1:84.4–7 and also in Proclus' *Theologia Platonica* 3.8 (ed. Saffrey-Westerink, 3.30.21–23), each time in conjunction with a reference, predictably, to the *Philebus* (23C7-D8, 30C4, 61C ff.).

18. Porphyry, *Life of Pythagoras* 36, 49–51; Iamblichus, *On the Pythagorean Life* 27.130–131. Cf. Plato, *Timaeus* 53C ff. (famously) and Proclus, *In Euclidem* 1.36. For the complex role of the triangle in Ficino's psychology, see Allen, "Marsilio Ficino, Daemonic Mathematics and the Hypotenuse of the Spirit," in *Natural Particulars: Nature and the Disciplines in Renaissance Europe*, ed. A. Grafton and N. Siraisi (Boston: MIT Press, 1999), pp. 121–137.

19. I.e. the seven numbers in 1–2–4–8 and 1–3–9–27, the two quaternaries of the *Timaeus's* lambda. See n. 16 above.

20. On the successive hebdomads, see Macrobius, *In somnium Scipionis*

1.6.66–76 (ed. Willis, pp. 31–32), and on the *septenarius* in general, see 1.6.45–77.

21. Note that Ficino's arithmological tradition privileges the odd numbers since they stem from one itself, which is held not to be a number.

22. I.e. numbers with no factors, numbers (especially squares) that are the products of two factors, and numbers (especially cubes) that are the products of three factors; cf. Allen, *Nuptial Arithmetic*, pp. 52–53.

23. Ibid., pp. 62–63. Note that 4:2 is the same proportion for Ficino as 2:4 and indeed 4:8, i.e. a double proportion, and likewise for other proportions. Note too that concord, consonance, harmony, and even melody are synonymous in this argument.

24. For these musical proportions, based as they are originally on Plato's *Timaeus* 35C2–36A3, see Macrobius, *In somnium Scipionis* 1.6.43–44, 2.1.13–25 (ed. Willis, pp. 26, 97–98), and Plutarch, *De musica* 22–23 = *Moralia* 1138C–1139F. Cf. Ficino's own *In Timaeum* 28–36 (*Opera*, pp. 1451–1461v).

25. Plutarch, *De animae procreatione in Timaeo* = *Moralia* 1028B; Calcidius, *In Timaeum*, ed. Waszink, p. 148.12–19; Macrobius, *In somnium Scipionis* 2.3.14–15 = *Porphyrii in Platonis Timaeum fragmenta*, ed. Sodano, p. 63.5–21; Proclus, *In Timaeum*, ed. Diehl, p. 265.8–29.

26. In Theon of Smyrna's *Expositio rerum mathematicarum ad legendum Platonem utilium* 38 (ed. Hiller), this is the eighth quaternary.

27. This all derives from Plato, *Phaedrus* 246AB; cf. Ficino's own *In Phaedrum* 2 and 7 (ed. Allen, p. 77, 99, 101), and, for an analysis, Allen, *Platonism*, pp. 216–217 and chapter 5, passim. For the higher and lower horses as four of the *Sophist*'s five genera of being — and here Ficino seems to have a quadriga rather than a biga in mind — see Chapter 2, para. 3 above, and Allen, *Icastes*, chap. 2, especially pp. 59–64.

28. For the music of the spheres, see Aristotle's refutation in *De caelo* 2.9.290b12–291a25 (plus the notices in *Metaphysics* 1.5.986a2, 14.6.1093b4), along with the notices in Porphyry, *Life of Pythagoras* 30–31 (ed. Des Places); Iamblichus, *On the Pythagorean Life* 15.65 (ed. Dillon-Hershbell,

pp. 88–90); and Macrobius, *In somnium Scipionis* 1.5.15, 19.22 ff. (ed. Willis, pp. 17, 77).

29. Marcel refers us to Iamblichus' *De mysteriis* 1.5.16–17, which merely separates demons from heroes; but in separating higher demons and heroes from lower ones Ficino is introducing a subtler distinction.

30. *Identitas* is a scholastic neologism not a classical term.

31. *Phaedrus* 246E-248A and in general 246A-257A (the mythical hymn); see Ficino's *In Phaedrum* 11.4–11 (ed. Allen, pp. 122–129), and Allen, *Platonism*, chaps. 4–6.

32. *Phaedrus* 247B-E.

33. Ibid. 248A-249C, 250D-254E. See Ficino's *In Phaedrum* summae 23, 31 (ed. Allen, pp. 158–161, 184–189), and in general Allen, *Platonism*, chap. 7.

34. *Phaedrus* 248C-E; see Ficino's *In Phaedrum* summa 24 (ed. Allen, pp. 164–169),

35. Ibid. 249A-C.

36. Ibid. 257A; see Ficino's *In Phaedrum* 1–2 (ed. Allen, pp. 72–79).

37. Proclus, *In Parmenidem*, Book 3 (ed. Cousin, col. 808). Marcel's other reference to Proclus — to the *In Timaeum* 3.252 — runs up against the problem that Ficino had no access to this later part of Proclus' commentary. By the followers of Proclus, Ficino has in mind Ammonius (Hermias' son), Damascius, Simplicius, and Olympiodorus.

38. Plotinus, *Enneads* 4.8.7–8. See Ficino, *Platonic Theology* 12.4.10.

39. A crux: alternatively "order" might refer, not to an angelic choir, but to an arrangement — "whether this happens with a lesser or greater degree of order;" or again to the "order" of divine souls (mentioned in 17.3.3 above) who proceed from species to species.

40. Zoroaster, frag. O8 (in Bidez-Cumont, *Les mages hellénisées* 2:150–153); see Ficino, *Platonic Theology* 4.2.5. For palingenesis in Ficino and Augustine's attack on it in his *City of God* 12.12,14,18, 20–21; 22.28, see Allen, "Life as a Dead Platonist," in *Marsilio Ficino: His Theology, His Philosophy, His Legacy*, pp. 159–178; and Hankins, "Ficino on *Reminiscentia* and the

Transmigration of Souls." The term appears, interestingly, in Matthew 19:28 and Titus 3:5.

41. *Pimander* 13.1,10–16.

42. *Statesman* 269C-274D, and especially 273DE. See n. 58 below.

43. *Timaeus* 41D ff. See *Platonic Theology* 17.2.12 above.

44. *Republic* 10.617D-621D.

45. Ibid. 620A1–3.

46. Ibid. 617E1, 4–5. Cf. Plotinus, *Enneads* 3.4.3.

47. Ibid. 617E3.

48. Playing on *disponere, componere*, and *deponere*.

49. *Republic* 10.617B4; cf. *Phaedrus* 248C2: "the ordinance of Adrastia" (which for Ficino is "the law of Providence"). See Ficino's *In Rempublicam* (*Opera*, pp. 1434–35) and *In Phaedrum* 8.2, 10.10–12 and summae 19, 24 and 38 (ed. Allen, pp. 103, 116–119, 151, 163, 199); also his *Platonic Theology* 18.10.2 below.

50. *Republic* 617B-D, 620DE.

51. Ibid. 620D-621A.

52. Ibid. 621A.

53. Aeneas of Gaza, *Theophrastus* 12.1 (ed. Colonna).

54. Hermias, *In Phaedrum* 170.16–19 (ed. Couvreur); and Proclus, *In Rempublicam* 16 (ed. Kroll, 2:309.3–341.4) — Proclus' most extensive discussion; idem, *In Timaeum* 5 (ed. Diehl, 3:294.22–295.32). But again Ficino knew neither of these later portions of the two commentaries.

55. Plato, *Phaedrus* 248C-249B — cf. Ficino's *In Phaedrum* summa 25 (ed. Allen, pp. 168–171) — and *Republic* 10.615AB. See also Allen *Platonism*, pp. 177–178.

56. Hermias, *In Phaedrum* 169.2–12 (ed. Couvreur).

57. Alternatively *numero* could be referring to a scholastic notion of individuation, and mean that the soul must not be thought to return to a man who is numerically the same in every material respect, as distin-

guished from a man who merely has what Ficino calls two sentences later "the same species of life."

58. *Statesman* 269C-274D. Cf. n. 42 above.

59. Cf. Ficino's *Platonic Theology* 4.2.5.

60. Psalm 12:8 "in circuitu impii ambulant."

61. Cicero, *Academica* 1.45–46, 2.33; Augustine, *Contra Academicos* 2.6.14–15, 3.17.37–19.42. See Allen, *Synoptic Art*, pp. 56–62.

62. See Allen, *Synoptic Art*, pp. 69, 74–77.

63. Notably in *Phaedo* 70C ff., 81C-E, 113A, *Meno* 81BC, *Phaedrus* 248C ff., *Republic* 10.617D ff., *Timaeus* 41E ff., 90E ff., *Laws* 10.903D ff., 904E, and *Seventh Letter* 335C.

64. Orpheus, *Hymn* 25 (to Proteus); Empedocles, frags. 8, 9, 17, 21, 35, 115, and, best of all, 117 (ed. Diels-Kranz 31 B); Heraclitus, frag. 15 (ed. Diels-Kranz 22 B).

65. Iamblichus, *On the Pythagorean Life* 14.63, refers both to Pythagoras' own previous lives and to his arousing the memory of an earlier life in others he encountered.

66. *Apud* Nemesius, *De natura hominis* 51.117–118 (*PG* 40.584).

67. *Apud* Augustine, *City of God* 10.30 passim, 12.21.61–68, 13.19.39–41, 22.12.56–64; also Aeneas of Gaza (*PG* 85.893). Note that these and other fragments of Porphyry's lost *De regressu animae* were culled and edited by J. Bidez in his *Vie de Porphyre*, pp. 27*-44*); see especially frag. 11 (pp. 38*-41*); in the new collection, *Porphyrii Philosophi Fragmenta* (ed. Smith); these are now frags. 298, 300, and 301. We recall that Plotinus, the master of Porphyry and Ficino, did accept transmigration (see *Enneads* 1.1.11, 3.4.2, 4.3.9, 12.35–39, 5.2.2.1–10, 6.7.6–7), though not without some irony in 3.4.2 in the allotment of lives.

68. See n. 67 above.

69. Proclus, *In Rempublicam* 2.101–132 (ed. Kroll). Cf. n. 54 above.

70. Hermias, *In Phaedrum* 170.16–19 (ed. Couvreur). Cf. n. 54 above.

71. Cf. *Platonic Theology* 16.5.3–4, 17.3.5–8 above.

72. I.e., in the fact and in the implications of the transmigration of

souls. See Augustine's strictures cited in *City of God* 10.29–30; cf. nn. 40 and 67 above.

73. See n. 63 above.

74. Diogenes Laertius, *Lives* 3.6–8, 52; Cicero, *Tusculan Disputations* 1.17.39; Apuleius, *De Platone* 1.2–3; Olympiodorus, *In Alcibiadem* 2.89–92; Jerome, *Apologia adversus libros Rufini* 3.40 (*PL* 23.486–87).

75. On Plato's Pythagoreanism in general—a Neoplatonic commonplace—see Cornelia J. de Vogel, *Pythagoras and Early Pythagoreanism* (Assen, 1966), pp. 202–207; and specifically in Ficino, Allen, *Icastes*, pp. 73–81, and "Marsilio Ficino on Plato's Pythagorean Eye" (= No. VII in *Plato's Third Eye*), pp. 173–177, with further references. Of significance is Ficino's assumption that the three Eleatics, Parmenides, Zeno and Melissus, were all Pythagoreans.

76. Zeno, the follower of Parmenides, is the opening speaker in the *Parmenides*, which from the viewpoint of the Neoplatonists and of Ficino is the master dialogue.

77. Aristotle's *Politics* 2.6.1264b26 says the *Laws* is "a later work" and Plutarch, *On Isis and Osiris* 48 = *Moralia* 370F, says that Plato was already an old man when he wrote it. Cf. Ficino's *Vita Platonis* and his epitome for *Laws* 1 (*Opera*, pp. 766.2, 1488).

78. *Second Letter* 314C. Cf. Ficino's epitome (*Opera*, pp. 1530–32).

79. *Seventh Letter* 341C. Cf. Ficino's epitome (*Opera*, pp. 1534–35).

80. *Timaeus* 28B6 ff., 37C-38B, 41A. The issue depends on the interpretation here of the Greek words *genesis* and *gignesthai* "to come into being" and their cognates.

81. Genesis 1.1; *Pimander* 3.1–3, 8.2–4, 10.10,14, 11.2–3; *Asclepius* 40.

82. *Apud* Proclus, *In Timaeum* 2 (ed. Diehl 1:276.30–277.7, 283.27 ff. [Atticus only], 289.6–13 [Severus], 326.1 ff., 381.26, 382.12, 384.4 ff.). Cf. Plutarch, *De animae procreatione in Timaeo* = *Moralia* 1013E ff.

83. *Apud* Eusebius, *Praeparatio Evangelica* 9.6.9, 11.10.14; and Clement of Alexandria, *Stromateis* 1.22.150 (in Des Places' edition of Numenius' fragments this is frag. 8). The same ref. appears in Ficino's letters to

Giovanni Niccolini and to Braccio Martelli (*Opera*, pp. 855.1, 866.3) and elsewhere.

84. *Apud* Proclus, *In Timaeum* 2 (ed. Diehl 1:277.8–32, and in general 276.10–282.22).

85. *De natura mundi* 93a (ed. Marg, p. 119). Cf. Proclus, *In Timaeum* 2 (ed. Diehl, 1:283.19 ff.).

86. *Epinomis* 981E-982A.

87. *Timaeus* 41AB.

88. *Laws* 6.781E-782A.

89. Aristotle, *De caelo* 1.10.279b4–280a23 and ff. (but at 2.1.383b27 ff. Aristotle argues for heaven's eternity).

90. *Laws* 10.892A-C, 896BC.

91. See para. 7 of Aquinas's *Summa contra gentiles* 2.83 which cites Origen's *De principiis* 2.9.6–7 (Crouzel-Simonetti 1: 365–371).

92. *Laws* 9.872D-873A; cf. 10.903D, 904E-905A.

93. *Laws* 7.818BC.

94. *Phaedrus* 249B3–4; cf. n. 104 below.

95. *Timaeus* 42C3–4.

96. *Republic* 10.620C2–4 "clothing itself in the body of an ape."

97. *Phaedo* 113A.

98. Ibid. 113D-114B, 114D (on the reasonability but non-verifiability of such a "story" that one takes "a noble risk" in believing).

99. Ibid. 114BC.

100. *Epinomis* 992B-D.

101. *Gorgias* 523B-526B (cf. *Protagoras* 324B-D), *Theaetetus* 176D-177A, *Republic* 10.614D-616A (cf. 2.363DE).

102. *Gorgias* 525B-D; cf. n. 101 above.

103. *Republic* 10.615C-616A. Note that Ardiaeus, like other incurably wicked men, is never allowed to escape through hell's mouth.

104. *Phaedrus* 249B3–4; cf. n. 94 above.

105. *Laws* 10.904A-905A, especially 904DE; cf. *Phaedo* 67AB, 82C-83B, 84AB.

106. *Republic* 9.588B-589B (though Socrates does not introduce a dragon/snake till 590B1).

107. Ibid. 588E-589A. Socrates makes no mention of a cudgel; rather he declares that an unjust man is subject to the beasts and cannot control them, while a just man should take charge of the beasts like a farmer who trains the cultivated plants but checks the uncultivated; he must care for them and make an ally of the lion's nature (589B1–4).

108. Ibid. 590A9-B1.

109. Ibid. 588E-589A.

110. In his *Republic* epitome, Ficino argues that souls migrate into the feelings (*affectus*) and habits of beasts, but not into their bodies (*Opera*, p. 1427).

111. Is kite (*milvus* in Latin) a mistake for the ape (*pithêkon*) of 590B9, given that *mimus* aptly renders *pithêkon* in the sense of trickster? Cf. *Phaedo* 82A: "wolves and hawks and kites."

112. *Phaedrus* 230A.

113. *Phaedrus* 246A-256E (the charioteer myth).

114. Parmenides, frag. 28 B1.1–30 (ed. Diels-Kranz), i.e., the proem to his hexametrical *Poema* "On Nature" (preserved in Sextus Empiricus, *Adv. Math.* 7.3). Here Parmenides describes a visionary chariot ride drawn by two mares up through the gates of Night and Day accompanied by the daughters of the Sun. His and Plato's chariot visions have been linked together since late antiquity; see Leonardo Tarán, *Parmenides: A Text with Translation, Commentary, and Critical Essays* (Princeton, 1965), p. 18. Ficino refers to the *Poema* on a number of occasions and especially in his *Parmenides* commentary.

115. Timaeus Locrus, *De natura mundi* 225 (ed. Marg, p. 151).

116. *Aurea dicta* 70–71 (tr. Ficino, *Opera*, p. 1979); Ficino had quoted it earlier in his *De voluptate* 4 (*Opera*, p. 994).

117. Orpheus, *Hymns* 57.1 (ed. Ricciardelli, p. 150), "To Terrestrial Mercury."

118. *Pimander* 10.7–8 (poetically described), 19–20 (condemned).

119. Ibid. 10.20–21 (though the eternity of the punishment of the wicked is not "clearly" asserted).

120. Ibid. 10.22.

121. Ibid. 10.18–19, 23–25 (summarized).

122. *Oracula Chaldaica* no. 3 (ed. Tambrun-Krasker [= Des Places, frag. 157], with commentary on p. 68). Cf. Plato, *Phaedo* 81E-82A, on the animals that vicious men come to resemble.

123. *Phaedo* 81CD; [Pseudo-] Olympiodorus [i.e. Damascius], *In Phaedonem* 1.349–360 (ed. Westerink 2: 190–192).

124. Ibid.

125. Pliny the Younger, *Letters* 7.27.

## BOOK XVIII

1. *Platonic Theology* 6.12.

2. Ibid. 2.4.4.

3. Apud Proclus, *In Parmenidem* 3 (ed. Cousin, 800.20–801.5). In Des Places' edition of the *Chaldaean Oracles*, this is frag. 37. Ficino's rendering of the enigmas differs, incidentally, from that by Glen Morrow and John Dillon in their *Proclus' Commentary on Plato's 'Parmenides'* (Princeton, 1987), pp. 168–169.

4. *Timaeus* 29E-30A.

5. *Pimander* 10.2–3, 13.2; *Asclepius* 8, 11, 26.

6. These two lines conclude the Orphic fragment (Kern's frag. 21a) known as the *Hymn to Jove* cited at the close of [Pseudo-]Aristotle, *De mundo* 7.401a28 ff.; they are also cited separately by Proclus, *In Timaeum* 2 (ed. Diehl, 1:325.10–11). See also the close of the longer version of the hymn (Kern's frag. 168) in Eusebius, *Praeparatio evangelica* 3.9.2 (ed. Sirinelli et al.).

7. *Timaeus* 31AB, 36E-38B, 52B.

8. Macrobius, *In somnium Scipionis* 1.21.23–25 (ed. Willis, pp. 88–89).

9. Ibid. 1.21.25.

10. Ibid. 1.21.26.

11. *In Timaeum* 2 (ed. Diehl 1:293.14–295.12) and so for the remainder of the paragraph.

12. E.g. *Platonic Theology* 11.4.15 and 14.7.6–7 (for which see n. 175 below).

13. *Timaeus* 29D-30B.

14. Ibid. 41AB.

15. *Pimander* 8.3–4, 10.10.

16. Apud Eusebius, *Praeparatio evangelica* 9.27.6 (ed. Sirinelli et al.). Artapanus was a Jewish historian of the second century BC. In his *De christiana religione* 26 (*Opera*, p. 29), Ficino writes more circumspectly that Artapanus merely showed that "the deeds attributed to Trismegistus were in fact by Moses and in Moses' books, and furthermore that Moses was called Mercury and also Musaeus" (again from Eusebius, *Praeparatio* 9.27.3).

17. See Aquinas, *Summa contra Gentiles* 2.81.3, who cites Avicenna and Algazel.

18. Reference unknown, but cf. Plotinus, *Enneads* 3.1, 3.4.6, 4.3.17.

19. Here and in the arguments to follow, Ficino will use *procreare* as an equivalent to *creare*; it is here usually rendered simply as "create."

20. I.e., Aquinas and his followers who argued that each angel was itself an individual species.

21. *Philebus* 30A.

22. *Timaeus* 34C-37C, 41A-E.

23. *De amore* 2.3 (ed. Laurens, p. 27).

24. Marcel notes that Ficino's *Di Dio et anima* (ed. Kristeller, *Supplementum Ficinianum* 2:138–139) attributes this celebrated definition to Hermes Trismegistus, and that Ficino probably took it from Alain de Lille's

*Regula de sacra theologia* 7:447 (*PL* 210.627AB — chapter title and text). It also appears in the *Book of the 24 Philosophers* as *propositio* ii (ed. C. Baeumker, *Studien und Charakteristiken zur Geschichte der Philosophie*, 1927, p. 208), written around 1200 but attributed to Hermes; and it is in Vincent of Beauvais's *Speculum naturale* 1.4, and Nicholas of Cusa's *De docta ignorantia* 1.12, 3.11 and *De ludo globi* 2. See Wind, *Pagan Mysteries*, p. 227 and note.

25. Psalm 19:5 (AV 19:4).

26. Zoroaster, *Oracula Chaldaica* nos. 14, 15ab (ed. Tambrun-Krasker, p. 2 [= Des Places frags. 104, 158] with Pletho's commentary on pp. 10–12, and with extensive editorial commentary on pp. 89–107); Hermes Trismegistus, *Pimander* 13.3–16. These references are clarified by the argument in paragraphs 3, 4 and 6 below.

27. Aristotle, *De generatione animalium* 2.3.736b27 ff.

28. Ibid., 2.3.736b29 ff.

29. In *Platonic Theology* 15.2.2.

30. Aristotle, *De generatione animalium* 2.3.737a17–18, i.e., the conclusion to the argument in 736a35–737a18.

31. For an analysis of this and the following paragraphs, see Allen, *Platonism*, pp. 218–220. Marcel refers us to Proclus's *In Timaeum* (ed. Diehl 2:72, 3:298–299), *In Rempublicam* 16 (ed. Kroll, 2:145–146, 154–155), but Ficino had no access to the last three of these four passages; and *Elements of Theology*, props. 196–209 (ed. Dodds).

32. *Phaedrus* 246A-248B, 253C ff.; cf. Ficino, *In Phaedrum* 7 (ed. Allen, pp. 96–101 — with analysis in *Platonism*, chap. 4).

33. *Timaeus* 41E2.

34. *Oracula Chaldaica* no. 14 (ed. Tambrun-Krasker [= Des Places, frag. 104], with Pletho's commentary on pp. 10–12, and extensive editorial commentary on pp. 89–103); see n. 26 above. This is one of Ficino's favorite oracles.

35. This is a gloss on the oracle just cited at n. 34 above.

36. For example *Platonic Theology* 15.12.4 (at n. 87).

37. *Timaeus* 69C-E.

38. *Oracula Chaldaica* no. 15a (ed. Tambrun-Krasker, p. 2 [= Des Places, frag. 158], with Pletho's commentary on pp. 12, and editorial commentary on pp. 104–106); see n. 26 above.

39. *Enneads* 4.4.29, adapted. The rest of the paragraph summarizes Plotinus' argument. But see n. 57 below.

40. Ficino is playing on the subtle senses of *mittere: emittere, dimittere, immittere*. It is just possible that he intended *dimittere* and *immittere* antonymically: "order it to go away" v. "let it back in."

41. *Pimander* 13.4–16.

42. Ibid. 13.3.

43. Olympiodorus, *In Phaedonem*, 82.15–17 (ed. Westerink 1: 178–180). Apollonius (d. *ca.* AD 98) was a wandering Neopythagorean philosopher-sage whose life and miracles were described by Philostratus and Hierocles in anti-Christian biographies deliberately modelled on those of the Gospels.

44. E.g. Macrobius, *In somnium Scipionis* 1.11.11–12 (ed. Willis, p. 47); and more especially Proclus, *Theologia Platonica* 3.5 (ed. Saffrey-Westerink, 3:18.24–19.15) and *Elements of Theology* props. 196, 205, 207–10 (ed. Dodds). The most important analysis is Proclus' *In Timaeum* 5 (ed. Diehl 3: 297.17–299.9), but again Ficino did not know this fifth book.

45. Plato, *Timaeus* 41D8-E1, 42D4–5.

46. See similar statements by Ficino earlier in the *Platonic Theology*, e.g. 4.1.12–16, 15.16.13, 16.6.1–2, 10. Marcel refers us to Proclus, *In Rempublicam* 16 (ed. Kroll 2:96), but again Ficino only knew the first twelve treatises.

47. *Timaeus* 41E1–3.

48. Macrobius, *In somnium Scipionis* 1.12.1–2 (ed. Willis, p. 48).

49. Or perhaps "to grace" with a play on *Charites* — the three Graces, Aglaia, Euphrosyne and Thalia.

50. Macrobius, *In somnium Scipionis* 1.12.14–15 (ed. Willis, p. 50).

51. Ibid.

52. Is Ficino calling for a new church council to be held to revisit the is-

sue of the descent of souls, declared unorthodox by the Council of Chalcedon in 451? See Hankins, "Ficino on *Reminiscentia* and the Transmigration of Souls."

53. See Plotinus, *Enneads* 3.4 passim, "On our allotted guardian spirit," focusing as it does on Plato's *Phaedo* 107D and *Republic* 10.617.

54. *Symposium* 197AB, *Protagoras* 320D, *Statesman* 271D-272B, *Critias* 109BC.

55. *Laws* 4.713C-714A.

56. Plato, *Phaedrus* 240A, 259A, as glossed by Ficino's *In Phaedrum* summae 9 and 35 (ed. Allen, pp. 136–139, 194–195); Hermeias, *In Phaedrum* 163.24–27 (ed. Couvreur). For Ficino and Platonic demonology, see Allen, *Platonism*, chap. 1, especially pp. 7–31.

57. *Enneads* 4.4.29; cf. 4.3.22, 4.5.6–7. See n. 39 above.

58. *Phaedo* 107D-108C, 113D-114C.

59. Pythagoras, *Golden Sayings* 70–71 (ed. Thom) — the concluding lines.

60. *Phaedo* 80C-84B; *Gorgias* 524B-D.

61. I.e., Plotinus, *Enneads* 4.7.13–14; cf. n. 63 below (4.7 is one of Ficino's favorite Plotinian treatises, not surprisingly given its title, "On the immortality of the soul").

62. *Timaeus* 41D-42B. Cf. n. 45 above

63. Plotinus, *Enneads* 4.7.15.

64. Above all, Plato, *Republic* 6.508 ff.

65. For the spark, see Plato, *Seventh Letter* 341CD and 344B, though Plato maintains there that it can endure. On its suddenness, see *Symposium* 210E, and on the fire within us, *Philebus* 29BC. Cf. Ficino's *Platonic Theology* 11.3.21 and n. 15.

66. E.g., *Platonic Theology* 14.7.6.

67. *Phaedrus* 246A-257A; cf. Ficino's *In Phaedrum* 7–11 (ed. Allen, pp. 96–129; analyzed in Allen, *Platonism*, chaps. 5–6).

68. *Phaedrus* 247E. Cf. Ficino's *In Phaedrum* summa 24 (ed. Allen,

pp. 158–159), along with *De voluptate* 1, *De amore* 7.14 (ed. Laurens, pp. 240–244), and *In Philebum* 1.34 (ed. Allen, pp, 218–227).

69. *Statesman* 269C-274D.

70. II Corinthians 4:16. Ficino frequently quotes this verse.

71. Recalling the phrasing of the *Phaedrus* 247A4–5; cf. Ficino's *In Phaedrum* summa 19 (ed. Allen, pp. 150–151).

72. *Symposium* 210D-212B (with the image of "the open sea of beauty" at 210D4).

73. Referring surely to the heavenly "nectar" of *Symposium* 203B and *Phaedrus* 247E.

74. *Epinomis* 992BC.

75. *Phaedrus* 245BC, 249DE, 265A-C; see Allen, *Platonism*, chap. 2.

76. Cf. Ficino's letter to Lorenzo "Quid est felicitas" (ed. Gentile, pp. 201–210 as no. 115). See the discussion in Hankins, *Humanism and Platonism*, 2: 317–350.

77. E.g., Dionysius the Areopagite, *Celestial Hierarchy* 6.2–9.4 (PG 3.200D-261D) — the principal authority; and Aquinas, *Summa contra gentiles* 3.80. See Ficino's own *De christiana religione* 14 and *De raptu Pauli* 6 (*Opera*, pp. 19, 699–700); also his *Platonic Theology* 12.7.8 (and nn. 90–91) above.

78. See especially Proclus, *Theologia Platonica* 3.14, and *In Parmenidem* 6.1090–91. But Ficino discovered Proclus' ontology replete with triads within triads and saw nines everywhere in the Platonic tradition (as the number of the Muses, the celestial spheres, and the months of gestation, and so on). See for example his analysis of the nine lives in the *Phaedrus* 248C-E (*In Phaedrum* summae 24, 33 [ed. Allen, 164–167, 190–191]); his Neoplatonic understanding of the crucial second part of the *Parmenides* as consisting of nine hypotheses (see Allen, "Ficino's Theory of the Five Substances and the Neoplatonists' *Parmenides*," now in *Plato's Third Eye* as no. VIII); and his exposition of the role of nine (and its square and cube) in the ninth book of the *Republic* at 587E ff. (see Allen, *Nuptial Arithmetic*, pp. 73–74). Moreover, there were the six nines of Plotinus' *Enneads*.

79. Cf. Ficino's argument at 8.27 below.

80. Plato, *Timaeus* 38C-39D, *Republic* 10.616D-617B.

81. The old edition of the Orphic fragments by Eugenius Abel (Leipzig 1885, repr. Hildesheim 1971), p. 272, treats this passage of Ficino as a unique testimonium and labels it under *dubia* as "fragment 320"; it is omitted from Kern's 1922 edition of the fragments. But see n. 169 below, where the same opinion is attributed to Orpheus.

82. I.e., the seven planetary spheres, the sphere of the fixed stars, and the primum mobile (equated here with the crystalline sphere) as in Dante's *Paradiso*.

83. As in the nine circles proper of Dante's *Inferno*.

84. Matthew 5:3-11 — the nine beatitudes.

85. The reference here is to the nine hypotheses of the second part of the *Parmenides* where — from a Neoplatonic perspective — Plato is exploring what can and cannot be predicated of the One (the Good). See n. 78 above.

86. Dionysius the Areopagite, *Mystical Theology* 1.1 (PG 3.997B) and passim.

87. *In eiusmodi vero cognitione . . . substantiam cognoverimus*; cf. Aquinas, *Summa contra Gentiles* 3.50.2276 (Collins, No. 74).

88. Cf. Aquinas, *Summa contra Gentiles* 3.50.4-5 (not in Collins).

89. *Proinde quo quid naturali . . . multo minus illae*; cf. Aquinas, *Summa contra Gentiles* 3.50.2281 (Collins, No. 75A).

90. Cf. Aristotle, *De caelo* 2.11.291b13: "nature does nothing without reason or in vain."

91. *Quoniam vero naturalis . . . videre non potest*; cf. Aquinas, *Summa contra Gentiles* 3.51.2284-85 (Collins, No. 75B).

92. *Sed ne quis absurdum putet . . . iubet emendum*; cf. Aquinas, *Summa contra Gentiles* 3.51.2287 (Collins, No. 76*). The reference is to Revelation 3:18: "I counsel thee to buy of me gold tried in the fire, that thou mayest be rich."

93. *Ad hoc autem ut mens . . . ignis evadit*; cf. Aquinas, *Summa contra Gentiles* 3.52.2291 (Collins, No. 77).

94. *Praeterea nihil potest ad . . . non urentem*; cf. Aquinas, *Summa contra Gentiles* 3.53.2301 (Collins, No. 78*). Note that prior to the sixteenth century, comets were considered sublunary (atmospheric) phenomena on the basis of Aristotle's *Meteorology* 1.6.342b25–7.345a10.

95. *Negabit forte aliquis . . . proportio est*; cf. Aquinas, *Summa contra Gentiles* 3.54.2304–5 (Collins, No. 79A).

96. *Nos autem respondebimus . . . ad causam*; cf. Aquinas, *Summa contra Gentiles* 3.54.2312 (Collins, No. 79B).

97. *Denique infinitas ipsa Dei . . . vires proprias elevare*; cf. Aquinas, *Summa contra Gentiles* 3.54.2316 (Collins, No. 80*).

98. *Neque tamen putandum est . . . inde formatur*; cf. Aquinas, *Summa contra Gentiles* 3.55.2321 (Collins, No. 81*).

99. *Quid ergo? Numquid . . . perspectus est Deus*; cf. Aquinas, *Summa contra Gentiles* 3.55.2323 (Collins, No. 82A).

100. *Platonic Theology* 13.4–5.

101. *Accedit ad haec quod . . . quilibet intellectus*; cf. Aquinas, *Summa contra Gentiles* 3.56.2326–27 (Collins, No. 82B).

102. *Nemo vero diffidere debet . . . sublimia rapiuntur*; cf. Aquinas, *Summa contra Gentiles* 3.57.2332 (Collins, No. 83).

103. *Praeterea suprema mentium . . . angelus rapiatur*; cf. Aquinas, *Summa contra Gentiles* 3.57.2333 (Collins, No. 84).

104. *Denique si mentium generi . . . naturaliter exoptatum*; cf. Aquinas, *Summa contra Gentiles* 3.57.2334 (Collins, No. 85*).

105. Cf. Ficino's argument at 8.11 above.

106. *Possunt autem aliae mentes . . . suaviusque fruuntur*; cf. Aquinas, *Summa contra Gentiles* 3.58.2337 (Collins, No. 86*).

107. *Proinde si mentium finis est . . . quandoque formetur*; cf. Aquinas, *Summa contra Gentiles* 3.59.2346 (Collins, No. 87).

108. *Quidnam prohibet intellectum . . . mirifice roboretur*; cf. Aquinas, *Summa contra Gentiles* 3.59.2347 (Collins, No. 88).

109. *Praeterea intellegibile genus . . . iuncto producit*; cf. Aquinas, *Summa contra Gentiles* 3.59.2348 (Collins, No. 89).

110. *Rursus quamvis alius perfectius . . . distincte discernunt*; cf. Aquinas, *Summa contra Gentiles* 3.59.2349 (Collins, No. 90).

111. Ibid. 2.100.2 (not in Collins).

112. Ibid. 2.100.4 (not in Collins).

113. Ibid. 2.100.5 (not in Collins).

114. *Cum mentes illic unica Dei . . . manendo conspiciunt*; cf. Aquinas, *Summa contra Gentiles* 3.60.2355–56 (Collins, No. 91).

115. *Rursus si perpetua intellegentia . . . translata dicatur*; cf. Aquinas, *Summa contra Gentiles* 3.61.2359 (Collins, No. 92).

116. *Merito quidem, nempe mens . . . aeternis aeterna*; cf. Aquinas, *Summa contra Gentiles* 3.61.2362 (Collins, No. 93).

117. *Denique quonam pacto visio . . . semper habendum*; cf. Aquinas, *Summa contra Gentiles* 3.61.2361 (Collins, No. 94) — notice the return here to the preceding paragraph.

118. *Praeterea ubi naturalia sub se . . . existimet carituram*; cf. Aquinas, *Summa contra Gentiles* 3.62.2367 (Collins, No. 95).

119. *Adde quod quicquid naturaliter cuidam . . . prorsus evadere*; cf. Aquinas, *Summa contra Gentiles* 3.62.2368 (Collins, No. 96).

120. Virgil, *Eclogues* 2.65.

121. *Timaeus* 29E, *Phaedrus* 247A.

122. *Enneads* 4.3.18.

123. Hermeias, *In Phaedrum* 68.27, 69.18 (ed. Couvreur).

124. Avicenna, *Metaphysics* 9.7 (ed. Van Riet, *Liber*, p. 520). Cf. n. 130 below.

125. On the Milky Way see Macrobius, *In somnium Scipionis* 1.12.3–4, 15.1–7 (ed. Willis, pp. 48–49, 61–62).

126. See *Enneads* 5.7.1,3 where Plotinus examines the Stoic doctrine of recurrent world-periods, a doctrine embraced by his closest associate Amelius, in the course of arguing, in this treatise at least, for the existence of Ideas of particulars. Proclus opposes Plotinus' argument in his *In Parmenidem* 3.7 (ed. Cousin, pp. 824–825). Ficino seems to have been un-

aware of their disagreement. On the related topic of transmigration, see n. 157 below.

127. That is, their souls will return in the same bodies as distinct from being reincarnated in other bodies.

128. *Statesman* 270D-271B.

129. See the reference in Ficino's address to Pope Sixtus IV in the sixth book of his *Letters* (*Opera*, p. 813.2); also his *Consiglio contro la pestilenza*, ch. 23 (ed. E. Musacchio, Bologna 1983, p. 109).

130. Avicenna, *Metaphysics* 9.7 (ed. Van Riet, *Liber*, p. 520). Cf. n. 124 above.

131. The following four proofs are borrowed from Aquinas, *Summa contra Gentiles* 4.79.1-3 (not in Collins).

132. Cf. Aquinas, *Summa contra Gentiles* 4.80.1-3 (not in Collins).

133. I Corinthians 15:54-55 ("Absorta est mors in victoria"). Cf. Psalms 23:4, 68:18, 107:14-16; Isaiah 25:8; Hosea 13:14; Romans 6:4-10; and Revelation 21:4. Cf. Aquinas, *Summa contra Gentiles* 4.82.6,10 (not in Collins).

134. Cf. Aquinas, *Summa contra Gentiles* 4.85.1-4 (not in Collins).

135. Given the link with the poets in the second half of the sentence (see the next note), Ficino is probably referring to Plato's notion of the philosopher's quest for the golden age — for which see *Cratylus* 397E-398C, *Laws* 4.713B-714A, and above all the myth in the *Statesman* 269C-274D. More generally, he is referring to such mysteries in the *Oracula Chaldaica* as "Do not soil the pneuma or give depth to what is plane" (see n. 34 above) and to those in the *Pimander* 10.18-25, 11.20, and 13.13, and *Asclepius* 6. Marcel refers us by contrast to *Pimander* 13.9 ff., *Phaedrus* 252C-253, and *Timaeus* 43A-44C.

136. E.g. Hesiod, *Works and Days* 106-20; Virgil, *Eclogues* 4.4-10; Ovid, *Metamorphoses* 1.89-112.

137. Cf. Aquinas, *Summa contra Gentiles* 4.85.5 (not in Collins).

138. Ibid. 4.86 (not in Collins).

139. For Ficino's conceptions of Hades and Hell in this chapter, see Robert Klein, "L'enfer de Ficin," in *Umanesimo e esoterismo: Atti del V convegno*

*internazionale di studi umanistici,* ed. Enrico Castelli (Padua, 1960), pp. 47–84.

140. *Phaedrus* 248C2: "the ordinance of Necessity," which for Ficino is "the law of Providence;" see his *In Phaedrum* 8.2, 10.10–12 and summae 19, 24 and 38 (ed. Allen, pp. 103, 116–119, 151, 163, 199); and cf. *Platonic Theology* 17.3.9 above. Ficino knew, incidentally, that [Pseudo-]Aristotle's *De mundo* 401b7 ff. had equated God with, *inter alia*, Necessity, Fate, and Adrastia. On man's ultimate rewards and punishments, cf. Plato's *Phaedo* 80D-81D, *Gorgias* 525C-E, *Republic* 10.613AB, 619C-E, and *Laws* 4.716CD.

141. E.g., in Plotinus, *Enneads* 4.3.15.

142. The Platonists here are probably Porphyry and Proclus. See Ficino's notes in the eighth book of his letters on Porphyry as a spokesman for Plotinus (*Opera*, pp. 876–879, especially 878.2,3), and even more importantly his epitome of Porphyry's *De abstinentia*, and especially of the second book which treats in detail of sacrifices, demons and prayers (ibid., pp. 1932–39, especially 1934–37). See too his translation of Proclus's *De sacrificio et magia* (ibid., pp. 1928–1929).

143. *Republic* 10.615E ff., *Phaedo* 113E-114B; ps. Hermes Trismegistus, *Pimander* 1.23.

144. *Gorgias* 526D.

145. *Gorgias* 527AB, *Theaetetus* 176B-177B, *Republic* 10.614B, 621BC.

146. *Republic* 2.361B-362C, 364B ff., 366E ff.

147. *Theaetetus* 176BC. (C1: *dikaiotatos*)

148. Ibid., 177A-B.

149. Plato, *Eighth Letter* 355A1 (though Plato says that the unwise have pleasure, *hêdonê*, not desire, as their god).

150. Ibid., 354E: "moderate slavery consists in being the slave of God, immoderate, in being the slave of men"; or *Laws* 6.762E (epitomized).

151. For this whole line of argument, see Plato, *Republic* 4.430D-432A; and, for the terminology of temperance, continence, etc., see Aristotle, *Nicomachean Ethics* 7 passim.

152. See *Platonic Theology* 18.4.3–7 above, with references to *Phaedrus*

247B and *Timaeus* 41DE, 44DE, 69C. See also Allen, *Phaedran Charioteer*, pp. 250–251n; idem, *Platonism*, pp. 97–98, 101–102, 218–220 (an analysis of 18.4).

153. Avicenna, *De anima* 4.1 (ed. Van Riet, pp. 4–6).

154. See Aristotle, *De anima*, Book 2 passim for the nutritive and other powers of the soul: sensation, imagination, reason, memory.

155. Anon., *Argonautica orphica* 1142 (ed. Vian, p. 157). *Aidao pulai* echoes Homer's *Iliad* 5.646, 9.312, and *Odyssey* 14.156; and *dêmos oneirôn* echoes the *Odyssey* 24.12.

156. *Republic* 7.534CD.

157. Herodotus, *Histories* 2.123, claims the doctrine of transmigration was originally Egyptian and one passage in the *Corpus Hermeticum* (which Ficino supposed an ancient body of Egyptian texts), namely 10.7–8, seems to affirm metempsychosis, though at 10.19 the same treatise declares "it is not allowed for a human soul to fall down into the body of an unreasoning animal." However, Ficino encountered the doctrine principally in: a) the pre-Socratics, especially Pythagoras (*apud* Diogenes Laertius, *Lives* 8.4, 36, and Porphyry, *Life of Pythagoras* 19) and Empedocles, frags. 115, 117, and especially 127 (*apud* Diogenes Laertius, *Lives* 8.77); b) Plato, *Phaedo* 81E-82B, 113A; *Phaedrus* 248D, 249B, *Republic* 10.618A, 620A-D; and *Timaeus* 42BC, 91D-92C; and c) Plotinus, *Enneads* 3.4.2.17–31; 3.4.6.17–18; 4.3.12.35–39; 5.2.2.1–10; and 6.7.6–7. Furthermore, from Augustine's *City of God* 10.30, he knew that Porphyry had rejected the doctrine by interpreting Plato's allusions figuratively. And independently he knew that Iamblichus and Proclus had done the same. Cf. Ficino's *Platonic Theology* 17.3.10, 17.4.3–4 above, and Hankins, *Plato*, 1: 358–59; idem, "Ficino on *Reminiscentia* and the Transmigration of Souls."

158. Hermes Trismegistus, *Asclepius* 24, 37; Plotinus, *Enneads* 4.3.11.

159. Orpheus, *Hymns* 69.2 (to the Erinyes); idem, *Argonautica orphica* 968–70 (ed. Vian, p. 145). Cf. Virgil, *Aeneid* 6.571, 10.761 (Tisiphone), 7.324, 341, 415 (Alecto), 12.846 (Megaera); and Ovid, *Metamorphoses* 4.451–511.

160. Plato, *Phaedo* 108AB, 114AB combined with *Republic* 10.615E-616A; and Plotinus, *Enneads* 3.4.6.10–18; 4.8.5.10–24.

161. *Hymn* 73, "To the Daemon" (ed. Ricciardelli, p. 186).

162. Not identified.

163. Proclus, *In Timaeum* 4 (ed. Diehl 3:157.26–158.23). But Ficino did not know this fourth book of the commentary.

164. Echoing Virgil's *Aeneid* 1.118 "in gurgite vasto."

165. Hermes, *Asclepius* 28; Plato, *Phaedo* 107D-108C, 112A-114B. See n. 174 below.

166. Pseudo-Olympiodorus (i.e. Damascius), *In Phaedonem* 2.81.2 (ed. Westerink, 2: 362–366), glossing *Phaedo* 111D-114B.

167. *Phaedo* 113E and in general 113D-114B; cf. *Republic* 10.615D-616A.

168. *Phaedo* 114BC but in the light of Pseudo-Olympiodorus' glossing? (See n. 166 above.)

169. See n. 81 above. This testimonium is also listed by Abel as an Orphic fragment (*dubia* 321), and also rejected by Kern. Ficino is perhaps making an inference from pseudo-Olympiodorus (Damascius) 1.497 (ed. Westerink 2: 252) coupled with the passage at 2.131–145 (ed. Westerink 2: 362), where the myth of the underworld is attributed to Orpheus.

170. *Platonic Theology* 18.7.12 above.

171. Virgil, *Georgics* 4.480.

172. A formula from the general Confession in the Mass.

173. Virgil, *Aeneid* 6.724–751 (the famous speech of Anchises) and especially 733–743 (on purgation); cf. Augustine, *City of God* 21.13.

174. Hermes Trismegistus, *Asclepius* 28; Plato, *Phaedo* 112A-114B and *Republic* 614C-616A (punishment in Hades), *Timaeus* 69D, 86E ff. (the passions). See n. 165 above.

175. *Platonic Theology* 14.7.6–7. Along with a letter to Lotterio Neroni of 3 December 1480 in his sixth book of *Letters* (*Opera*, pp. 836.2–839), a letter which in fact incorporates para. 7, this is one of Ficino's most memorable passages on life as a dream. See n. 12 above.

176. An extrapolation from Matthew 24:42–44, 25:13, 26:40–45, Mark 13:35–37, 15:37–41, and Luke 22:45–46; cf. Luke 12:37–40 and 1 Peter 5:8. Note that in Compline, the last of the day offices, the antiphon for the *Nunc dimittis* is "Salva nos, Domine, vigilantes: custodi nos dormientes ut vigilemus cum Christo et requiescamus in pace."

177. Matthew 26:46; John 14:31.

178. Plato, *Timaeus* 42A-C; *Gorgias* 524B-525C; *Republic* 9.588C-589B, 10.611A-612A; Origen, *De principiis* 1.6.3, 2.1.3, 3.6.3 (ed. Crouzel-Simonetti, 1:200–204, 238, 3:241).

179. Aquinas, *Summa contra Gentiles* 3.61 (not in Collins).

180. Ficino is alluding to Greek [pseudo-]etymologies of the names: Acheron from *achos* (pain) and *rhoê* (river), the Styx from *stugos* (hatred or object of hate), Tartarus from *taragma* (confusion) or *tarassein* (to disturb/trouble), Phlegethon from *phlegethein/phlegein* (to scorch, to burn up), and Cocytus from *kôkutos* (wailing/shrieking).

181. *Republic* 10.615C1–2: "And other things not worthy of record he said of those who had just been born and lived but a short time. . . ."

182. Avicenna, *Metaphysics* 9.6 (ed. Van Riet, p. 504)

183. *Timaeus* 29E-30B; Timaeus Locrus, *De natura mundi* 205 (ed. Marg, p. 119).

184. The *lux* versus *lumen* distinction is Augustinian; see the opening of the following paragraph. Ficino's *De sole* 12 (*Opera*, pp. 973–974) speaks of three kinds of brightness (*lumen*) emanating from the Sun: a white light, a red light, and a mixed light, while *lux* refers to light before any emanation.

185. Acts 17:28 "For in Him we live and move and have our being, as certain of your own poets have said."

186. This is the same disclaimer prefacing the whole work (in this edition, Vol. I, p. 1).

## INTRODUCTION TO PLATONIC THEOLOGY

1. This whole *argumentum* appears in Ficino's second book of *Letters* (*Opera*, pp. 706.4–716.1). See Note on the Text.

2. This preface reappears as the first paragraph of two in a letter addressed to Lorenzo in Ficino's third book of *Letters* (*Opera*, p. 737.2). The last sentence was added in the later (1491) redaction of the text. See Note on the Text.

3. Ibid. This breakdown reappears as the second paragraph.

4. Aristotle, *De caelo* 1.9.278a10–16; also 8.277b15 ff.

5. Averroes, *De substantia orbis* 2 (Juntine edition, 1562–74, vol. 9: 5v-8v).

6. Proclus, *Theologia Platonica* 3.5 (ed. Saffrey-Westerink, 3:18.24–19.15). Cf. Ficino's *Platonic Theology* 18.4.7 and accompanying note 44.

7. We have opted for the Laurenziana MSS. 83.11 and 83.12 reading, which is clearly required by the sense, contra Marcel's *quantitate* (adopted by Blum et al. in their edition); see Note on the Text.

8. Cf. Plato, *Timaeus* 29B, *Republic* 616E; Plotinus, *Enneads* 2.1.7–8 (and 2.1 in general along with Ficino's commentary, *Opera*, pp. 1593–1604).

9. Cf. Aristotle, *Metaphysics* 7.1.1028a25–6.1032a10.

10. This paragraph was added in the 1491 redaction and left unnumbered.

11. Again, cf. Aristotle, *Metaphysics* 7.31029a10–26.

12. *Formosus* means both "formed" and "possessing beauty."

13. Genesis 1:2 "And the earth was without form and void, and darkness was upon the face of the deep." Augustine, *Confessions* 12.8.8, is just one of countless references to this verse.

14. Genesis 1:3–4.

15. Epistle of St. James 1:17: "the Father of lights."

16. Again *formositas* means "having form and beauty."

17. "Constrained," translating *contrahere*, a scholastic term signifying contraction or confinement within certain boundaries, usually applied to the presence of universals in particulars.

18. "Plane" translates *superficies*: having length and breadth. Ficino thinks of the intellectual soul as a plane or surface as compared to the solidity of

the body: as such it is analyzable in terms of plane geometry. See Allen, *Nuptial Arithmetic*, pp. 93–100.

19. This refers to line 8 of the Orphic *Hymn of Jove* (ed. Kern, *Orphica*, frag. 168) known to Ficino from a Porphyry citation in Eusebius' *Praeparatio evangelica* 3.9.2 (see the earlier reference in Ficino's *Platonic Theology* 18.1.7 at n. 6 above). In 1492 Ficino included his translation of it (and of the Orphic *Palinode* he also found in Eusebius, op. cit. 3.12, Kern's frag. 247) in a letter to his friend Martin Prenni(n)ger (Martinus Uranius), now in his 11th book of *Letters* (*Opera*, p. 934.2 — the phrase "Nox simul atque dies" is line 5). Note that Jupiter is equated here with God.

20. Psalm 139:12: "Quia tenebrae non obscurabuntur a te, et nox sicut dies illuminabitur: sicut tenebrae eius, ita et lumen eius." Ficino is adapting the *eius* of this verse.

21. Cf. Aristotle, *Metaphysics* 2.1.993b10–11: "For as the eyes of bats are to the blaze of day, so is the reason in our soul to the things which are by nature most evident of all." Cf. n. 31 below. Ficino has substituted an owl for bats!

22. *Letter* 7.341CD, 343E–344B. Cf. Ficino, *Platonic Theology* 11.3.21 at n.15.

23. Timaeus Locrus, *De natura mundi* 1–2; cf. Plato, *Timaeus* 28B–30D.

24. Echoing John 1.1–3, 9.

25. E.g. *Philebus* 31BC, 46A–47E, 50A–D and passim; *Laws* 5.732E-734A.

26. Cf. Ficino, *De amore* 6.19 (ed. Laurens, p. 203).

27. Cf. Ficino, *De amore* 2.8 (ed. Laurens, p. 47).

28. Virgil, *Aeneid* 6.129–130.

29. A compounding of John 15.11 and 16.22. Ficino calls Christ "the master of life" also in the *Platonic Theology* 18.10.17 above.

30. Virgil, *Aeneid* 6.730–734.

31. Aristotle, *Metaphysics* 2.1.993b10–11. Cf. note 21 above.

32. Avicenna, *Metaphysics* 9.7 (ed. Van Riet, p. 514), paraphrased. This

text is not a commentary on Aristotle's *Metaphysics* but an independent work by Avicenna.

33. Virgil, *Aeneid* 6.745–747: Ficino is adapting the last line (which has been variously rendered) to his own argument about the mind's release (and adopting the more usual *aurae* for *aurai*).

34. The edition of Blum et al. cites Plotinus, *Enneads* 1.1.10.7; Proclus, *Elements* 186 (ed. Dodds).

35. Blum et al. cross-reference us to Ficino, *Opera*, p. 1551 (*In Plotinum* I.7), but the Themistius reference awaits identification.

36. See Plato, *Phaedrus* 248C-249C, and Plotinus, *Enneads* 3.4; also Ficino's *In Phaedrum* summae 24–25 (ed. Allen, pp. 162–173 ) and *Platonic Theology* 17.4, passim.

37. Ficino is pitting *verissime* against the *verisimiliter* of the preceding sentence.

38. See especially Aquinas, *Summa contra gentiles* 2.83. Cf. Ficino's *Platonic Theology* 18.9.4.

39. Contra the *immortali* of the *Opera*, Marcel, and Garin, the sense requires the *in mortali* of the Turin MS; cf. Figliucci's vernacular rendering "in questo mortal corpo."

40. *Phaedo* 65B-67D, 79CD, 83AB summarized and presented here as lemmata (with Ficino's own glossing in parentheses).

41. *nervus* in classical Latin can variously mean "nerve," "sinew," "string" (of a musical instrument), "bowstring" or "bow itself" or the "cords" controlling a puppet. Cf. Ficino's *Platonic Theology* 12.4.8 at n. 51.

42. The *utor/fruor* distinction occurs memorably throughout Augustine's *Confessions*.

# Outline of Ficino's Platonic Theology

As the structure of the *Platonic Theology* is only partly reflected in its book and chapter divisions, we give here an outline of the work's overall plan, following for the most part cues given in the text itself.

I. Books I-IV.   Ficino's immortality proofs and answers to questions in the later books of the *Theology* presuppose and are founded upon his general systematic account in these first four books of God, creation and the place of the soul within creation. These reverse the usual order of the medieval *summa*, itself founded on Neoplatonic models. The medieval *summa* generally deals in hierarchical order beginning with God and moving down through creation in general, angelic and human nature; it then follows the flow of the divine creative act back to its source by treating the redemption of human nature, understood as that nature's return via reason, love, and grace to the source of its being. Ficino begins instead with what is known *quoad nos*, i.e. with the material world known to the senses, and ascends through the five grades of reality to God. He then descends again to the level of soul and discusses its nature and species. His system thus follows a psychological or heuristic rather than an ontological or generative order.

A.   Book I.   Ascent to God through the four created substances: *body* (inert extended matter), form divided in body or *quality* (an active principle of change), *rational soul* (active, both divided in body and undivided, mobile), and *angel* (active, undivided and immobile). See 1.1.2. The ascent is also a philosophical itinerary, from pure corpuscularism (as in the Democriteans, Cyrenaics and Epicureans), to a higher awareness of an active shaping power in bodily nature (as in, for Ficino, the Stoics and Cynics), to recognition of the existence of a more excellent form beyond body which is the seat of the rational soul (as in Heraclitus, Varro, Manilius), to realization of an unchangeable mind beyond changeable soul (as in

319

Anaxagoras and Hermotimus), and finally to the light of truth itself, God (as in Plato and the Platonists).

B. Book II. God.

1. The divine essence: God is unity, truth, and goodness.

2. What God is not. Why there is not an infinity of equal gods on the same metaphysical level; why there is not an infinity of gods arranged hierarchically.

3. The divine attributes: God's power is infinite; He is everlasting; omnipresent; the source of motion and the immediate cause of all change; God acts by His being; He understands infinite things; His understanding is infinite; He has will and acts through will; His will reconciles freedom and necessity; God is loving and provident.

C. Book III. Descent through the grades of being and comparison of the grades among themselves. Ficino establishes the soul's status as the third and middle essence, "the link that holds all nature together," giving life to things below it, and knowing itself and things both above and below it.

D. Book IV. The three species of soul: the world soul; the souls of the twelve spheres, including planetary and elemental spheres; the souls of living creatures within and distinct from those spheres. The souls of the spheres cause circular motion in accordance with the laws of fate.

II. Books V-XIV. Immortality proofs. See 1.1.3: After describing the nature of soul and its place in creation, Ficino says that he is going to seek to establish that the condition and nature of the soul is such as he has described, "firstly by general arguments (*rationes communes*), secondly by specific proofs (*argumentationes propriae*), thirdly by signs (*signa*), and lastly by resolving questions (*solutiones quaestionum*)."

A. Book V. The rational soul's immortality is shown from *rationes communes* — i.e., the general metaphysical principles and characteristics of soul as third essence. These include: the fact that it is capable of self-induced circular motion but is unchanging in its substance; its natural attraction both to divine and material things; its ability to rule matter while remaining independent of it; its indivisibility; the relation of essence and existence in soul; the nature of soul as pure form; the self-subsistence of soul; its dependence on and resemblance to its divine cause; the fact that the soul is not potential with respect to existence and is directly dependent on God for its existence; the fact that it is the principle of life, and a power inherently superior to body.

B. Books VI-XII. The rational soul's immortality shown from *rationes propriae*, i.e. particular arguments. These *rationes propriae* consist of more detailed demonstrations of some of the *rationes communes* in II.A.

1. Book VI.1 Introductory interlude. This takes the form of a dialogic intervention by Giovanni Cavalcanti, the only one in the *Theology*, revealing for the first time that the previous five books had been a disputation held at the country home of Giovanni Cavalcanti in the presence of Cavalcanti, Cristoforo Landino, Bernardo Nuzzi and Giorgio Antonio Vespucci. Cavalcanti lays out five possible views of the nature of soul and demands that Ficino explain why the Platonic one is correct. These views include various Presocratic and Stoic views, i.e., that the soul is a pneumatic or a fine-material substance or that the soul is a quality dependent on material potencies. The fifth and highest view is that of Plato and the ancient theologians, "in whose footsteps Aristotle, the natural philosopher, for the most part follows" : namely that the soul is divine, i.e. "something indivisible, wholly present to every part of the body and produced by an incorporeal creator such that it depends only on the power of that agent," and not on any material potency. Ficino is challenged to refute the four materialists and prove the view of Plato.

2. Book VI.2.   Ficino's response: Refutation of the materialists by analysis of the soul's three *officia* or roles: acting in the body (the vegetative power), acting through the body (the sensitive power) and acting through itself (the intellective power). Ficino argues that the "vulgar philosophers" who hold to materialism have been misled by "perverse custom" and the influence of the body, and he devises educational thought-experiments drawn from Avicenna, Plato's analogy of the Cave in *Republic* 7 and other sources to reveal the true nature of the soul as "invisible, life-giving, sentient, intelligible, intelligent, independent of body, active of its own accord, heat-giving, life-giving, sentient, capable of attaining things above, a substantial unity." The argument in II.B.2 is described as a "first foray, a sort of prelude" or protreptic to purge the mind of the vulgar of their "wretched lack of trust" which keeps them from acknowledging the realm of immaterial spirit.

3. Books VI.3-VIII.   Return to the main argument of the *Theology*. Ficino takes up in turn the *rationes propriae* which will demonstrate the *rationes communes* in greater detail, beginning with the *ratio communis* of the soul's *indivisibility in body*. Other *rationes* are then addressed in ascending hierarchical order. The soul's indivisibility in body (and therefore its immortality) is demonstrated from its three *officia* (or *virtutes*, powers) as described in II.B.2, arranged hierarchically from lowest to highest.

> a. Book VI.4–13. The soul's lowest or *vegetative* powers, of nutrition, locomotion and growth, already show why the soul cannot be material or be form-in-matter: soul is a principle of activity that applies to all bodily parts; it is not spatially divided.

> b. Book VII. Proofs that the soul is not divisible from the power of *sensation*: general proofs from the nature of sensation itself and specific proofs from the soul's complexions and the harmony of its humors.

c. Book VIII. Proofs that the soul is not indivisible as inferred from the nature of *intellection*. Topics include the intellect's relation to truth; the nature of the intellective power in itself; its instruments (i.e., intelligible species); its operations; the objects of intellection (i.e., universals); the possibility of communication as such; the incorporeal way the mind is modified by form; the goals of intellection; the infinite force of the intellective power.

4. Book IX. Immortality proofs based on a second *ratio communis*: the soul's *independence of body*.

5. Book X. Immortality proofs based on *general structural or aesthetic principles*, i.e. the fitness of immortality, given the soul's relationship to the things below and above it in the order of nature. Answers are given to objections from Epicurus, Lucretius, and the Stoic Panaetius.

6. Book XI. Immortality proofs based on the soul's *eternal and immaterial objects*, i.e., the Ideas. The nature of the Ideas. Confirmation of their nature by signs. Answers to Epicureans, Skeptics, and Peripatetics.

7. Book XII.1–4. Immortality proof based on *relationship of the mind to God*; its being formed by God. The general structure of the argument is as follows: if the mind is formed by the Divine Mind, it is immortal; but it is in fact formed by the Divine Mind for such-and-such a reason, therefore etc. Ficino then answers a possible objection: why are we not ordinarily conscious of being formed by the Divine Mind?

8. Book XII.5–7. Three confirmations of the arguments in II.B.1–7 derived from a consideration of sight, hearing, and the mind. These confirmations take the form of extensive quotations from Augustine. This provides a bridge to the next section on signs.

C. Books XIII-XIV. Immortality shown by 'signs' (rather than reasons)

1. Book XIII. The soul shown to be immortal by signs of the soul's power over things beneath it and its own body, for example in psychosomatic phenomena, in phantasy, prophecy, the arts, and in the performance of miracles. The magical powers of the soul.

2. Book XIV. Twelve signs from the soul's imitation of what is above it: i.e. the soul's desire to be like God. Remarks on the nature and universality of religion. Answer to the Lucretians.

III. Books XV-XVIII. Resolution of five questions relating to the soul's immortality.

A. Book XV. Question 1: Is there one soul for all mankind? This book contains an exhaustive refutation of Averroes, and is in a sense the centerpiece of the entire work, in that it draws extensively on Ficino's prior exposition and argumentation.

B. Book XVI.1–6. Question 2: Why then did God put souls in bodies at all? Answers to Epicureans.

C. Book XVI.7. Question 3: Why do rational souls experience tumultuous emotions?

D. Book XVI.8. Question 4: Why do rational souls depart unwillingly from bodies? I.e., why is there fear of death if souls are just returning to their true home, and departing from the miseries of this life?

E. Books XVII-XVIII. Question 5: What is the status of soul before entering the body and after leaving it? The creation and composition of souls; their kinds and their circuits (i.e., their descents and ascents).

1. Book XVII. Excursus on issues of interpretation: what is the true Platonic position on transmigration?

a. Book XVII.2–3. The interpretation of the last two ancient Platonic academies.

b. Book XVII.4. The interpretation of Plato of the first four academies, and the two better academies. The doctrine of the transmigration of souls is condemned.

2. Book XVIII.1–2. Excursus on the nature of creation in general, presenting and defending "the theology common to the Hebrews, Christians, and Arabs," i.e. (a) that the world was created at a certain moment of time; (b) that angels were created from the beginning; (c) that new immortal souls are continuously created in time. Ficino's goal is to establish a wider theological framework, creation in general, for his discussion of point (c): the continuous or sequential creation of individual souls in time.

XVIII.1. Arguments that the world was created in time.

XVIII.2. Arguments for the creation of angels and souls in time.

3. Book XVIII.3. The creation of human souls in time. Arguments for the continuous, sequential creation of souls by God. The creation of souls is regulated by Providence, not by chance sexual unions. Why souls had to be created successively rather than all at once.

4. Book XVIII.4–7. The descent of souls.

a. Book XVIII.4. The descent of the soul into the body. The aethereal vehicle of the soul. The theory that the soul has three vehicles, celestial, aerial, and elemental.

b. Book XVIII.5. In what part of heaven souls are created. The influence of the stars and their configurations on the soul in its descent.

c. Book XVIII.6. Physical generation in the body; the soul's attendant genius; our souls' need for the protection of higher powers.

d. Book XVIII.7. Infusion of the soul into the mid-point of the body, the heart, and the soul's relation with the body's heat, its spirit, its humors and heavier members.

5. Book XVIII.8–12. The ascent of souls, or more broadly, what happens to the soul and its body after death.

a. Book XVIII.8. The state of *pure souls* after separation from the body, i.e., the souls of the blessed. The capacity of the rational soul to see the light of God; capacity of the soul to love God's light. The ninefold degrees of blessedness; the changelessness of the pure soul; the nature of its union with God; that even the lowest species of soul — the human rational soul — is capable of union with God; ranking of souls in heaven; rest of reason in the vision of God; rest of the will in the love of God.

b. Book XVIII.9. On the *bodies of pure souls* after death, i.e. the resurrection of the body, prefigured in pagan religion and confirmed by the three modern religions, Christianity, Judaism and Islam. Four proofs of the Resurrection from "Christian theologians", i.e. Thomas Aquinas. Further arguments from the order of nature.

c. Book XVIII.10. The state of the *impure soul*. Platonic and Christian doctrines of rewards and punishments compared; the four ways of living life; the possibility that impure souls without fixed habits of evil can attain blessedness after death; the doctrine of the afterlife and hell in the ancient theologians.

d. The middle state of rational souls that are *neither pure nor impure*. What happens to children who die before they are capable of making a choice of life; what happens to persons who are mentally defective.

e. Concluding exhortation to live for eternity, not for this life.

# Concordance

ぁ§ぁ

| Allen-Hankins | Opera | Marcel |
|---|---|---|
| Proem | 106 | I: 35 |
| 1.1 | 107 | I: 38 |
| 1.2 | 107 | I: 40 |
| 1.3 | 109 | I: 44 |
| 1.3.10 | 111 | I: 48 |
| 1.3.20 | 113 | I: 53 |
| 1.4 | 114 | I: 56 |
| 1.5 | 115 | I: 58 |
| 1.5.10 | 118 | I: 64 |
| 1.6 | 119 | I: 67 |
| 2.1 | 122 | I: 73 |
| 2.2 | 123 | I: 75 |
| 2.2.10 | 124 | I: 79 |
| 2.3 | 125 | I: 80 |
| 2.4 | 126 | I: 82 |
| 2.5 | 127 | I: 84 |
| 2.6 | 127 | I: 85 |
| 2.6.10 | 129 | I: 90 |
| 2.7 | 130 | I: 91 |
| 2.8 | 132 | I: 97 |
| 2.9 | 133 | I: 98 |
| 2.10 | 134 | I: 103 |
| 2.11 | 135 | I: 105 |
| 2.11.10 | 137 | I: 109 |
| 2.12 | 138 | I: 112 |
| 2.12.10 | 140 | I: 117 |
| 2.13 | 141 | I: 118 |
| 2.13.10 | 144 | I: 126 |
| 3.1 | 145 | I: 128 |

| Allen-Hankins | Opera | Marcel |
|---|---|---|
| 3.1.10 | 147 | I: 132 |
| 3.2 | 149 | I: 137 |
| 4.1 | 152 | I: 144 |
| 4.1.10 | 154 | I: 149 |
| 4.1.20 | 158 | I: 158 |
| 4.1.30 | 161 | I: 165 |
| 4.2 | 161 | I: 166 |
| 4.2.10 | 164 | I: 172 |
| 5.1 | 165 | I: 174 |
| 5.2 | 165 | I: 175 |
| 5.3 | 166 | I: 176 |
| 5.4 | 166 | I: 176 |
| 5.4.10 | 167 | I: 180 |
| 5.5 | 168 | I: 181 |
| 5.6 | 169 | I: 184 |
| 5.7 | 170 | I: 185 |
| 5.8 | 170 | I: 187 |
| 5.9 | 172 | I: 191 |
| 5.10 | 173 | I: 194 |
| 5.11 | 174 | I: 196 |
| 5.12 | 175 | I: 199 |
| 5.13 | 177 | I: 203 |
| 5.13.10 | 179 | I: 207 |
| 5.14 | 180 | I: 209 |
| 5.15 | 182 | I: 214 |
| 5.15.10 | 184 | I: 219 |
| 6.1 | 186 | I: 223 |
| 6.2 | 187 | I: 225 |
| 6.2.10 | 189 | I: 230 |
| 6.2.20 | 192 | I: 236 |
| 6.3 | 192 | I: 238 |
| 6.4 | 193 | I: 239 |
| 6.5 | 193 | I: 240 |
| 6.6 | 194 | I: 242 |

| ALLEN-HANKINS | OPERA | MARCEL |
|---|---|---|
| 6.7 | 194 | I: 243 |
| 6.8 | 195 | I: 245 |
| 6.9 | 196 | I: 246 |
| 6.10 | 197 | I: 248 |
| 6.11 | 197 | I: 249 |
| 6.12 | 198 | I: 251 |
| 6.12.10 | 200 | I: 256 |
| 6.13 | 201 | I: 259 |
| 7.1 | 203 | I: 263 |
| 7.2 | 204 | I: 265 |
| 7.3 | 204 | I: 267 |
| 7.4 | 205 | I: 268 |
| 7.5 | 206 | I: 270 |
| 7.6 | 207 | I: 274 |
| 7.7 | 208 | I: 276 |
| 7.8 | 208 | I: 277 |
| 7.9 | 209 | I: 278 |
| 7.10 | 209 | I: 279 |
| 7.11 | 210 | I: 280 |
| 7.12 | 210 | I: 281 |
| 7.13 | 211 | I: 282 |
| 7.14 | 211 | I: 283 |
| 7.15 | 211 | I: 284 |
| 8.1 | 212 | I: 285 |
| 8.2 | 214 | I: 290 |
| 8.2.10 | 215 | I: 293 |
| 8.3 | 216 | I: 296 |
| 8.3.10 | 218 | I: 299 |
| 8.4 | 218 | I: 300 |
| 8.4.10 | 220 | I: 304 |
| 8.4.20 | 223 | I: 310 |
| 8.5 | 223 | I: 311 |
| 8.6 | 224 | I: 313 |
| 8.7 | 224 | I: 314 |

| Allen-Hankins | Opera | Marcel |
|---|---|---|
| 8.8 | 225 | I: 315 |
| 8.9 | 225 | I: 316 |
| 8.10 | 226 | I: 317 |
| 8.11 | 227 | I: 320 |
| 8.12 | 227 | I: 320 |
| 8.13 | 227 | I: 321 |
| 8.14 | 228 | I: 323 |
| 8.15 | 229 | I: 324 |
| 8.16 | 230 | I: 328 |
| 8.16.10 | 231 | I: 331 |
| 9.1 | 232 | II: 8 |
| 9.2 | 233 | II: 10 |
| 9.3 | 234 | II: 12 |
| 9.4 | 236 | II: 18 |
| 9.4.10 | 238 | II: 23 |
| 9.5 | 241 | II: 30 |
| 9.5.10 | 243 | II: 33 |
| 9.5.20 | 245 | II: 39 |
| 9.5.30 | 247 | II: 44 |
| 9.6 | 248 | II: 44 |
| 9.7 | 249 | II: 47 |
| 10.1 | 251 | II: 51 |
| 10.2 | 252 | II: 54 |
| 10.2.10 | 254 | II: 59 |
| 10.3 | 256 | II: 62 |
| 10.4 | 258 | II: 68 |
| 10.5 | 259 | II: 71 |
| 10.6 | 262 | II: 76 |
| 10.7 | 263 | II: 80 |
| 10.8 | 265 | II: 83 |
| 10.8.10 | 267 | II: 88 |
| 10.9 | 268 | II: 89 |
| 11.1 | 269 | II: 91 |
| 11.2 | 270 | II: 93 |

| ALLEN-HANKINS | OPERA | MARCEL |
|---|---|---|
| 11.3 | 271 | II: 97 |
| 11.3.10 | 274 | II: 103 |
| 11.3.20 | 275 | II: 106 |
| 11.4 | 277 | II: 110 |
| 11.4.10 | 280 | II: 116 |
| 11.4.20 | 283 | II: 123 |
| 11.5.1 | 284 | II: 126 |
| 11.5.10 | 287 | II: 133 |
| 11.6 | 288 | II: 134 |
| 11.6.10 | 290 | II: 139 |
| 11.7 | 293 | II: 145 |
| 11.8 | 293 | II: 147 |
| 12.1 | 295 | II: 150 |
| 12.1.10 | 297 | II: 154 |
| 12.2 | 298 | II: 158 |
| 12.3 | 299 | II: 160 |
| 12.4 | 301 | II: 166 |
| 12.4.10 | 304 | II: 172 |
| 12.5 | 305 | II: 174 |
| 12.5.10 | 307 | II: 178 |
| 12.6 | 308 | II: 181 |
| 12.6.10 | 310 | II: 186 |
| 12.7 | 310 | II: 187 |
| 12.7.10 | 312 | II: 192 |
| 13.1 | 314 | II: 196 |
| 13.2 | 316 | II: 201 |
| 13.2.10 | 318 | II: 206 |
| 13.2.20 | 320 | II: 211 |
| 13.2.30 | 323 | II: 217 |
| 13.3 | 325 | II: 223 |
| 13.3.10 | 327 | II: 228 |
| 13.4 | 328 | II: 229 |
| 13.4.10 | 330 | II: 235 |
| 13.5 | 333 | II: 241 |

| ALLEN-HANKINS | OPERA | MARCEL |
|:---:|:---:|:---:|
| 14.1 | 335 | II: 246 |
| 14.2 | 337 | II: 250 |
| 14.2.10 | 339 | II: 255 |
| 14.3 | 339 | II: 256 |
| 14.4 | 341 | II: 260 |
| 14.5 | 341 | II: 261 |
| 14.6 | 344 | II: 266 |
| 14.7 | 345 | II: 269 |
| 14.8 | 347 | II: 273 |
| 14.9 | 349 | II: 279 |
| 14.10 | 351 | II: 283 |
| 14.10.10 | 353 | II: 289 |
| 14.10.20 | 356 | II: 296 |
| 15.1 | 357 | III: 8 |
| 15.1.10 | 358 | III: 11 |
| 15.2 | 360 | III: 16 |
| 15.2.10 | 362 | III: 21 |
| 15.2.20 | 365 | III: 27 |
| 15.3 | 365 | III: 28 |
| 15.4 | 366 | III: 29 |
| 15.5 | 367 | III: 33 |
| 15.6 | 369 | III: 38 |
| 15.7 | 370 | III: 40 |
| 15.7.10 | 372 | III: 45 |
| 15.8 | 373 | III: 47 |
| 15.9 | 375 | III: 51 |
| 15.10 | 376 | III: 54 |
| 15.10.10 | 378 | III: 59 |
| 15.11 | 378 | III: 59 |
| 15.11.10 | 380 | III: 63 |
| 15.12 | 381 | III: 65 |
| 15.12.10 | 382 | III: 69 |
| 15.13 | 383 | III: 71 |
| 15.13.10 | 385 | III: 75 |

| Allen-Hankins | Opera | Marcel |
|---|---|---|
| 15.14 | 385 | III: 76 |
| 15.15 | 386 | III: 78 |
| 15.16 | 387 | III: 80 |
| 15.16.10 | 389 | III: 85 |
| 15.17 | 390 | III: 88 |
| 15.17.10 | 392 | III: 92 |
| 15.18 | 393 | III: 95 |
| 15.19 | 395 | III: 99 |
| 15.19.10 | 397 | III: 104 |
| 16.1 | 398 | III: 105 |
| 16.1.10 | 399 | III: 109 |
| 16.1.20 | 401 | III: 113 |
| 16.2 | 403 | III: 116 |
| 16.3 | 403 | III: 117 |
| 16.4 | 404 | III: 119 |
| 16.5 | 404 | III: 120 |
| 16.6 | 406 | III: 125 |
| 16.6.10 | 408 | III: 131 |
| 16.7 | 409 | III: 131 |
| 16.7.10 | 411 | III: 136 |
| 16.8 | 413 | III: 142 |
| 17.1 | 416 | III: 148 |
| 17.2 | 416 | III: 149 |
| 17.2.10 | 418 | III: 154 |
| 17.3 | 420 | III: 158 |
| 17.3.10 | 422 | III: 163 |
| 17.4 | 423 | III: 165 |
| 17.4.10 | 425 | III: 172 |
| 18.1 | 427 | III: 175 |
| 18.1.10 | 429 | III: 180 |
| 18.2 | 430 | III: 183 |
| 18.3 | 431 | III: 185 |
| 18.3.10 | 433 | III: 190 |
| 18.4 | 434 | III: 192 |

| ALLEN-HANKINS | OPERA | MARCEL |
|:---:|:---:|:---:|
| 18.5 | 435 | III: 196 |
| 18.6 | 436 | III: 198 |
| 18.7 | 437 | III: 199 |
| 18.8 | 437 | III: 200 |
| 18.8.10 | 439 | III: 206 |
| 18.8.20 | 442 | III: 212 |
| 18.8.30 | 443 | III: 216 |
| 18.9 | 445 | III: 220 |
| 18.9.10 | 447 | III: 224 |
| 18.10 | 448 | III: 227 |
| 18.10.10 | 450 | III: 231 |
| 18.10.20 | 452 | III: 237 |
| 18.11 | 452 | III: 238 |
| 18.12 | 454 | III: 243 |

## CONCORDANCE TO ARGUMENTUM
## IN PLATONICAM THEOLOGIAM

| ALLEN-HANKINS | OPERA | MARCEL |
|:---:|:---:|:---:|
| 1 | 736 | III: 267 |
| 5 | 737 | III: 268 |
| 10 | 738 | III: 271 |
| 15 | 740 | III: 275 |
| 20 | 741 | III: 278 |
| 25 | 743 | III: 282 |
| 30 | 744 | III: 285 |
| 35 | 745 | III: 288 |

# Corrigenda

❧❦❧

## VOLUME 1

p. 11, line 17: "and it is no empty belief" (*nec vana fides*) is from Virgil, *Aeneid* 4.12

p. 325, note 18: Aristotle, *De caelo* 1.9.277b26–278b9; *Metaphysics* 14.2.1088b14–28

p. 329, note 28: Stählin

p. 332, note 3: Ficino, *In Philebum* (ed. Allen, pp. 384–424)

p. 333, note 11: Praeterea,

p. 333, note 17: In his *Platonic Theology* (ed. Saffrey-Westerink 6: 45.5), Proclus says "Jupiter particular" is the "second Jupiter" of *Gorgias* 523A, not the first, the demiurgic Jupiter of the *Timaeus*; see Allen, *Platonism*, pp. 126–28

p. 334, note 22: *Stromata* 5.8.48 (ed. Stählin, 2.358.11)

p. 338, sub Walker: Campanella

## VOLUME 2

p. 95, line 27: not be destroyed; but in reality it is destroyed rather than

p. 123, line 3: Cavalcanti

p. 127, line 7: When we were dining

p. 263, title, line 1: undivided

p. 329, line 15: way

p. 379, note 5: 2.7.198a14

pp. 383–4, notes 11, 17, 19: these Macrobius references are to the *In somnium Scipionis* 1.14.19–20 (ed. Willis, p. 59); similarly in note 31 to Book VIII (p. 390)

p. 385, note 30: incrementi: *read* decrementi

p. 390, note 26 (last line): 2.1445

p. 391, note 39: *Laws* 10.894b–896a

## VOLUME 3

p. 32, line 11–p. 34, line 3: "Naturali enim existimatione . . . sortita sunt speciem": see the parallel passage in Ficino's *Second Sermon* (*Opera*, p. 477)

p. 36, line 5–p. 56, line 10: "Praecipue vero ex hoc . . . qui violentia non pulsatur": see the parallel passage in Ficino's *Disputatio contra iudicium astrologorum* in M, f. 22v (see Kristeller, *Supplementum Ficinianum* 2.14–15)

p. 101, lines 15–16: whose power and activity changes

p. 219, line 13: to become the matter or seat of

p. 238, line 11–p. 240, bottom line: "Quis neget animum . . . omnium rationibus praediti": see the parallel passage in Ficino's *De amore* 6.12 (ed. Laurens, pp. 177–181)

p. 267, line 8: by night, full of stars, fills a rivulet with the images

p. 293, line 15: using them beforehand [NOT from nature]

p. 319, line 8: cannot: *read* can not

p. 342, line 24: 1995 [NOT 1965]

p. 344, note 13: *Quaere*

p. 345, note 27: *De vita animae immortali*

p. 346, note 47: *De sensu et sensibilibus*

p. 347, note 56: pseudo-Quintilian

p. 350, note 37: *In Phaedrum*, summa 19

p. 353, note 33: the quotation from the *De christiana religione* continues for another six lines down to *sui ipsius imaginem* (on p. 262 bottom line)

## VOLUME 4

p. 176, lines 11–24: "Unum illud est . . . persimiles ordine": see the parallel passage in the first book of Ficino's *Letters* (ed. Gentile, no. 123.128–141)

p. 222, lines 13–23: "quemadmodum in libro *De amore* . . . ut deus evadat": see the parallel passage in the first book of Ficino's *Letters* (ed. Gentile, no. 41.11–22)

p. 255, line 28: for they would strive in vain

p. 276, line 12–p. 278, line 15: "Experimur in nobis . . . umbrae volitant": see the parallel passage in the sixth book of Ficino's *Letters* (*Opera*, p. 837.2)

p. 292, line 21–p. 294, line 24: "Nullum enim bruta prae se . . . excepta religione, mutantur": see the parallel passage in Ficino's *De christiana religione* (*Opera*, p. 2)

p. 318, line 4–18; p. 318, line 2up–p. 320, line 4/5: "quia deum nemo vere . . . quam inquirendo" "Praeterea cognoscendo . . . reliquum superesse": see the parallel passages in the first book of Ficino's *Letters* (ed. Gentile, no. 115.100–113, 182–188)

p. 336, note 62: animum

p. 342, note 12: *Praeparatio*

p. 345, lines 4–5: *remove parentheses*

p. 350, note 30: The letter is no. 52 in Gentile's edition

p. 350, note 33: The Soul as Rhapsode

p. 354, note 89 (last line): Prenninger

p. 361, note 44: Cf. Plato, *Meno* 100A

p. 361, note 46: non exaudiat

p. 361, note 49: animum

## VOLUME 5

p. 5, line 16: men would be the same or superfluous qualities would be in the

p. 97, line 21: accord us that mind

p. 160, lines 7–11: "Si mens adeo divina est . . . semper et putet": see the parallel passage in the first book of Ficino's *Letters* (ed. Gentile, no. 39.22–25)

p. 164, lines 1–7: "Quotiens unitatem . . . respuere et odisse": see the parallel passage in the first book of Ficino's *Letters* (ed. Gentile, no. 39.28–32)

p. 203, chapter heading: men would be the same, or superfluous qualities would be in

p. 265, line 6: are: *read* is

p. 335, note 27: (ed. Van Riet, pp. 71–88)

p. 340, note 101: (ed. Crawford, p. 399.362–369)

p. 340, note 110 (ed. Crawford, pp. 362–366)

p. 343, note 21: the Proclus reference is to *In Timaeum* 3 (ed. Diehl, 2: 130.1–29). There is a similar Janus reference in Ficino's letter to Jacopo Bracciolini (ed. Gentile, no. 107.31–32)

# Bibliography

Allen, Michael J. B. *The Platonism of Marsilio Ficino: A Study of His "Phaedrus" Commentary, Its Sources and Genesis.* Berkeley and Los Angeles: University of California Press, 1984.

———. *Icastes: Marsilio Ficino's Interpretation of Plato's "Sophist".* Berkeley and Los Angeles: University of California Press, 1989. Contains studies of Ficino's ontology and an edition of the *In Sophistam.*

———. *Nuptial Arithmetic: Marsilio Ficino's Commentary on the Fatal Number in Book VIII of Plato's "Republic."* Berkeley and Los Angeles: University of California Press, 1994. Includes studies of Ficino's numerology and his theories of Platonic prophecy and time.

———. *Plato's Third Eye: Studies in Marsilio Ficino's Metaphysics and Its Sources.* Aldershot: Variorum, 1995. Various studies.

———. *Synoptic Art: Marsilio Ficino on the History of Platonic Interpretation.* Florence: Olschki, 1998. Includes chapters on Ficino's views on ancient theology, on Socrates, on the later history of Platonism, on the war with the poets, and on dialectic.

Allen, Michael J. B., and Valery Rees, with Martin Davies, eds. *Marsilio Ficino: His Theology, His Philosophy, His Legacy.* Leiden: E. J. Brill, 2002. A wide range of new essays.

Collins, Ardis B. *The Secular Is Sacred: Platonism and Thomism in Marsilio Ficino's Platonic Theology.* The Hague: Nijhoff, 1974.

Copenhaver, Brian P., and Charles B. Schmitt. *Renaissance Philosophy.* Oxford: Oxford University Press, 1992. Excellent introduction to the context.

Field, Arthur. *The Origins of the Platonic Academy of Florence.* Princeton: Princeton University Press, 1988. Fine, detailed study of Ficino's formative years.

Hankins, James. *Plato in the Italian Renaissance.* 2 vols. Leiden: E. J. Brill, 1990. A synoptic account of the Platonic revival.

———. "Ficino, Avicenna and the Occult Powers of the Soul." In *Tra antica sapienza e filosofia naturale. La magia nell' Europa moderna.* Ed.

Fabrizio Meroi with Elisabetta Scapparone, 2 vols., 1: 35–52. Florence: Olschki, 2006. Discusses themes in *Platonic Theology*, Book XIII.

———. "Ficino on *Reminiscentia* and the Transmigration of Souls." In the acts of the conference, *Enigmi della memoria: essere, conoscere, ricordare*," Istituto Nazionale di Studi sul Rinascimento, Florence, 15–17 December 2005 (Florence: Leo S. Olschki, forthcoming). Discusses themes in *Platonic Theology*, Book XVII.

———. *Humanism and Platonism in the Italian Renaissance.* 2 vols. Rome: Edizioni di Storia e Letteratura, 2003–2004. Includes nineteen studies on Ficino and Renaissance Platonism.

———. "Socrates in the Italian Renaissance." In proceedings of the conference "Images and Uses of Socrates," July 18–21, 2001, King's College, London. Ed. Michael Trapp. Aldershot, England, and Burlington, Vt.: Ashgate, forthcoming.

Katinis, Teodoro. "Bibliografia ficiniana: Studi ed edizioni delle opere di Marsilio Ficino dal 1986." In *Accademia* 2 (2000): 101–136. A bibliography from 1986 to 2000; updated annually.

Kristeller, Paul Oskar. *Marsilio Ficino and His Work after Five Hundred Years.* Florence: Olschki, 1987. An essential guide to the bibliography.

———. *Medieval Aspects of Renaissance Learning*, ed. and tr. Edward P. Mahoney. 2nd ed. New York: Columbia University Press, 1992.

———. *The Philosophy of Marsilio Ficino.* New York: Columbia University Press, 1943; repr. Gloucester, Mass.: Peter Lang, 1964. The authoritative study of Ficino as a formal philosopher.

———. *Renaissance Thought and Its Sources.* New York: Columbia University Press, 1979. Pays special attention to Platonism.

———. *Studies in Renaissance Thought and Letters.* Rome: Edizioni di Storia e Letteratura, 1956. Important essays on Ficino's context and influence.

———. *Studies in Renaissance Thought and Letters III.* Rome: Edizioni di Storia e Letteratura, 1993. More essays on Renaissance Platonism and on individual Platonists.

Members of the Language Department of the School of Economic Science, London, trs. *The Letters of Marsilio Ficino.* 7 vols. to date. London: Shepheard-Walwyn, 1975–.

Toussaint, Stéphane, ed. *Marcel Ficin ou les mystères platoniciens*. Les Cahiers de l'Humanisme, vol. 2. Paris: Les Belles Lettres, 2002.

Trinkaus, Charles. *In Our Image and Likeness: Humanity and Divinity in Italian Humanist Thought*. 2 vols. London: University of Chicago Press, 1970. Wide-ranging analysis of a Christian-Platonic theme.

Walker, D. P. *Spiritual and Demonic Magic from Ficino to Campanella*. London: The Warburg Institute, 1958; repr. Pennsylvania State University Press, 2000. A seminal study.

Wind, Edgar. *Pagan Mysteries in the Renaissance*, rev. ed. New York: Norton, 1968. A rich book on Platonism's influence on Renaissance mythography, art and culture.

# Cumulative Index of Sources

❧❦❧

References are by book, chapter, and paragraph number. Numbers preceded by "App" refer to the *Introduction to Platonic Theology* in the Appendix to volume 6. An asterisk (*) indicates that the passage is cited more than once in the given paragraph.

Aeneas of Gaza
  *Theophrastus* (PG 85)
    892: 17.3.10
    893: 17.4.3, 17.4.4
Aëtius
  *Placita* (ed. Diels)
    1.3: 11.6.6
Alain de Lille
  *Regula de sacra theologia* (PL 210)
    7.477 (627a–b): 18.3.12
Albertus Magnus
  *De causis* (*Opera*, vol. 10)
    p. 532: 4.1.25
Alexander of Aphrodisias
  *De anima* (CAG, ed. Bruns)
    2.21, 22–24: 15.1.2
    2.81–82, 108: 15.11.10
    2.107–108: 15.12.2
  *De intellectu* (ed. Théry)
    pp. 74–77, 82: 15.11.10
Pseudo-Alexander of Aphrodisias
  *Problemata medica* (ed. Ideler)
    2 prologus: 15.1.2*
Algazel
  *Destructio* (ed. Marmura)
    8: 15.5.8
  *Metaphysica*

I, tract. 1, ch. 10–11: 15.2.1
II, tract. 4, ch. 4: 9.5.25
V, tract. 5, ch. 1–2: 9.5.25
Apuleius
  *De deo Socratis*
    11: 16.5.4
    passim: 13.2.33
  *De Platone et eius dogmata*
    1.2–3: 17.4.4
  *Argonautica Orphica*
    968–70: 18.10.13
    1142: 18.10.11
Aristotle
  *Categoriae*
    5.3b25–28: 7.9.1
    8.10b12–17: 7.9.1
    8.10b12–15: 1.2.4
  *De anima*
    1.2.405a: 1.1.2*
    1.2.405b2: 6.1.3
    1.2.405b5: 6.1.3
    1.4.408b1–32: 15.7.1
    1.4.409a4–7: 15.3.2
    2: 18.10.8
    2.1–3: 15.7.10
    2.1.412a20–22: 15.7.10
    2.2.413a7: 15.11.11

343

# Cumulative Index of Subjects

꽃5?

References are by book, chapter, and paragraph number. Italicized roman numerals refer to pages in the translator's introduction (Volume 1). Numbers preceded by "App." refer to the *Introduction to Platonic Theology* in the Appendix to volume 6.

# Cumulative Index of Names

ক৺৺৳

References are by book, chapter, and paragraph number. "Pr" refers to the Proem. Numbers preceded by "App" refer to the *Introduction to Platonic Theology* in the Appendix to volume 6.

*Publication of this volume has been made possible by*

The Myron and Sheila Gilmore Publication Fund at I Tatti
The Robert Lehman Endowment Fund
The Jean-François Malle Scholarly Programs and Publications Fund
The Andrew W. Mellon Scholarly Publications Fund
The Craig and Barbara Smyth Fund
for Scholarly Programs and Publications
The Lila Wallace–Reader's Digest Endowment Fund
The Malcolm Wiener Fund for Scholarly Programs and Publications

*Preparation of this volume was supported in part by a grant
to Michael J. B. Allen from the UCLA Academic Senate*